Philip Sidney, William Gray

The Miscellaneous Works of Sir Philip Sidney

Philip Sidney, William Gray

The Miscellaneous Works of Sir Philip Sidney

ISBN/EAN: 9783337058395

Printed in Europe, USA, Canada, Australia, Japan

Cover: Foto ©ninafisch / pixelio.de

More available books at **www.hansebooks.com**

THE
MISCELLANEOUS WORKS
OF
SIR PHILIP SIDNEY

Of this edition of Miscellaneous Works of
Five hundred copies are printed,—Two hundred *for*
England, and Two hundred and fifty for America

THE

MISCELLANEOUS WORKS

OF

Sir Philip Sidney, knt

WITH A LIFE OF THE AUTHOR AND
ILLUSTRATIVE NOTES

By WILLIAM GRAY, Esq.

OF MAGDALEN COLLEGE, AND THE INNER TEMPLE

' Live ever, sweet book! he who wrote thee was the secretary of eloquence, the breath of the Muses, and the honey-bee of the daintiest flowers of wit and art.

GABRIEL HARVEY

LONDON
WILLIAM W. GIBBINGS
18 BURY STREET, W.C.
1893

WOULD I HAD FALL'N UPON THOSE HAPPIER DAYS,
THAT POETS CELEBRATE, THOSE GOLDEN TIMES,
AND THOSE ARCADIAN SCENES, THAT MARO SINGS,
AND SIDNEY, WARBLER OF POETIC PROSE.
Cowper's Task.

EDITOR'S PREFACE.

N presenting Sir Philip Sidney's Miscellaneous Works to the world, it will be unnecessary to trouble the reader with many prefatory remarks. It is enough for us to state that all our Author's published writings, with the exception of the Arcadia and the Psalms, have been collected from various quarters and embodied in this volume; and that several of his MS. letters now make their appearance for the first time, from the originals preserved in the British Museum.

We have assiduously compared the text of the different editions of Sidney's productions, and have in innumerable instances been able to correct the gross inaccuracies of preceding copies. On this head we would particularly direct our censure against the reprint of the Defence of Poesy superintended by Dr. Joseph Warton, which, though it abounds in the most grotesque and inexcusable blunders, seems to have been implicitly followed in a more recent publication.

We have not presumed to introduce into our volume any portion of the Version of the Psalms, which is commonly attributed to the united labours of Sir P. Sidney and the Countess of Pembroke; since it is impossible to decide, with any degree of certainty, what part of this paraphrase belongs to Sir Philip, and what to his accomplished sister: and besides, a beautiful edition of these interesting compositions was published only a few years ago, by Mr. Weller Singer, in his "Select Early English Poets."

For a reason which we have stated at p. 326, we have printed the sixteen letters, placed at the end of this volume, without making the slightest alteration in their orthography; but in all the other writings of our Author, we have taken the liberty of adapting the spelling to the standard now in use: and, though we may encounter some little blame on this account from the rigid lovers of antiquity, we are persuaded that we have rendered a service to the general reader. The orthography of the fathers of our literature was invariably most whimsical and uncertain. Sir John Fenn has mentioned an instance in the Paston Letters, where the same word is spelt three different ways within the short space of two lines; and many other examples of similar caprice might be produced, were it necessary. "Every writer," says Dr. Henry, "contented himself with putting together any combination of letters that occurred to him at the time, which he imagined would suggest the word he intended to his readers, without ever reflecting what letters others used, on former occasions, for that purpose."

It is perhaps superfluous to add more, but we cannot resist making a short quotation from Dr. Johnson's Preface to his Dictionary, where he says, "If the language of theology were extracted from Hooker and the translation of the Bible; the terms of natural knowledge from Bacon; the phrases of policy, war, and navigation from Raleigh; the dialect of poetry and fiction from Spencer and SIDNEY; and the diction of common life from Shakespeare, few ideas would be lost to mankind, for want of English words in which they might be expressed."

CONTENTS.

	PAGE
LIFE	1
Defence of Poesy	59
Astrophel and Stella	125
Miscellaneous Poems	211
The Lady of May	263
Valour Anatomized in a Fancy	281
Letter to Queen Elizabeth	287
A Discourse in Defence of the Earl of Leicester	305
Letters reprinted from the Sidney Papers, Seward's Biographiana, etc.	325
Letters from the Unpublished Originals in the British Museum	343

THE LIFE

OF

SIR PHILIP SIDNEY.

THE LIFE

OF

SIR PHILIP SIDNEY.

HE life of Sir Philip Sidney is one of the most faultless and interesting of which our history can boast. His ancient lineage, and varied acquirements, his gallant bearing in the field, and the melancholy close of his career while yet in the very blaze of his glory, have all contributed to endear his name, and to throw a halo around his memory. By his contemporaries he appears to have been regarded as the "glass of fashion and the mould of form," as the Bayard of England "sans peur et sans reproche," the mirror of the knighthood, and the flower of chivalry. Whether he betook himself, accordingly, to the camp, the court, or the grove, he never failed to become "the cynosure of all neighbouring eyes," the paragon whom the warrior sought to rival in the brilliancy of his exploits, and the fair to bind with love-knots to the triumphal car of beauty.

This accomplished person was born on the 29th of November, 1554, at Penshurst, in West Kent, a seat which had been granted to his ancestors by the munificence of Edward the Sixth. The mansion, and the beautiful and romantic scenery with which it is surrounded; "the broad beech, and the chestnut shade;" and

> That taller tree, which of a nut was set
> At his great birth, where all the muses met;*

have each been rendered classic by Ben Jonson, in the celebrated lines of his Forest, where he has taken occasion to introduce them. It has been supposed that the Sidney family were originally of French extraction, and that they came over into England about the reign of Henry the Second, to whom William de Sidney was chamberlain. At all events, the grandfather of Sir Philip, who was cousin, through his mother, to Charles Brandon, Duke of Suffolk, held some offices of dignity and importance in the household of Henry the Eighth, and had the honour of being celebrated among the commanders who were present at the bloody fight of Flodden. He left an only son, Henry, the parent of our author, who received the honour of knighthood, and was subsequently appointed Ambassador to France by his amiable sovereign, Edward the Sixth, with whom he was connected by the closest ties of early intimacy and regard. The characters of Sir Henry and his consort, who was eldest daughter to the ambitious and unfortunate John Dudley, Duke of Northumberland, have been thus delineated by Fulke Greville, Lord Brooke, who was the kinsman, companion, and biographer of their son. "Sir Henry Sidney," he says, "was a man of

---

* This "sacred mark," as Waller reverently denominates it, was cut down in 1768; but it will ever "live in description, and look green in song."

excellent natural wit, large heart, sweet conversation, and such a governor as sought not to make an end of the state in himself, but to plant his own ends in the prosperity of his country. On the other side, Lady Mary Sidney, as she was a woman by descent of great nobility, so was she by nature of a large ingenious spirit. Whence as it were even racked with native strengths, she chose rather to hide herself from the curious eyes of a delicate time, than come upon the stage of the world with any manner of disparagement, the mischance of sickness having cast such a veil over her excellent beauty, as the modesty of that sex doth many times upon their native and heroical spirits."

On the death of his royal master and patron, who breathed his last in his arms, Sir Henry Sidney withdrew from the court to his paternal residence at Penshurst, and thus escaped the complicated miseries in which his father-in-law was involved, by his fruitless attempt to place the Lady Jane Grey upon the throne. It was during this retirement from public life that the subject of our memoir first saw the light; and he received the name of Philip out of compliment to the lately married husband of Queen Mary, by whom Sir Henry was appointed her vice-treasurer, and advanced to other high preferments. He was afterwards nominated President of Wales in the beginning of Elizabeth's golden reign, and thence translated to the embarrassing situation of Lord Deputy of Ireland; important trusts which he discharged with the greatest ability and moderation. "What Tacitus observes of Agricola's excellent conduct in Britain," says Arthur Collins, "is matched by Sir Henry Sidney's in Ireland. In his military capacity also, considered as a Roman, he obtained the 'opima spolia,' in killing, with his own hand, James Macconnel, the principal leader of the Scots; an honour snatched but by three in that state, greedy of glory, viz: Romulus, Cassius, and Marcellus; and lastly, as a thorough-paced Roman, he consumed his patrimony in the nation's service, and was on his death buried, like Valerius, at the public expense."

The early years of his son Philip were singularly indicative of his future eminence, and were illustrated by many traits of natural genius and industry. "Of his youth," observes Lord Brooke, "I will report no other wonder but this, that though I lived with him, and knew him from a child, yet I never knew him other than a man; with such staidness of mind, lovely and familiar gravity, as carried grace and reverence above greater years. His talk ever of knowledge, and his very play tending to enrich his mind; so as even his teachers found something in him to observe, and learn, above that which they had usually read or taught. Which eminence by nature, and industry, made his worthy father style Sir Philip, in my hearing, (though I unseen,) 'lumen familiæ suæ.' "

After having remained some considerable time, and made unwonted progress in ancient learning, at the grammar-school of Shrewsbury, young Sidney was removed to Oxford, of which his maternal uncle, the famous Robert Dudley, Earl of Leicester, then held the office of chancellor; and he was entered at Christ Church in 1569, under the tuition of Dr. Thomas Thornton,[*] an elegant and accomplished scholar. Here

---

[*] This amiable divine had it recorded upon his tomb, that he was "the tutor of Sir Philip Sidney." Lord Brooke, also, had

again, as formerly, his assiduity and acuteness more than justified the exalted estimate of his talents which his juvenile precocity had excited. "He cultivated," we are informed, "not one art, or one science, but the whole circle of arts and sciences; his capacious and comprehensive mind aspiring to preëminence in every part of knowledge attainable by human genius or industry." And, not satisfied with the liberal opportunities of adding to his acquirements which his present alma mater afforded, he appears at a later period to have transferred his residence to the sister seminary of Cambridge, where he continued to prosecute his studies with unabated ardour and success.

During his abode at the university, a matrimonial alliance seems to have been proposed by Lord Leicester, between his nephew, young as he was, and the eldest daughter of Sir William Cecil, by his second wife, Mildred Coke. But it appears soon afterwards to have been broken off, by the wily old treasurer, on account of certain reasons and misunderstandings to which no clue can now be found; and this gifted lady was, in consequence, most unhappily espoused to Edward de Vere, Earl of Oxford.

In the month of May, 1572, Mr. Sidney obtained a license from the Queen to travel beyond the seas, in order that he might perfect his knowledge of the continental tongues. The period of his absence was limited to two years; and he set out on his journey, with several others of distinguished rank, in the train of the Earl of Lincoln, then Lord Admiral of England, and Am-

the following inscription placed over his grave : "Fulke Greville, servant to Queen Elizabeth, counsellor to King James, and friend to Sir Philip Sidney."

bassador Extraordinary to the Court of France. Whilst he sojourned at Paris, his deportment attracted the marked attention and approval of the reigning monarch, Charles the Ninth, who honoured him with the appointment of Gentleman in Ordinary of his chamber; but whatever regard our traveller might have entertained for this inhuman and perfidious sovereign was, we presume, sufficiently extinguished, after a very short duration, by having witnessed, and nearly suffered in, that most savage act of religious bigotry, the fiendlike massacre of St. Bartholomew. At the same time a far more grateful and flattering acquisition was made by him in the friendship and sincere respect of the gallant Henry of Navarre, which he was then so fortunate as to secure by his winning manners and address.

The disturbed and infuriated condition of the French empire at this epoch, and more particularly the danger to which all of Hugonot principles were exposed by attempting to remain within its territories, induced Mr. Sidney to hurry onwards into less perilous lands; and he therefore now passed successively through Germany, Hungary, Italy, and Belgium. He appears, from the accounts of his biographers, to have uniformly acquired the affection and permanent esteem of the many virtuous and learned persons whom he happened to encounter in the course of his journeyings; and, from among the number of these literati, he entered into the strictest bonds of amity at Frankfort, with the celebrated Hubert Languet, minister of the Elector of Saxony, and the admired companion of Melancthon, who chanced to lodge under the same roof where he had taken up his temporary abode. From this invaluable associate Sidney derived much important information relative to the government, the usages, and the laws of different nations; not to mention the various other branches of erudition in which that universal scholar was so exactly versed, a circumstance to which our author has very feelingly alluded in one of the poems to be found in the " Arcadia." We have it, moreover, on the authority of Lord Brooke, that Languet actually quitted his several functions, without prospect of hire or reward, for the purpose of becoming, as he quaintly expresses it, " a nurse of knowledge to this hopeful young gentleman," and the attached companion of the greater portion of his travels. A regular correspondence was kept up by the friends after their unavoidable separation; and the Latin epistles of the sage, which were first published at Frankfort and subsequently at Edinburgh, have received the highest encomiums for their classic purity and elegance.

Sir Philip neglected no opportunity that was offered to him on his route of increasing his stock of accomplishments, which was already so extraordinary. At Vienna he received lessons in horsemanship, and the several martial exercises of the age; at Venice he held intercourse with all the brightest spirits of the proud republic, then in the zenith of its magnificence; and at Padua he again applied himself, with all his early assiduity, to the acquisition of geometry, astronomy, and the other branches of study usually prosecuted in that yet flourishing university. Here, also, he had the singular felicity of forming an acquaintance with Tasso, who had been for some time known to the world as a distinguished cultivator of the Muses, and whose splendid and immortal effort, the "Gierusalemme Liberata," was then partly executed, and rapidly advancing towards its completion. It would be unfair, however, not to mention that this acquaintance between Sidney and the Italian bard has been entirely discredited by a rigid critic, inasmuch as Tasso appears to have been residing at Ferrara and Venice during the year in which Sir Philip was studying at Padua. But we may be pardoned, perhaps, for following Dr. Zouch in stating an incident in our author's biography which has been generally received as true.

Sidney was prevented from visiting Rome by the earnest dissuasions of his mentor, Languet—who seems to have been sadly alarmed lest the religious principles of his young correspondent should suffer any serious injury from a near intercourse with the scarlet lady, her abominations, and her active emissaries—and our author, accordingly, returned to his native country in 1575, after a separation from his relatives of exactly three years' duration.

Soon after his arrival he made his debut in fashionable life, and straightway became the delight of every circle that was favoured with his acquaintance and familiar intercourse. Indeed, " he was so essential," if we may believe Fuller, "to the English court, that it seemed maimed without his company, being a complete master both of matter and language." Queen Elizabeth herself received him with the most flattering civilities ; "and called him," says Zouch, " *her* Philip, in opposition, it is alleged, to Philip of Spain, her sister's husband." Perhaps our author was in no small degree indebted for this last mark of condescension and endearment to his close relationship, and confidential union, with the haughty favourite Leicester. But, be that as it may, Sir Philip was nominated Ambassador to

Vienna in 1576, to condole with the Emperor Rodolph on the demise of his father, Maximilian the Second; and we are farther informed, that this distinguished appointment proceeded directly from the discernment and personal suggestion of his royal mistress.

In the discharge of his diplomatic duties, which likewise embraced the formation of an alliance between all the Protestant states of Europe against the increase of Romish power, and the cruel tyranny of the Spaniards, Mr. Sidney acquitted himself with adroitness, and to the entire satisfaction of his employers; and he returned once more to England in 1577, crowned with additional laurels, and furnished with a deeper knowledge of mankind. Among the number of his new admirers, and warm congratulators on his success, he had the pleasure of enumerating Lord Burleigh, the political enemy of his family, and the experienced Sir Francis Walsingham, to whom he had been previously known in private life, and with whom friendship was ultimately cemented by the still dearer ties of kindred.

Though in the commencement of 1576, Sir Philip's connection and influence had been materially increased by the marriage of his sole surviving sister* with Henry, Earl of Pembroke; yet for several years subsequent to his return from his German embassy he appears neither

* This accomplished lady evinced no inconsiderable poetic capacity, and is well known as the subject of Ben Jonson's famous epitaph; beginning,

        Underneath this sable herse
        Lies the subject of all verse;
        Sidney's sister, Pembroke's mother:
        Death, ere thou hast killed another
        Fair, and learn'd, and good as she,
        Time shall throw a dart at thee.

to have made any advance in his public career, nor to have held any office of trust or honor in the state, except the trifling and merely nominal one of the Royal Cupbearer. It is possible, however, and indeed we gather as much from the letters of Languet, that this may have proceeded from his own temporary disinclination to active labour, and that he preferred devoting his leisure to the happy privacy which he celebrates in his poems, and to the literary exercises in which he never relaxed, or conceived for a moment that he had attained the goal of his ambition. But we must admit, at the same time, that we think it still more probable his promotion may have been retarded from the machinations of Lord Burleigh, part of whose policy it was, as we are informed by Lord Bacon, in the Cabala, that "able men should be by design and of purpose suppressed."

About the period in question, Sidney stood manfully forward to defend the character of his father, who had been charged with some act of arbitrary authority in his government of Ireland; and he not only succeeded in conciliating the Queen, over whom the enemies of his house had gained much influence, but also completely reinstated his parent in the good opinion of the virtuous and the impartial. This affair had nearly involved him in a dangerous quarrel with Thomas, Earl of Ormond, to whom he imputed the insidious practices by which her majesty's affections had been alienated; but, fortunately, the dispute terminated, when the first excitement had a little subsided, by the intervention of friends, and the mutual concessions of the parties. The danger, however, to which his father was still exposed, from the active malice of his adversaries, prevented Sidney from accepting a flattering invitation, which he received in 1578, from John Casimir, the Count Palatine of the Rhine,* to join him in his meditated warfare against the King of Spain in the Netherlands. The venerable Lord Deputy fully appreciated the affectionate solicitude which had induced his beloved defender to remain in England; and he thus speaks of Sir Philip in a letter to his second son, Robert, with all that fondness and pride which the possession of such an offspring might well excite and justify. "Follow the advice," he says, "of your most loving brother, who, in loving you, is comparable with me, or exceedeth me. Imitate his virtues, exercises, studies, and actions; he is a rare ornament of his age, the very formular that all well-disposed young gentlemen of our court do form also their manners and life by. In truth, I speak it without flattery of him or myself, he hath the most virtues that ever I found in any man. I saw him not these six months, little to my comfort. You may hear from him with more ease than from me. In your travels, these documents I will give you, not as mine, but his practices. Seek the knowledge of the estate of every prince, court, and city, that you pass through. Address yourself to the company, to learn this of the elder sort, and yet neglect not the younger. By the one you shall gather learning, wisdom, and knowledge; by the other, acquaintance, languages, and exercise. Once again I say, imitate him."

* This prince visited England in the autumn of 1578, for the purpose of gaining supporters to his hitherto unfortunate cause, the defence of the United Provinces. He was accompanied on this occasion by Hubert Languet, who was principally induced to take the journey, that he might once more enjoy the society and conversation of his friend Sidney.

It is pleasing to remark that Robert Sidney did not derogate from his illustrious parentage, or show himself unworthy of his brother's regard. He was an able envoy, and a gallant soldier. His bravery at the battle of Zutphen procured him the honour of knighthood from his uncle Leicester, on the 7th of October, 1586. He was advanced to the dignity of Lord Sidney, Baron of Penshurst, on the accession of James the First to the English throne; and was subsequently created Viscount L'Isle in 1605; and elevated to the earldom of Leicester in 1618.*

In 1572, Catherine de Medicis had proposed joining England to France, by forming a matrimonial union between Elizabeth and her son Henry, the Duke of Anjou. This project, however, was for the time counteracted by the zealous efforts of the Hugonot chiefs; but it was not long afterwards revived by the emissaries of France, though a new suitor was now brought forward in the person of the Duke of Alençon, the youngest son of Catherine, who subsequently succeeded to the title of Anjou, on the elevation of his brother to the throne of Poland. To this match Elizabeth herself, whether from policy or inclination, at first lent no unwilling ear; and the circumstance filled the realm with undisguised alarm and distress. The Protestant party in the kingdom, how discordant soever on other topics, unanimously combined in a strenuous opposition to the scheme. Both Burleigh and Leicester covertly, and Sir Walter Mildmay, Sir Ralph Sadler, and numerous influential persons openly, lent their cordial

* There was also another brother, Thomas, who rose to the rank of colonel, and whose name is handed down as being a very valiant commander.

endeavours to break off the treaty, and to bring disgrace upon its supporters; and Sir Philip Sidney addressed a remonstrance to the powerful and "throned vestal," in which he ably pointed out the evils that were likely to arise from a connection with the unpopular house of Valois. This production, bearing the date 1580, which is alleged to have had the effect of diverting the Queen from her intentions, has received a very lofty meed of praise from Mr. Hume, and has been more recently characterized by that delightful writer, Miss Lucy Aiken, as "at once the most eloquent and the most courageous piece of that nature which the age can boast. Every important view of the subject," she adds, " is comprised in this letter, which is long, but at the same time so condensed in style, and so skilfully compacted as to matter, that it well deserves to be read entire; and must lose materially either by abridgment or omission."

The next affair of consequence that our hero became engaged in, was one in which he was eminently qualified to gain the noblest distinctions. A joust with sword and lance was celebrated in 1580, in the presence of Elizabeth, and all the retainers of her court. Philip, Earl of Arundel, and Sir William Drury were the challengers; Edward Vere, Earl of Oxford, Frederick, the fourth Lord Windsor, Mr. Philip Sidney, and fourteen other gallants, the defenders. What farther part Sidney took in this great trial of skill has been nowhere recorded; but we may easily imagine that *he* would not pass unnoticed in the tilt-yard, who has been described by his contemporary, Spenser, as

──────────── the president
Of nobleness and chevalree.

All we can learn, however, relative to the conclusion of the combat is, that the victory was adjudged, by her majesty, to the Earl of Oxford.

With this haughty peer, who has been already mentioned as having become the husband of Sir Philip's destined bride, Anne Cecil, our author was about this time involved in a quarrel which attracted the deepest attention, not only over England, but likewise in every court in Europe. The story is thus circumstantially related in the scarce and curious volume of Lord Brooke, and is a remarkable instance of the aristocratic privileges, and pride of place, that were then conceded to our magnates.

"Sidney," says his lordship, "being one day at tennis, a peer of this realm, born great, greater by alliance, and superlative in the prince's favour, abruptly came into the tennis-court, and, speaking out of these three paramount authorities, he forgot to intreat that which he could not legally command. When, by the encounter of a steady object, finding unrespectiveness in himself (though a great lord) not respected by this princely spirit, he grew to expostulate more roughly. The returns of which style coming still from an understanding heart, that knew what was due to itself, and what it ought to others, seemed (through the mist of my lord's passions, swollen with the wind of his faction then reigning) to provoke in yielding. Whereby the less amazement or confusion of thoughts he stirred up in Sir Philip, the more shadows this great lord's own mind was possessed with; till at last with rage (which is ever ill-disciplined) he commands them to depart the court. To this Sir Philip temperately answers, that if his lordship had been pleased to express desire in milder characters, perchance he might have led out those, that he should now find would not be driven out with any scourge of fury. This answer (like a bellows) blowing up the sparks of excess already kindled, made my lord scornfully call Sir Philip by the name of puppy. In which progress of heat, as the tempest grew more and more vehement within, so did their hearts breathe out their perturbations in more loud and shrill accent. The French commissioners, unfortunately, had that day audience in those private galleries whose windows looked into the tennis-court. They instantly drew all to this tumult; every sort of quarrels sorting well with their humours, especially this. Which Sir Philip perceiving, and rising with inward strength, by the prospect of a mighty faction against him, asked my lord, with a loud voice, that which he heard clearly enough before. Who (like an echo, that still multiplies by reflections) repeated this epithet of puppy the second time. Sir Philip resolving in one answer to conclude both the attentive hearers, and passionate actor, gave my lord a lie impossible (as he averred) to be retorted; in respect all the world knows, puppies are gotten by dogs, and children by men. Hereupon those glorious inequalities of fortune in his lordship were put to a kind of pause, by a precious inequality of nature in this gentleman. So that they both stood silent a while, like a dumb show in a tragedy, till Sir Philip, sensible of his own wrong, the foreign and factious spirits that attended, and yet, even in this question between him and his superior, tender to his country's honour, with some words of sharp accent, led the way abruptly out of the tennis-court, as if so unexpected an accident were not fit to be decided any further in that place. Whereof the great lord making another sense, continues his play, without any advantage of reputation, as by the standard of humours in those times it was conceived. — A day Sir Philip remains in suspense, when hearing nothing of, or from the lord, he sends a gentleman of worth to awake him out of his trance; wherein the French would assuredly think any pause, if not death, yet a lethargy of true honour in both. This stirred a resolution in his lordship to send Sir Philip a challenge. Notwithstanding, these thoughts in the great lord wandered so long between glory, anger, and inequality of state, that the lords of her majesty's council took notice of the differences, commanded peace, and laboured a reconciliation between them. But needlessly in one respect, and bootlessly in another. The great lord being (as it should seem) either not hasty to adventure many inequalities against one, or inwardly satisfied with the progress of his own acts; Sir Philip, on the other side, confident he neither had nor would lose, or let fall, any thing of his right. Which her majesty's council quickly perceiving, recommended this work to herself. — The Queen, who saw that by the loss or disgrace of either she could gain nothing, presently undertakes Sir Philip; and, like an excellent monarch, lays before him the difference in degree between earls and gentlemen; the respect inferiors owed to their superiors; and the necessity in princes to maintain their own creations, as the degrees descending between the people's licentiousness, and the anointed sovereignty of crowns; how the gentleman's neglect of the nobility taught the peasant to insult upon both. — Whereunto Sir Philip, with such reverence as became him, replied: first, that place was never intended for privilege to wrong; witness herself, who, how sovereign soever she were by throne, birth, education, and nature, yet was she content to cast her own affections into the same moulds her subjects did, and govern all her rights by their laws. Again, he besought her majesty to consider that although he [Oxford] were a great lord by birth, alliance, and grace, yet he was no lord over him [Sir Philip]; and, therefore, the difference of degrees between free-men, could not challenge any other homage than precedency. And by her father's act (to make a princely wisdom become the more familiar) he did instance the government of King Henry the Eighth, who gave the gentry free and unreserved appeal to his feet, against the oppression of the grandees; and found it wisdom, by the stronger corporation in number, to keep down the greater in power; inferring else, that if they should unite, the over-grown might be tempted, by still coveting more, to fall, as the angels did, by affecting equality with their Maker."

In this spirited manner did our author exhibit his sense of his own dignity, and vindicate the rights and independence of an English commoner. Neither was her majesty offended by the bold truths which he uttered; and we are further informed by Collins, the editor of the Sidney Papers, that Sir Philip did not think it proper to obey her commands, but rather retired for a season to the abode of the Countess of Pembroke at Wilton, where he whiled away his time in planning and composing the Arcadia. This work, however, was not completed, nor made public, during his life; but was collected together, after his decease, and given to the press, by his sister, and hence it obtained the name of the Countess of Pembroke's Arcadia. It has even been stated, that, had he survived, "his design was to have arranged the whole anew; and it is asserted on the authority of Ben Jonson, in his conversation with Mr. Drummond of Hawthornden in Scotland, in the year 1619, that he intended to change the subject by celebrating the prowess and military deeds of King Arthur."* Whatever truth there may be in the latter part of this anecdote, there can be no doubt that the Arcadia suffered severely in being deprived of the finishing touches and corrections of its author; and, indeed, it is not a little wonderful, considering all the disadvantages under which it laboured, that we find it so perfect and so comparatively faultless as it now appears; for he tells us himself, in his dedication to the Countess, that it was written on loose sheets of paper, most of it in her presence, and the rest sent to her in the same way as fast as it was done; and he is alleged to have requested, with considerable earnestness, on his death-bed, that this " charm of ages," as Dr. Young rightly calls it, might be committed wholly to the flames.†

* Both Milton and Dryden also intended to have made the achievements of King Arthur and his heroes, the first great theme of their song. These mighty warriors, therefore, must be considered as peculiarly unfortunate in having become the victims of Sir Richard Blackmore's graceless muse.

† " They that knew him well," says Lord Brooke, " will truly confess this Arcadia of his to be, both in form and matter, as much inferior to that unbounded spirit of his, as the industry and images of other men's works are many times raised above the writers' capacities; and besides acknowledge, that howsoever he could not choose but give them aspersions of spirit and learning from the father, yet that they were scribbled rather as pamphlets, for the entertainment of time and friends, than any account of himself to the world. Because if his purpose had been to leave his memory in books, I am confident, in the right use of logick, philosophy, history, and poesie, nay even in the most ingenious of mechanical

Such was the origin and history of a production which was received, at the epoch that gave it birth, with the most inordinate favour; but which has since been subjected to much contradictory, and some sneering and unamiable, criticism. This is partly to be attributed to the peculiar nature of the work itself, and partly to the exaggerated expectations of the individuals who have undertaken to examine it. Yet it is proper to mention, that while on the side of praise we find arrayed nearly all the brightest ornaments of our literature, on the other we discover Horace Walpole,* and Mr. Hazlitt, almost unsupported and alone. This is a powerful fact; and, perhaps, exhibits as much unanimity as can reasonably be expected in lauding the merits of any author, however distinguished and deserving.

arts, he would have shewed such tracts of a searching and judicious spirit, as the professors of every faculty would have striven no less for him than the seven cities did to have Homer of their sept. But the truth is, his end was not writing, even while he wrote, nor his knowledge moulded for tables and schools; but both his wit and understanding bent upon his heart, to make himself, and others, not in words or opinion, but in life and action, good and great."

* The Quarterly reviewer of Dr. Zouch's Memoirs of Sidney gives this peevish "catcher of passing ridicules," as he describes himself, the following severe and richly-merited chastisement. "The universal favourite of this age," says the writer referred to, " was Sir Philip Sidney, the most accomplished character in our history, till Lord Orford startled the world by paradoxes, which attacked the fame established by two centuries. Singularity of opinion, vivacity of ridicule, and polished epigrams in prose, were the means by which this nobleman sought distinction; but he had something in his composition more predominant than his wit; a cold unfeeling disposition, which contemned literary men at the moment that his heart secretly panted to share their fame; while his peculiar habits of society deadened every impression of grandeur in the human character."

The Arcadia, with some admixture of the heroic, was an imitation of the pastoral romance; one of the earliest forms of prose fiction which was cultivated by the ancients. Even the stories of chivalry, exquisitely described by Ben Jonson, as " niches filled with statues to invite young valours forth," amid all the rough turmoil and warlike prowess in which they revel, were not devoid of stray scenes, in which rural beauty and innocence were duly appreciated and represented. The Eclogues of Virgil, of which the darkest eras were not ignorant, are supposed by Mr. Dunlop to have been mainly instrumental in fostering this taste; and his idea is materially corroborated by the circumstance that the pastoral compositions of the middle ages usually appeared under a similar form with the work of the Augustan poet. The Troubadours and Trouveurs, however, were by no means successful in this style of writing; their love adventures were full of sameness, and their delineations of nature were generally pointless and affected. It was, therefore, an enterprise of small difficulty for Boccaccio to excel their feeble attempts in his prose Idilium of Ameto, which the historian of fiction conceives to have been the prototype of the Arcadia of Sannazzaro, "written towards the end of the fifteenth century, and which, though it cannot be itself considered as a pastoral romance, yet appears to have first opened the field to that species of composition." This production, it would seem, was, like the Consolations of Boëthius, a combination of prose and verse; and, similar in that respect, became the form of all succeeding narratives of the same class. But, as this early model was totally destitute of any fable that could create an interest for the characters introduced, much room was left for the improvements and perfecting ingenuity of later authors. This desideratum, accordingly, was in part supplied by George of Montemayor in his Diana, one of the few precious tomes spared by the curate in the friendly conflagration of Don Quixote's library, and from certain incidents in which, Shakespeare most probably borrowed his plot of the Twelfth Night, and the story of Proteus and Julia in the Two Gentlemen of Verona. Beaumont and Fletcher are likewise imagined to have derived from the same source, the first conceptions which they wrought up into the celebrated drama of Philaster. By Gaspard Gil Polo, Cervantes in his Galetea, and numerous other continuators and imitators of Montemayor, the pastoral romance was considerably advanced in point of consistency and keeping; while Honre d'Urfé* in France, and Sir Philip Sidney in England, contributed many additional charms, and extended its popularity still more widely by the novel attractions with which they adorned it.

The Arcadia of the latter, with all the imperfections that can be laid to its charge, is a rich mint of deep feeling and of varied excellence. It displays a fancy, it is

* D'Urfé's book, according to Boileau, was an accurate recital of the author's personal gallantries and adventures in love, the various real characters being disguised under the names of shepherds and shepherdesses. "The style," he adds, "was florid and animated, and the characters imagined with skill, and admirably diversified and sustained. The popularity of this publication gave rise to many imitations. Tales were rapidly produced, consisting of ten or twelve bulky volumes apiece. The most popular were those of Gomberville, Calprenade, Desmarais, and Scuderi. But endeavouring to improve upon their original, and to elevate their characters, these writers fell into the most inconceivable puerility. The world, however, ran mad after these absurdities."

true, which often ran riot amid the diversity of its creations, and a taste that sometimes erred from the infinite seductions to which it was exposed. But the work invariably makes atonement by the stately eloquence of its descriptions, and by the delicious incense which it offered up to the cause of virtue and true heroism.

"Against the criticisms of its detractors," says an elegant and enthusiastic writer in the Retrospective Review, "the best defence will be found in the production itself, to which we confidently refer our readers. That it has many faults we do not deny; but they are faults to which all the writers of his time were subject, and generally in a greater degree. It has been said that his language is very quaint; but we may safely ask, what author is there of his age in whose language there is in reality so little of quaintness? Let us remember a work which the Arcadia contributed more than any thing else to consign to oblivion; a work which for a long time was in high fashion and celebrity; and the style of which is, perhaps, more elaborately and systematically bad, than that of any work in the whole extent of literature. We mean Lilly's Euphues. With it let us compare Sir Philip Sidney's Arcadia — the style he introduced, with the style he contributed to banish — and we shall then regard him as the restorer of the purity of our language, and as meriting our eternal gratitude and respect. The language of the Arcadia is, indeed, as much superior to that of the Euphues, as is the varied melody of the nightingale to the monstrous harshness of the jay. — Another radical fault in the Arcadia, is the defect of the species of writing of which it is a part — the heroic and pastoral romance, either disjunctively or commixed. But, so far from lowering, this primary disadvantage ought rather to increase our admiration of his genius, who has been able to give attraction to so preposterous a kind of composition. Who would not applaud the ingenuity of him, who could engraft with success the apricot on the sloe, or the nectarine on the crab? When we see a structure irregular and clumsy, but built of massy gold; however we may censure its defective plan, yet surely we must admire the richness of its materials. ———— The feeling which the perusal of the Arcadia excites, is a calm and pensive pleasure, at once full, tranquil, and exquisite. The satisfaction we experience is not unsimilar to that of meditation by moonlight, when the burning fervor of the day has subsided, and every thing which might confuse or disorder our contemplation is at rest. All is peaceful and quiet, and clear as a transparency. The silvery glittering of the language, the unearthly loftiness of its heroes, the etheriality of their aspirations, and the sweet tones of genuine and unstudied feeling which it sounds forth, all combine to imbue our souls with a soft and pleasing melancholy. We feel ourselves under the spell of an enchanter, in the toils of a witchery, too gratifying to our senses to be willingly shaken off, and therefore resign ourselves without resistance to its influence. By it we are removed to other and more delightful climes; by it we are transported to the shady groves of Arcady and the bowery recesses of Tempe; to those heavenly retreats, where music and melody were wafted with every sighing of the breeze along their cool and translucid streams. We find ourselves in the midst of the golden age, with glimpses of the armed grandeur of the age of chivalry. We find ourselves in a period of conflicting sights and emotions, when all that was lovely in the primitive simplicity of the one, and all that was fascinating in the fantastic magnificence of the other, were united and mingled together; where the rustic festivity of the shepherd was succeeded by the imposing splendour of the tournament, and the voice of the pastoral pipe and oaten reed were joined with the sound of the trumpet and the clashing of the lance."

The least defensible blemishes of the Arcadia are the flatness of its comic humour, and the truly mediocre character of the poetry with which it is interspersed. The latter fault, however, as may very easily be perceived, proceeded less from a want of talent or a deficiency in poetic temperament, than from the inveterate and studied affectation of the author. Sidney was too fond of imitating the Italian conceits, and the extravagant devices with regard to versification, which were then so much in vogue; and in his attempts to introduce the Greek and Latin measures into our language, in which, by the way, he was countenanced by no less a personage than Sir Walter Raleigh, he was not a whit more successful than a recent experimentalist in the same line. His poems of this sort seem throughout, to borrow a picturesque description of Spenser's, "either like a lame gosling that draweth one leg after her, or like a lame dog that holdeth one leg up."

Yet these, his weakest points, are not to be judged with the correct severity of modern criticism, but are rather to be palliated and excused as the common foibles of the age in which he lived. We learn from Dr. Farmer's excellent Essay on Shakespeare, that "Gabriel Harvey* desired only to be epitaphed, *the inventor of*

---

* Gabriel Harvey was " the most special friend " of both Sidney and Spenser, and is supposed to have been the medium through *the English hexameter*, and for a while every one would be halting on Roman feet; but the ridicule of Joseph Hall, in one of his satires, and the reasoning of Daniel in his Defence of Rhyme, against Campion, presently reduced us to our old Gothic."* Even Spenser was seriously affected by the prevailing mania for dactyles and spondees after the manner of the ancients. "I am of late," he says in one of his letters to Harvey, "more in love with my English versifying than with rhyming." By versifying he means here adapting English verse to Latin prosody; and he takes occasion, in the same epistle, to pass a high encomium on the unmelodious numbers of his friend.

The very passages in Sir Philip's volumes, accordingly, which we now reprobate most severely, were, perhaps, those which attracted the greatest amount of contemporary admiration; and this conjecture, indeed, is pretty clearly established by the fact, that we find Sir W. Temple, in an age far more scrupulous and advanced, declaring, without qualification, our author to be "the greatest poet and the noblest genius of any that have left writings behind them, or published in

---

which these two great men first became acquainted. He was a fellow of Trinity Hall, Cambridge, and took a Doctor of Law's degree in 1585.

* This absurd innovation was also humorously exposed by Nash in his Four Letters confuted, 1592. "The hexameter verse," he says, "I grant to be a gentleman of an ancient house, (so is many an English beggar,) yet this clime of ours he cannot thrive in; our speech is too craggy for him to set his plough in; he goes twitching and hopping in our language like a man running upon quagmires, up the hill in one syllable, and down the dale in another; retaining no part of that stately smooth gait, which he vaunts himself amongst the Greeks and Latins."

our's or any other language; a person born capable not only of forming the greatest idea, but leaving the noblest example, if the length of his life had been equal to the excellence of his wit and his virtues." Such was the calm decision of a man of genius when all the fleeting prejudices in Sidney's favour must have entirely passed away. To this we may add that the critics of his own time undertook to illustrate the whole art of rhetoric from his pages; and that from a perusal of them, both our elder and our modern poets have derived many of their happiest and their sweetest conceptions.

"The Arcadia," says Mr. Dunlop, "was much read and admired by Waller and Cowley, and has been obviously imitated in many instances by our early dramatists. The story of Plangus in the Arcadia is the origin of Shirley's Andromana, or Merchant's Wife. That part of the pastoral where Pyrocles agrees to command the Helots, seems to have suggested those scenes of the Two Gentlemen of Verona, in which Valentine leagues himself with the outlaws. An episode in the second book of the Arcadia, where a king of Paphlagonia, whose eyes had been put out by a bastard son, is described as led by his rightful heir, whom he had cruelly used for the sake of his wicked brother, has furnished Shakespeare with the underplot concerning Gloster and his two sons, in King Lear. There are in the romance the same description of a bitter storm, and the same request of the father that he might be led to the summit of a cliff, which occur in that pathetic tragedy.— The Arcadia was also, as we learn from Milton, the companion of the prison hours of Charles the First, whom that poet, in his Iconoclastes, reproaches with having stolen the prayer of Pamela, to insert in his

Ikon Basilikè. But whether the King actually fell into this inadvertence, or whether his antagonist procured the interpolation of the passage, that he might enjoy an opportunity of reviling his sovereign for impiety, and of taunting him with literary plagiarism, has been the subject of much controversy among the biographers of the English bard."

In 1581, the assistance of Mr. Sidney was warmly solicited by Don Antonio, Prior of Crato, who had laid claim, not long previously, to the contested crown of Portugal, and actually assumed the vacant title of King; but his application was disregarded, though couched in terms the most flattering, and our author preferred sitting in Parliament for his native county of Kent. His name appears at this period as a member of a committee to frame such laws as would secure the kingdom against the Pope and his adherents.

He was engaged, during the same year, in a splendid military spectacle, which was exhibited in compliment to the ambassadors of the Duke of Anjou, who had perseverance enough again to cross the Channel, that they might renew their royal master's earnest overtures of marriage. On this occasion the Earl of Arundel, Lord Windsor, Mr. Philip Sidney, and Mr. Fulke Greville, presented themselves as champions, and challenged all comers to the combat. The equipments of our hero, and his associates, have been minutely described in Stow's continuation of Old Hollinshed, and are well worthy of a perusal by all those who take delight in the antique splendour of the tournament, or whose fancy loves to dwell on the forgotten usages of chivalry.

The gaiety of the English court was soon after increased by a personal visit from the amatory French grandee; but, though he was received by the Queen with the most gracious condescension, he experienced in the end a decisive refusal of his offers, which, perhaps, proceeded considerably more from the advisers of Elizabeth, than from her own heart. There can certainly be no doubt that her vanity, at the least, would have derived its dearest gratification from a longer continuance of her princely suitor's assiduities; for her highness's characteristics appear to have been thoroughly understood, and summed up, by Thuanus, when he remarks, "ambiri, coli ob formam, et amoribus, etiam inclinata jam ætate, videri voluit." The reasons of state, however, were too manifold and too urgent to permit her coquetry the unlimited indulgence which it craved; and the Duke was attended on his return to the Netherlands, in the course of a few months, by the Earl of Leicester, Lord Hunsdon, Mr. Philip Sidney, Sir Walter Raleigh, and a numerous and illustrious train of nobles and gentlemen, who accompanied him the length of Antwerp, by the special command of her majesty.

It is supposed, that for a season immediately following the stirring events which we have just been recording, Sir Philip Sidney devoted himself to a life of contemplative retirement. Part of the fruits of his meditation was his much celebrated Defence of Poesy, one of the noblest tributes ever offered to the allurements of the Muse. It belongs, in fact, to the small number of those happy creations which he alone could either have produced or devised, who has been touched and purified with the sacred fire of true genius. Originally designed as an answer to certain diatribes of the Puritans — a sect which was then springing rapidly into notice, and beginning to signalize itself by an austere and fierce aversion to all the elegant recreations of society and of mind — it remains an imperishable monument of the digested learning of its author, and of the engaging facility with which he could turn his talents to account. It has been aptly described, in his own words, as the "sweet food of sweetly uttered knowledge;" as the outpouring and register of those "high-erected thoughts" which are solely to be found seated in their purity "in a heart of courtesy." At the same time it contains few of those mannerisms, and studied affectations of his day, with which, it must be confessed, his larger work is often deformed. This is, on the contrary, a plain and practical treatise, seeking above all things to carry conviction by its illustrations and its arguments, and making fancy and ornament entirely subservient to the cause of persuasion and of truth. Yet the imaginative genius of the author frequently bursts forth in all its splendour, and strews his didactic path with a galaxy of the most brilliant conceptions. He seems here to follow religiously the memorable advice with which his muse favoured him on another occasion — "look in thy heart and write."

Viewing this production in a different light, it acquires an additional interest. It was, as it were, the flourish of trumpets, or the richly varied overture "in linked beauties long drawn out," which preceded the appearance of Shakespeare, and his fellow bards, on the dramatic scene.* It smoothed down the asperities of feel-

---

* Though the first edition of the Defence did not issue from the press till 1595, there is every reason to suppose, as Mr. Collier has remarked, that the Arcadia, and all Sir Philip's other productions, were handed about in manuscript long before their formal publication; since we find in Puttenham's Art of Poetry, which was

ing with which their performances might have been assailed by a powerful religious party in the state, and prepared the way for those magnificent effusions of human intellect which have secured to the reign of Elizabeth one of the most glorious pages in the records of immortality. Previous to its publication; if we may implicitly credit Sidney's account, both poetry and its professors had been reduced to the lowest form of degradation in the popular esteem ; and some efficient auxiliary was required to secure them a patient and unbiassed audience, and to elevate them into that estimation which was necessary to give them a chance of success. This our author achieved for them by the convincing eloquence of his discourse,* and he has reaped his reward in the imperishable renown of ages. To quote, indeed,

printed in 1589, a reference to the Arcadia, which was not printed till the year following; and we have Sir John Harrington complaining, in his translation of the Orlando Furioso, of a sonnet which had been "left out in the printed book."

* Thomas Churchyard published, in 1595, a performance which he entitled " A praise of poetrie : some notes thereof drawn out of the Apologie," (Sidney's Defence was originally so called,) " the noble-minded knight, Sir Philip Sidney, wrate." This tractate has been reprinted in the Censura Literaria, vols. 3 and 4 ; and contains the following lines in allusion to the effects which our author's reasonings had produced.

> Good poets were in high esteem
>   When learning grew in price ;
> Their virtue and their verse did seem
>   A great rebuke to vice.
>
> With blunt, base people, of small sense,
>   They fall now in disdain ;
> But Sidney's book in their defence,
>   Did raise them up again :

the several eulogies of this Defence's merits, would be to cite every author who has mentioned it since its gifted composer lived. Even Walpole, the most inveterate detractor from Sir Philip's deserts, found nothing in it against which to level his ever-ready sarcasm. The scholar and the critic have been equally animated in its praises; and while the one has recommended it as being replete with Greek and Roman erudition, the other has held it up as a perfect model, at once of expression, and of logical method. "It is a work of love," says a reviewer in the first number of the Quarterly, "and the luminous order of criticism is embellished by all the graces of poetry." "As an essay on the nature, objects, and effects of poetry as an art," declares an able journal — the Retrospective, "it is beyond comparison the most complete work of the kind which we possess, even up to the present day. The truth is, that the Defence of Poesy has formed the staple of all the thousand and one dissertations on that art, with which our magazines and reviews have teemed during the last twenty years." "There are few rules and few excellencies of poetry, especially epic and dramatic," observes Dr. Joseph Warton, "but what Sir Philip Sidney, who had diligently read the best Latin and Italian commentaries on Aristotle's poetics, has here pointed out and illustrated with true taste and judgment."

Neither was the contemporary applause which attended the appearance of this tractate, less fervent than

> And sets them next divines in rank,
>   As members meet and fit
> To strike the world's blind boldness blank,
>   And whet the bluntest wit.

the effusions of more modern panegyric. Ben Jonson has coupled Sidney's name with that of the eloquent Hooker, as "great masters of wit and language, in whom all vigour of invention, and strength of judgment, met;" and the Defence is thus particularly alluded to in the Cambridge Lacrymæ, a series of elegies which the untimely death of Sir Philip called forth from that learned retreat of poesy and science. —

> Te Musa excoluit, finxit tibi pectora Virtus,
>   O decus, ô patriæ stella (Philippe) tuæ.
> Quid Musis poteras, docuit Defensio Musæ,
>   Arcadiæ docuit fabrica texta novæ.

To these may be subjoined a few perhaps not unjustly forgotten verses by George Wither, in the same laudatory strain, —

> This in Defence of Poesie to say
> I am compel'd, because that at this day
> Weakness and ignorance have wrong'd it sore:
> But what need any man therein speak more
> Than divine Sidney hath already done?
> For whom (though he deceas'd ere I begun)
> I have oft sighed, and bewail'd my fate
> That brought me forth so many years too late
> To view that worthy. —

Mr. Sidney applied by letter to Lord Burleigh, in the month of January, 1582, to be conjoined in the mastership of the ordnance with his gallant uncle, the Earl of Warwick; but we are informed that his solicitation in this instance was devoid of success, even although her majesty yielded "a gracious hearing unto it." It is by no means improbable, as we have already surmised, that the very uncommon abilities and accomplishments which our author possessed, may have been pleaded as a reason for not granting him any appointment whatever under the crown; at least we find these very matters seriously stated by Elizabeth, as a cause why Lord Bacon had been impeded in his professional advancement.*

In the course of the same year, overtures were made to his father by the persons at the helm of affairs, to undertake once more the administration of government

---

* "She did acknowledge," says the Earl of Essex in a letter to Mr. Francis Bacon, "you had a great wit, and an excellent gift of speech, and much other good learning. But in law, she rather thought you could make show, to the utmost of your knowledge, than that you were deep."—"If it be asked," observes Bishop Hurd, in remarking on this passage, "how the Queen came to form this conclusion, the answer is plain. It was from Mr. Bacon's having a great wit, an excellent gift of speech, and much other good learning."—Speaking of his friend Sidney, Lord Brooke has the following observations: "Nature guiding his eyes to his native country, he found greatness of worth and place, counterpoised there by the arts of power and favour; the stirring spirits sent abroad, as fuel to keep the flame far off, and the effeminate made judges of danger which they fear, and honour which they understand not." Spenser has also described the situation of a court suitor in the reign of Elizabeth, in stanzas which are too vivid not to have been the result of a harassing personal experience.

> Full little knowest thou, that hast not tried,
> What hell it is in suing long to bide,
> To lose good days that might be better spent,
> To waste long nights in pensive discontent,
> To speed to-day, to be put back to-morrow,
> To feed in hope, to pine with fear and sorrow;
> To have thy prince's grace, yet want her peers,
> To have thy asking, yet wait many years;
> To fret thy soul with crosses and with care;
> To eat thy heart through comfortless despair;
> To fawn, to crouch, to wait, to ride, to run,
> To spend, to give, to want,— to be undone.

in Ireland, which he had formerly discharged with such prudence and ability; and that venerable worthy would have had no objection again to burthen his advanced age with the irksome toils of office, provided his son would have consented to accompany him as an assistant, and put himself in the way of obtaining some reversionary advantage from the appointment. Yet, though the offer appears to have been increased in attraction by prospects of peerages and grants, it does not seem to have inspired Sir Philip with any inclination to embrace it.

During the subsequent year, our author became united in marriage to the only surviving daughter of his old friend Sir Francis Walsingham. She is mentioned as being a lady possessed of many amiable qualities, and as distinguished besides by "extraordinary handsomeness." It is probable, however, that she never acquired much more than the respect of her husband. His affections were long previously devoted to the Lady Penelope Devereux, the daughter of Walter, Earl of Essex; and a matrimonial treaty had at one time proceeded so far between their parents, as to lead Sir Edward Waterhouse, the common friend of the two families, to say, in a letter to Sir Henry Sidney, that "the breaking off of this match, if the default be on your parts, will turn to more dishonour than can be repaired with any other marriage in England." Notwithstanding this expostulation, however, broken off most certainly it was; but on which side the blame lay, if any really existed, it is utterly impossible, at this distance of time, to ascertain. One thing is pretty evident, that Sir Henry Sidney could never have been cordially disposed to the alliance; for we find him declaring, in a private communication to

Lord Leicester, where he has occasion to allude to Essex and the Earl of Ormond, that his correspondent should have found the former " as violent an enemy as his heart, power, and cunning would have served him to have been; and for their malice, I take God to record, I could brook neither of them both."

The Lady Devereux was afterwards married to Robert, Lord Rich; and it was she whom our author sought to commemorate under the feigned names of Philoclea in the Arcadia, and Stella in his poems of Astrophel. For the mode in which he has acquitted himself of his task in this latter instance, as far as moral feeling and propriety are concerned, Sidney has incurred the indignation and severe censure of Mr. Godwin, who, while he maintains that the series of songs and sonnets embodies " some of the finest examples in this species of composition that the world can produce," cannot tolerate the " making a public exhibition of such addresses to a married female, speaking contemptuously of the husband, and employing all the arts of poetical seduction to contaminate the mind, of the woman he adores." Mr. Godwin refers particularly to the fifty-second sonnet, and to the second and tenth songs, for the most flagrant specimens of the " grossness and carnality" which he considers himself bound to reprehend. These stanzas we have read over again and again, and though we imagine we may arrogate to ourselves as acute moral perceptions as belong to the apologist of Mary Wolstonecraft, we cannot perceive any of that shocking sensuality against which his virtuous fervour has been aroused and directed. No criminal intercourse was ever imputed to the parties; neither did their conduct or flirtations excite any sentiments of reproof in the age when they occurred. Nay, Sir Philip himself declares, that he "cannot brag of word, much less of deed," by which his charmer could be construed to have encouraged his flame; and the unhappy course of their loves, and the notoriously brutal character of Lord Rich, may be received as some excuse, if not as a perfect justification of the passionate, yet rarely indecorous, regard, which Sidney continued to express in his verses for the object of his earliest and most vehement attachment.*

But, though we cannot admit for a moment that the poetry of Sidney is debased by the vile alloy of licentiousness and pruriency, we are not blind to many other vices with which it may most justly be charged. Our author was styled, by Raleigh, the English Petrarch; and without doubt he derived many of his faults as well as excellencies from the bard of Arezzo, whom he frequently imitated both in his manner and in his exaggerated turn of expression. It was from this foreign prototype that he was probably smitten with the love of antithesis and conceit, and the other fashionable absurdities in which our best writers of sonnets then abounded. In seeking to embellish their essays by the choicest gems of thought, they were caught by far-fetched allusions and incongruous metaphors. As Sir Philip himself has felicitously enough described it, "Invention, Nature's child, fled step-dame Study's blows," and those who were thus deserted, strove to remedy their misfortune by

> Ennobling new-found tropes with problems old;
> Or, with strange similes enriched each line,
> Of herbs, or beasts, which Ind' or Afric hold.

* Lady Rich was married to a second husband, Charles Blount, Earl of Devonshire.

In this way they completely destroyed the chasteness and simplicity of their compositions, without adding aught of value to their brilliancy and effect; for one may almost apply to these conceits what Lord Bacon has observed of the discourses of philosophers on government, that "they are as the stars, which give little light because they are so high." But our author liberally compensated for his occasional aberrations from true taste, by frequent displays of a degree of elegance and facility to which few of his contemporaries, in the same species of writing, have succeeded in establishing any claim. At the same time he uniformly speaks of his own proficiency in the exalted art of song, with a modesty no less amiable than it is disarming to critical severity. And, if his sonnets possessed no other merit, it is in them that his various feelings, as they arose in his heart, are distinctly to be traced, and that we learn the little peculiarities by which his heroic character was discriminated and shaded. It is there that we are told of his constitutional melancholy, inherited in all likelihood from his mother; and of the "abstracted guise" which he was wont unconsciously to fall into in the largest companies, whereby many had been induced to suppose that he was wholly possessed by egotism and "bubbling pride"—a charge which he takes the opportunity most pointedly to deny, while he pleads guilty to a headlong ambition that made him "oft his best friends overpass."

On the 13th of January, 1583, our author received the honour of knighthood, at Windsor, as proxy to his acquaintance and admirer, John Casimir, the Prince Palatine of the Rhine, who was then invested with the most noble Order of the Garter.

We find Sidney engaged in 1584, in defending his uncle Leicester against one of the most inveterate and scurrilous libels which the religious dissensions of the times, prolific of animosity as they were, had produced. This was the famous tract entitled, "A Dialogue between a Scholar, a Gentleman, and a Lawyer;" and familiarly denominated "Father Parson's Green Coat," from the peculiar colour of its leaves; but afterwards still more generally known and circulated under the name of "Leicester's Commonwealth." It was understood to be the composition of Robert Parsons, a bigoted and intriguing Jesuit, and met with an immense popularity, both in England and abroad, among the numerous religious enemies and political rivals of the supercilious favourite. In its pages everything was raked together which the tongue of scandal had uttered to the disparagement of the exalted statesman whom it strove to overwhelm with obloquy;* and where that was silent, the imagination of the ecclesiastic was not slow in filling up the void, and in supplying materials which were characterized by all the venom and rancour that the most ruthless hatred could suggest.

Sir Philip's answer breathes far too much of the fierce and implacable spirit of his opponent. It is rather a cartel of defiance to his adversary, than a cool, deliberate refutation of the calumnies which had been advanced against the honour and fair fame of his relative. His wrath will not allow him to examine and repel the va-

---

* It was here that the story of the murder of his first wife was originally published, which Sir W. Scott has made the subject of his delightful tale of Kenilworth. The novelist has adhered strictly to the facts as they are stated in the annals of the times, and in Ashmole's Berkshire, and Lyson's Magna Britannia.

rious charges as they present themselves in detail; and nearly the whole of his eloquence is lavished on a topic in which general readers cannot now be supposed to take a very lively interest: the vindication of the ancient lineage of his maternal ancestors, the Dudleys. It was pretended, as we are told, that the Duke of Northumberland's father was not the son of John Dudley, a younger son of John Sutton, Lord Dudley; but of a totally different person of the same name, who was a Sussex mechanic; and this falsehood had sufficient currency and credit, at a later period, to impose upon the experience and accurate genealogical learning of Sir William Dugdale, though he ultimately discovered and corrected his mistake. When this is taken into account, and when we further recollect the strong prejudices of his age in favour of unsullied descent, we may pardon our author much of the diffuseness and acrimony into which his wounded feelings have here betrayed him. It was, in fact, assailing him on the very point from which his pride of birth derived its principal delight, and towards which he seems to have looked back as the surest support of his pretensions to hereditary distinction. "I am a Dudley in blood," he exclaims, "the Duke's daughter's son—my chiefest honour is, to be a Dudley." But it is to be regretted that he did not apply himself with more minuteness and patience to Lord Leicester's exculpation, and that he contented himself with pointing out a few of the inconsistencies and contradictions into which the libeller had fallen.

About the crisis of Sidney's life at which we have now arrived, he was inspired by an ardent desire to associate himself in a voyage of discovery with those hardy adventurers who were just beginning to exhibit that reckless intrepidity and skill, through which the navy of our country has since covered itself with glory. His active mind had long led him to take a warm interest in the discoveries and projects of Sir Martin Frobisher and his comrades. We see him withal expressing in a letter to Sir Edward Stafford, dated July 21, 1584, a sort of half inclination to join his fortunes with those of Sir Humphrey Gilbert, in a design, which the latter had for a considerable while meditated, of planting a colony in some unknown country; and in 1585, Sir Philip conceived the idea of conducting an expedition to attack the Spanish settlements in South America, conjointly with Sir Francis Drake, who had previously circumnavigated the globe, and acquired considerable riches and great celebrity from his achievements. In the present instance, however, Sidney had undertaken to equip the necessary armament with the assistance of thirty gentlemen "of great blood and state," whom he had won over to his cause, each having agreed to contribute the sum of one hundred pounds. He had likewise determined to take upon himself a principal share in the command as soon as the fleet should have quitted the shores of England, an office for which we should imagine his habits and acquirements hitherto could have done little to qualify him. Fulke Greville was the confidant, and had consented to become the companion, of his enterprise; and all their measures were concerted with the utmost secrecy and circumspection. Yet their preparations did not escape the prying eyes of Elizabeth; and her acuteness was probably assisted by private information from Drake, who appears to have become dissatisfied with the division of power to which, at the outset of the business, he had most cordially acceded.

A peremptory despatch, accordingly came down from the court to Plymouth, whither Sir Philip had conveyed himself to be in readiness for sailing, forbidding his departure, and commanding his immediate return to his family. But so determined was he to carry his designs into effect, that he caused the government messenger to be forcibly deprived, on his journey, by two soldiers in disguise, of the letters of recall with which he had been entrusted. This violent measure, however, was attended with no advantage to our author's schemes ; for an order was delivered to him personally, by a peer of the realm, holding out, on the one hand, the most severe threats of displeasure if he continued to persist in executing his projects; and, on the other, promising him an employment under his uncle in the Low Countries, provided he yielded a dutiful and instant obedience to the mandate of his sovereign. In such circumstances, therefore, no expedient was left for his adoption, but to pursue, quietly, the course thus chalked out by the higher powers.

The Queen certainly now owed him some distinguished appointment; especially, if it should be true, as has been often asserted, that she also prevented him, at this epoch, from being advanced to the regal dignity by the people of Poland. The crown of that kingdom, in which the monarchy was elective, had become vacant by the death of Stephen Bathori, the Prince of Transylvania; and it is related that Sir Philip Sidney was put in nomination by the States, and might have possessed a fair chance of success, had Elizabeth condescended to further or support his pretensions. But, according to Sir Robert Naunton, she was indisposed to the measure " not only out of emulation, but out of fear to lose the jewel of her times;" and, if Fuller may be believed to report more than the empty language of courtesy, our author was infinitely better pleased to be a subject of his present mistress "than a sovereign beyond the seas."

Her majesty having taken the Protestants of the Netherlands under her protection in 1585, and promised to dispatch a military force to their succour, Sir Philip Sidney was in that year nominated the Governor of Flushing. This place, from its advantageous position close to the mouth of the Scheld, was then considered to be one of the most important posts in the whole range of the United Provinces. Our author set out to enter upon the duties of his new situation, actuated by an anxious zeal for the interests which had been committed to his charge; and on the 18th of November he arrived at his destination, and was received with the respect to which his eminence and character entitled him. He was instantly declared colonel of all the Dutch regiments; and captain of two hundred English foot, and one hundred cavalry. He was soon afterwards followed by Lord Leicester, in command of a numerous reinforcement of auxiliary troops; and Sidney was straightway promoted to the rank of general of the horse under his uncle.

The Earl was very inadequate to fulfil the important offices which he had undertaken; and his operations were therefore conducted with singular indiscreetness and want of success. He was indebted, however, to his nephew for many prudent and salutary counsels; and for several instances of skilful and fortunate enterprise. It was by Sidney that the town of Axell was surprised and escaladed without the loss of so much as a single man; and if he failed, as he did, in seizing

Steenburg and Graveling, he was baffled by accidents which no degree of foresight could have anticipated. In the one case a sudden thaw occasioned the miscarriage of his assault; and in the other he was overreached by the treachery of the governor of the town, who had promised to deliver it up to him, as soon as the allied army should advance to the attack.

Sir Philip's father died on the 5th of May, and his mother on the 9th of August, 1586. But these domestic calamities he was not suffered long to deplore; for the premature termination of his own brilliant career was now close at hand. On the twenty-second of the succeeding September a small detachment of the English, consisting of little more than five hundred men, encountered a convoy of the enemy, amounting to three thousand troops, who were on their march to relieve Zutphen, a town in Guelderland, situated on the banks of the River Issel. A fierce and obstinate engagement, under the very walls of this fortress, was the result. The English, notwithstanding their great disparity in point of numbers, were completely victorious; but they considered their triumph was dearly purchased by the death of Sir Philip Sidney, the most distinguished hero of that hard-fought field. Early in the battle he had a horse killed under him, and had mounted another; he had, with daring intrepidity, rescued Lord Willoughby from the most imminent peril, and gallantly charged his opponents three times in one skirmish; when he received a musket-shot from the trenches, a little above his left knee, which "so brake and rifted the bone, and so entered the thigh upward, as the bullet could not be found before the body was opened." An eccentric feeling of emulation, caused by his having met the marshal of the camp only lightly armed, had induced Sir Philip to throw off his cuisses before going into action, and thus to leave exposed the parts of his frame which they protected, and where the ball from which he suffered unhappily took effect.*

While he was retiring from the place of combat a circumstance occurred that strongly evinced the natural excellence of his disposition, and which the late President West made the subject of a celebrated historical painting. It is recorded as follows by the affectionate pen of Lord Brooke. "The horse he rode upon," he says, "was rather furiously choleric, than bravely proud, and so forced him to forsake the field, but not his back, as the noblest and fittest bier to carry a martial commander to his grave. In which sad progress, passing

---

* George Whetstone, a sonneteer of the age, who had served in the Low Countries, and was eyewitness of Sir Philip's fall before Zutphen, has described the event in the following inharmonious, though by no means ungraphic stanzas, for which we are indebted to that learned and entertaining miscellany, the Poetical Decameron.

> But oh! to shade his glory with our woe,
> Hardy Sidney, much like to Mars in view,
> With furious charge did break upon the foe;
> A musket-shot his stately horse then slew;
> He horst again, the fight did soon renew:
> But fortune, that at his renown did spight,
> A billet sent that in his thigh did light.
>
> The wound was deep and shivered to the bone,
> His heart was good, and manly bare the cross;
> With courage stout he did suppress the moan,
> That many made that did behold his loss.
> Udall then lite, softly to lead his horse;
> "Let go," quoth he, "till I fall to the ground
> The foe shall miss the glory of my wound."

along by the rest of the army where his uncle the General was, and being thirsty with excess of bleeding, he called for drink, which was presently brought him; but as he was putting the bottle to his mouth, he saw a poor soldier carried along, who had eaten his last at the same feast, ghastly casting up his eyes at the bottle. Which Sir Philip perceiving, took it from his head before he drank, and delivered it to the poor man, with these words, 'Thy necessity is yet greater than mine.'"

The Earl of Leicester's grief, on account of the catastrophe which had befallen his nephew, was of the most passionate description. A letter of his to Sir Thomas Heneage, dated 23rd September, the day after the engagement, has been preserved and printed in the noble lord's memoirs, prefixed to the Sidney Papers. In it he details the mode in which our author received his fatal injury; and then proceeds to declare that this young man was his greatest comfort, next her majesty, of all the world; and, that if he could buy his life with all he had, to his shirt, he would give it. "How God will dispose of him," he continues, "I know not; but fear I must needs, greatly, the worst; the blow in so dangerous a place and so great; yet did I never hear of any man that did abide the dressing and setting his bones better than he did; and he was carried afterwards in my barge to Arnheim, and I hear this day, he is still of good heart, and comforteth all about him, as much as may be. God of his mercy grant him his life, which I cannot but doubt of greatly. I was abroad that time in the field, giving some order to supply that business, which did endure almost two hours in continual fight; and meeting Philip coming upon his horseback, not a little to my grief. But I would you had stood by to hear his most loyal speeches to her majesty; his constant mind to the cause, his loving care over me, and his most resolute determination for death, not a jot appalled for his blow, which is the most grievous that ever I saw with such a bullet; riding so long, a mile and a half, upon his horse, ere he came to the camp; not ceasing to speak still of her majesty; being glad if his hurt and death might any way honour her; for her's he was whilst he lived, and God's he was sure to be if he died; prayed all men to think that the cause was as well her majesty's as the country's; and not to be discouraged, 'for you have seen such success as may encourage us all; and this my hurt is the ordinance of God by the hap of the war.' Well, I pray God, if it be his will, save me his life; even as well for her majesty's service sake, as for mine own comfort."

His lordship's affectionate entreaties to the throne of mercy were unavailing. It is supposed that the bullet from which Sidney suffered had been poisoned. After lingering sixteen days in severe and unceasing pain, which he endured with all the fortitude and resignation of a Christian, symptoms of mortification, the certain forerunner of death, at length appeared, and Sir Philip then prepared, with undiminished and cheerful serenity, for his approaching dissolution. Though he was himself the first to perceive the fatal indications which the seat of his disease had begun to exhibit, he was able to amuse his sick-bed by composing an ode, unfortunately now lost, on the nature of his wound, which he caused to be sung to solemn music, as an entertainment that might soothe and divert his mind from his torments. Everything was done for him that medical skill could suggest, or the solicitude of his friends and the tenderness of his amiable wife, who had accompanied him into Zealand, could supply; but on the 16th day of October his complaints reached their crisis, and his gentle spirit took its flight to a world more worthy of its virtues. He breathed his last sigh in the arms of one whom he had long loved, his faithful secretary and bosom companion, Mr. William Temple.

His address to his brother, when he bade him a final adieu, is a noble outpouring of the heart, and is characterized by those many amiable sentiments and qualities which had dignified his conduct through life, and endeared him to society wherever it had been his fortune to wander. "Love my memory," he said, "cherish my friends; their faith to me may assure you they are honest. But above all, govern your will and affections by the will and word of your Creator; in me beholding the end of this world with all her vanities."

Thus perished, in the very prime of his days, and the zenith of his hopes, the man who was above all others the idol of his times,—"the soldier's, scholar's, courtier's, eye, tongue, sword." He was in many respects at once the Marcellus and the Mecænas of the English nation. He was the intimate friend, and most liberal benefactor of Spenser;* and that preëminent bard repaid

* The patient investigation of Mr. Todd, has proved that Spenser and Sidney were acquainted previously to the publication of the Shepherd's Calendar, in 1579, and of course long before the Fairy Queen appeared, or was, perhaps, so much as thought of. The common story, therefore, that this splendid poem was the first occasion of their intimacy, is utterly untrue. The anecdote also has been considered equally apocryphal, which describes Sir Philip as being so highly delighted with reading Spenser's delineation of the Cave of Despair, as to order him, after perusing a few stanzas, a payment of £50; "and that a continuation of the reading extended

his debt of gratitude and affection, by composing a pathetic elegy, wherein he bewailed his patron under Sidney's favourite and celebrated appellation of Astrophel. The two Universities, also, poured forth three volumes* of learned lamentation, on account of the loss of him whom they considered as being their brightest ornament; and indeed so far was the public regret, on this occasion, carried, that, for the first time in the case of a private individual, the whole kingdom went into mourning, and no gentleman of quality, during several months, ventured to appear in a light-coloured or gaudy dress, either in the resorts of business or of fashion. Certainly public affliction never did honour to a more amiable object; nor did the Muses ever shed their tears over the hearse of one who was more fervently devoted to their service; for his whole life, as it has been beautifully remarked by Campbell, was poetry put into action.

"Gentle Sir Philip Sidney," says Tom Nash in two sweetly-flowing sentences of his Pierce Penniless, "thou

---

Sir Philip's bounty to £200, which he directed his steward to pay the poet *immediately*, lest he should bestow the whole of his estate on the writer of such verses." There seems, however, to be some better foundation for the assertion, that the death of Sidney prevented the completion of the Fairy Queen, by depriving its author of both the means and the spirit to complete his design. It has been pretty generally admitted that he intended to represent our hero under the character of Prince Arthur.

* The several titles of these productions were, —

1. Academiæ Cantabrigiensis Lacrymæ, tumulo nobilissimi Equitis D. Philippi Sidneii sacratæ per Alexandrum Nevillum, Lond. 1587.

2. Peplus illustrissimi viri D. Sidnæi supremis honoribus dicatus, Oxon. 1587.

3. Exequiæ illustrissimi Equitis D. Philippi Sidnæi gratissimæ memoriæ ac nomini impensæ, Oxon. 1589.

knewest what belonged to a scholar; thou knewest what pains, what toil, what travel, conduct to perfection; well could'st thou give every virtue his encouragement, every art his due, every writer his desert, cause none more virtuous, witty, or learned than thyself. But thou art dead in thy grave, and hast left too few successors of thy glory, too few to cherish the sons of the Muses, or water those budding hopes with their plenty, which thy bounty erst planted."

"Indeed," observes Lord Brooke, "he was a true model of worth; a man fit for conquest, plantation, reformation, or what action soever is greatest and hardest amongst men: withal such a lover of mankind, and goodness, that whosoever had any real parts, in him found comfort, participation, and protection to the uttermost of his power; like Zephyrus, he giving life where he blew. The universities abroad, and at home, ac-

---

King James the First, likewise, honoured Sir Philip with an epitaph of his own composition, in English and Latin, of which we here subjoin the former version.

> Thou mighty Mars, the lord of soldiers brave,
> And thou Minerve, that does in wit excel,
> And thou Apollo, who does knowledge have
> Of ev'ry art that from Parnassus fell,
> With all your sisters that thereon do dwell,
> Lament for him who duly serv'd you all,
> Whom in you wisely all your arts did mell,
> Bewail, I say, his unexpected fall;
> I need not in remembrance for to call
> His race, his youth, the hope had of him ay,
> Since that in him doth cruel death appal
> Both manhood, wit, and learning every way;
>   But yet he doth in bed of honour rest,
>   And evermore of him shall live the best.

counted him a general Mecænas of learning; dedicated their books to him; and communicated every invention or improvement of knowledge with him. Soldiers honoured him, and were so honoured by him, as no man thought he marched under the true banner of Mars, that had not obtained Sir Philip Sidney's approbation. Men of affairs, in most parts of Christendom, entertained correspondency with him. But what speak I of these, with whom his own ways and ends did concur? since, to descend, his heart and capacity were so large, that there was not a cunning painter, a skilful engineer, an excellent musician, or any other artificer of extraordinary fame, that made not himself known to this famous spirit, and found him his true friend without hire, and the common rendezvous of worth in his time.———— Besides, the ingenuity of his nature did spread itself so freely abroad, as who lives that can say he ever did him harm; whereas there be many living that may thankfully acknowledge he did them good. Neither was this in him a private, but a public affection; his chief ends being, not friends, wife, children, and himself, but above all things the honour of his Maker, and the service of his prince or country."

"This is that Sidney," observes the venerable Cambden, "who as Providence seems to have sent him into the world to give the present age a specimen of the ancients; so did it, on a sudden, recall him, and snatch him from us, as more worthy of heaven than earth; thus where virtue comes to perfection it is gone in a trice, and the best things are never lasting. Rest then in peace, O Sidney, (if I may be allowed this address,) we will not celebrate your memory with tears, but admiration; whatever we loved in you, (as the best of authors speaks of that best governor of Britain,*) whatever we admired in you, still continues, and will continue, in the memories of men, the revolutions of ages, and the annals of time. Many, as inglorious and ignoble, are buried in oblivion; but Sidney shall live to all posterity. For, as the Grecian poet has it, virtue's beyond the reach of fate."

" He was not only of an excellent wit," relates, in his own confused and rambling way, the eminent antiquarian, John Aubrey, who was born not more than forty years after Sidney's decease, "but extremely beautiful; he much resembled his sister, but his hair was not red, but a little inclining; viz: a dark amber colour. If I were to find a fault in it, methinks 'tis not masculine enough; yet he was a person of great courage. He was much at Wilton with his sister, and at Ivy Church, (anciently a pleasant monastery, which adjoins to the park pale of Clarendon Park,) situated on a hill that overlooks all the country westwards and north, over Sarum and the plains, and into that delicious park (which was accounted the best of England) eastwards. It was, heretofore, a monastery; the cloisters remain still; 'twas called 'Cænobium Edrosium.' My great-uncle, Mr. T. Browne, remembered him; and said that he was wont to take his table-book out of his pocket, and write down his notions as they came into his head, when he was writing his Arcadia, (which was never finished by him,) as he was hunting on our pleasant plains. He was the reviver of poetry in those dark times, which was then at a very low ebb,—e. g. 'The pleasant Comedie of Jacob and Esau,' acted before King Henry Eighth's

---

* Tacitus of Agricola.

grace, where, I remember, is this expression, 'that the pottage was so good, that God Almighty might have put his fingers in't;'—'Gammer Gurton's Needle, etc.;' and in these plays there are not three lines but there is 'by God,' or, 'by God's wounds.' He was of a very munificent spirit, and liberal to all lovers of learning, and to those that pretended to any acquaintance with Parnassus; insomuch that he was cloyed and surfeited with the poetasters of those days."

"He was, if ever there was one," says the eloquent writer in the Retrospective already quoted, "a gentleman finished and complete, in whom mildness was associated with courage, erudition mollified by refinement, and courtliness dignified by truth. He is a specimen of what the English character was capable of producing, when foreign admixtures had not destroyed its simplicity, or politeness debased its honour. The very stiffness it then possessed had a noble original; it was the natural consequence of that state of society, when the degrees of order and subordination were universally observed and understood, when the social relations were not broken down by the encroaching power of innovation, and when each was as ready to pay as to exact his tribute of observance and respect. No lax discipline in morals had then interwoven itself with the manners of the great, nor was the court, as in the reign of Charles the Second, converted into a painted sepulchre, where the spirit, the gaiety, and the gilding without, could ill disguise the darkness and rottenness within: it was not, as in that court, a general national reservoir of iniquity, where all the degrees of order, and all the barriers of principle, were levelled and overthrown. The most accomplished members of the court of Queen Elizabeth were not less distinguished for the strictness of their moral principles, than for their polish and address as courtiers. Of such a stamp was Sir Philip Sidney, and such as he was, every Englishman has reason to be proud of him. He exalted his country in the eyes of other nations, and the country he honoured will not be ungrateful. England will ever place him amongst the noblest of her sons, and the light of chivalry, which was his guide and beacon, will ever lend its radiance to illuminate his tombstone, and consecrate his memory.——Let us remember that he died at the age of thirty-two; and, if the lives of Milton and Dryden had not been prolonged beyond that period, where would have been their renown, or where the poetical renown of their country."*

Sir Philip's body was brought to London and interred in St. Paul's Cathedral, notwithstanding the subjects of his late government entreated with the utmost earnestness that it might be suffered to remain among them, and, according to the continuator of Hollinshed, even offered, should their request be granted, " to erect for him as fair a monument as any prince had in Christendom, yea, though the same should cost half a ton of gold the building." His funeral was performed with great circumstance and pomp, the seven United Provinces sending each a representative to testify respect for his memory by their vicarious presence at his obsequies. A

* Had we not looked upon it as somewhat like " gilding refined gold," we might have extended these extracts from distinguished writers in commendation of the subject of our memoir to a much greater length. According to Mr. Todd, Oldys asserts, in his manuscript additions to Winstanley's Lives of the Poets, that he could muster up two hundred authors who had spoken in praise of Sir Philip Sidney.

simple tablet, which has long been removed, was put up in the choir of St. Paul's, bearing the subjoined inscription, imitated from the French of Isaac du Bellay.

> England, Netherlands, the heavens, and the arts,
> The soldiers, and the world, have made six parts
> Of the noble Sidney : for none will suppose,
> That a small heap of stones can Sidney enclose.
> His body hath England, for she it bred ;
> Netherlands his blood, in her defence shed ;
> The heavens have his soul, the arts his fame :
> All soldiers the grief, the world his good name.

Our author left behind him an only child, Elizabeth,* who was born in 1585, and became the wife of Roger Manners, the fifth Earl of Rutland. She died, however, in 1615, without leaving any issue, and was succeeded in her possessions by her uncle Robert, Viscount L'Isle, and Lord Sidney of Penshurst.

---

* It would appear by the following extracts from the Harl. MSS. 1641, with which we have been favoured through the kindness of that learned and assiduous antiquarian, Nicholas Harris Nicolas, Esq., that Queen Elizabeth honoured the christening of Sir P. Sidney's daughter with her presence.

Item. Paid to Richard Brakinburie one of thordinarye gent' Usshers of her Ma[ts] Chamber, to be by him distributed and geven by waie of Her Ma[tie] reward to the Nurse and Midwife, at the Cristeninge of S[r]. Philipp Sydney his doughter, to whom her Maiestie was Godmother, the some of c. shillings.

Item. Paid to Richard Brakinburye one of thordinary gent' Usshers of her Ma[tie] Chamber, for thallowance of himself, one grome of the Chamber, and one grome of the Wardrobe, for rydinge from the Court at Richmond to London, to make redie for Her Ma[tie] against the Cristininge of S[r]. Philipp Sydney his doughter, by the space of iiij[or] daies Mens' Novem' 1585, as appeareth by a bill signed by the Lo. Chamberlain, lxvj*s*, viiij*d*.

Her mother, Lady Sidney, survived her husband for a great many years; and entered into the married state a second time with the accomplished Robert Devereux, the famed Earl of Essex; by whom she had three children, a son and two daughters. After the brief career of her ill-fated lord had terminated on the scaffold in the year 1600, she embraced the Popish religion, and was espoused to a third husband, Richard de Burgh, fourth Earl of Clanricard in Ireland, a man of elegance and courage, who was created Earl of St. Albans in 1628. By him she became the mother of Honora, second wife of John, Marquis of Winchester; and of Ulric de Burgh, a zealous supporter of Charles the First, and the immediate successor of the Marquis of Ormond in his lieutenancy.

[We are induced to reprint the four following sonnets, addressed, in the quaint style of the times, to Sir Philip Sidney's soul, chiefly because they were prefixed to the first edition of the Defence, then called the "Apologie of Poetrie," which has now become extremely scarce, and also because they have hitherto been omitted in every subsequent republication of that treatise. They were the composition of Henry Constable, the author of the Diana, and various minor poems, of whom Antony Wood has said, borrowing the remark from Bolton's Hypercritica, that "No gentleman of our nation had a more pure, quick, and higher delivery of conceit." The subjoined specimen of his talents will not discredit this encomium.]

FOUR SONNETS

WRITTEN BY HENRY CONSTABLE TO SIR PHILIP SIDNEY'S SOUL.

I.

Give pardon, blessed soul, to my bold cries,
If they, importunate, interrupt thy song,

Which now, with joyful notes, thou sing'st among
The angel-quirister's of heav'nly skies:
Give pardon eke (sweet soul) to my slow cries,
   That since I saw thee now it is so long,
   And yet the tears that unto thee belong
   To thee as yet they did not sacrifice:
I did not know that thou wert dead before,
   I did not feel the grief I did sustain,
   The greater stroke astonisheth the more,
   Astonishment takes from us sense of pain;
I stood amaz'd, when others' tears begun,
And now begin to weep when they have done.

2.

Sweet soul, which now with heav'nly songs do'st tell
   Thy dear Redeemer's glory and his praise,
   No marvel though thy skilful Muse essays
   The songs of other souls there to excel;
For thou didst learn to sing divinely well,
   Long time before thy fair and glittering rays
   Increas'd the light of heav'n, for even thy lays
   Most heavenly were when thou on earth didst dwell:
When thou didst on the earth sing poet-wise,
   Angels in heav'n pray'd for thy company,
   And now thou sing'st with angels in the skies,
   Shall not all poets praise thy memory?
And to thy name shall not their works give fame,
Whereas their works be sweetened by thy name?

3.

Even as when great men's heirs cannot agree,
   So ev'ry virtue now for part of thee doth sue,

Courage proves by thy death thy heart to be his due,
    Eloquence claims thy tongue, and so doth courtesy;
Invention knowledge sues, judgment sues memory,
    Each saith thy head is his, and what end shall ensue
    Of this strife know I not, but this I know for true,
    That whosoever gains the suit, the loss have we;
We! I mean all the world, the loss to all pertaineth,
    Yea they which gain do lose, and only thy soul gaineth,
    For losing of one life, two lives are gained then:
    Honour thy courage mov'd, courage thy death did give,
Death, courage, honour makes thy soul to live,
Thy soul to live in heav'n, thy name in tongues of men.

4.

Great Alexander then did well declare
    How great was his united kingdom's might,
    When ev'ry captain of his army might,
    After his death, with mighty kings compare:
So now we see, after thy death, how far
    Thou do'st in worth surpass each other knight.
    When we admire him as no mortal wight,
    In whom the least of all thy virtues are:
One did of Macedon the king become,
    Another sat on the Egyptian throne,
    But only Alexander's self had all:
    So courteous some, and some be liberal,
Some witty, wise, valiant, and learned some,
But king of all the virtues thou alone.

THE
DEFENCE OF POESY.

The Defence of Poesy was most probably written about 1581. The first edition of it was printed in 4to. in 1595; and it was annexed to the third edition of the Arcadia in 1598. In 1787 it was reprinted separately by Dr. Joseph Warton, with observations on poetry and eloquence from Ben Jonson's Discoveries; and again in 1810 by Lord Thurlow. When Shakespeare's first play was composed, is a point which has exercised the ingenuity, rather than rewarded the diligence, of his numerous commentators. But it is pretty clearly ascertained that nothing of his was printed before 1597, when Romeo and Juliet, and Richard the Second and Third appeared. Spenser is conjectured to have begun his Fairy Queen about 1580.

THE

DEFENCE OF POESY.

WHEN the right virtuous E. W.* and I were at the Emperor's court together, we gave ourselves to learn horsemanship of Gio. Pietro Pugliano; one that, with great commendation, had the place of an esquire in his stable; and he, according to the fertileness of the Italian wit, did not only afford us the demonstration of his practice, but sought to enrich our minds with the contemplation therein, which he thought most precious. But with none, I remember, mine ears were at any time more laden, than when (either angred with slow payment, or moved with our learner-like admiration) he exercised his speech in the praise of his faculty.†

---

* This was Edward, the elder brother of Sir Henry Wotton. His name appeared at full length in the first edition of the Defence, and the initials were only substituted in the second, which accompanied the Arcadia. By Queen Elizabeth he was knighted in 1592, and nominated comptroller of her household; besides being honoured with various diplomatic employments at foreign courts. By James the First he was created Lord Wotton, Baron of Maherly in Kent, and appointed Lord Lieutenant of that county.

† The management of the horse is finely described by Sir Philip in the second book of the Arcadia.

He said, soldiers were the noblest estate of mankind, and horsemen the noblest of soldiers. He said, they were the masters of war, and ornaments of peace, speedy goers, and strong abiders, triumphers both in camps and courts; nay, to so unbelieved a point he proceeded, as that no earthly thing bred such wonder to a prince, as to be a good horseman; skill of government was but a "pedanteria" in comparison. Then would he add certain praises, by telling what a peerless beast the horse was, the only serviceable courtier, without flattery, the beast of most beauty, faithfulness, courage, and such more, that if I had not been a piece of a logician before I came to him, I think he would have persuaded me to have wished myself a horse. But thus much, at least, with his no few words, he drove into me, that self love is better than any gilding, to make that seem gorgeous wherein ourselves be parties.

Wherein, if Pugliano's strong affection and weak arguments will not satisfy you, I will give you a nearer example of myself, who, I know not by what mischance, in these my not old years and idlest times, having slipped into the title of a poet, am provoked to say something unto you in the defence of that my unelected vocation; which if I handle with more good will than good reasons, bear with me, since the scholar is to be pardoned that followeth the steps of his master.

And yet I must say, that as I have more just cause to make a pitiful defence of poor poetry, which, from almost the highest estimation of learning, is fallen to be the laughing-stock of children; so have I need to bring some more available proofs, since the former is by no man barred of his deserved credit, whereas the silly latter hath had even the names of philosophers used to the defacing of it, with great danger of civil war among the Muses.

And first, truly, to all them that, professing learning, inveigh against poetry, may justly be objected, that they go very near to ungratefulness to seek to deface that, which, in the noblest nations and languages that are known, hath been the first light-giver to ignorance, and first nurse, whose milk by little and little enabled them to feed afterwards of tougher knowledges. And will you play the hedge-hog, that being received into the den, drove out his host? or rather the vipers, that with their birth kill their parents? Let learned Greece, in any of her manifold sciences, be able to show me one book before Musæus, Homer, and Hesiod, all three nothing else but poets. Nay, let any history be brought, that can say any writers were there before them, if they were not men of the same skill, as Orpheus, Linus, and some others are named, who having been the first of that country that made pens deliverers of their knowledge to posterity, may justly challenge to be called their fathers in learning. For not only in time they had this priority (although in itself antiquity be venerable) but went before them, as causes to draw, with their charming sweetness, the wild untamed wits to an admiration of knowledge. So as Amphion was said to move stones with his poetry to build Thebes, and Orpheus to be listened to by beasts; indeed stony and beastly people; so among the Romans were Livius, Andronicus, and Ennius; so in the Italian language, the first that made it to aspire to be a treasure-house of science, were the poets Dante, Boccace, and Petrarch; so in our English were Gower and Chaucer;

after whom, encouraged and delighted with their excellent foregoing, others have followed to beautify our mother-tongue, as well in the same kind, as other arts.

This did so notably show itself, that the philosophers of Greece durst not a long time appear to the world but under the mask of poets; so Thales, Empedocles, and Parmenides sang their natural philosophy in verses; so did Pythagoras and Phocylides their moral counsels; so did Tyrtæus in war matters; and Solon in matters of policy; or rather they, being poets, did exercise their delightful vein in those points of highest knowledge, which before them lay hidden to the world; for that wise Solon was directly a poet, it is manifest, having written, in verse, the notable fable of the Atlantic Island, which was continued by Plato. And, truly, even Plato, whosoever well considereth, shall find, that in the body of his work, though the inside and strength were philosophy, the skin, as it were, and beauty, depended most of poetry. For all stands upon dialogues; wherein he feigns many honest burgesses of Athens speaking of such matters, that if they had been set on the rack, they would never have confessed them; besides, his poetical describing the circumstances of their meetings, as the well-ordering of a banquet, the delicacy of a walk, with interlacing mere tales, as Gyges's Ring, and others; which, who knows not to be flowers of poetry, did never walk into Apollo's garden.

And even historiographers, although their lips sound of things done, and verity be written in their foreheads, have been glad to borrow both fashion and, perchance, weight of the poets; so Herodotus entitled the books of his history by the names of the Nine Muses; and both he, and all the rest that followed him, either stole or usurped, of poetry, their passionate describing of passions, the many particularities of battles which no man could affirm; or, if that be denied me, long orations, put in the mouths of great kings and captains, which, it is certain, they never pronounced.

So that, truly, neither philosopher nor historiographer could, at the first, have entered into the gates of popular judgments, if they had not taken a great disport of poetry; which in all nations, at this day, where learning flourisheth not, is plain to be seen; in all which they have some feeling of poetry. In Turkey, besides their lawgiving divines they have no other writers but poets. In our neighbour-country Ireland, where, too, learning goes very bare, yet are their poets held in a devout reverence. Even among the most barbarous and simple Indians, where no writing is, yet have they their poets, who make and sing songs, which they call "Arentos," both of their ancestors' deeds and praises of their gods. A sufficient probability, that if ever learning come among them, it must be by having their hard dull wits softened and sharpened with the sweet delight of poetry; for until they find a pleasure in the exercise of the mind, great promises of much knowledge will little persuade them that know not the fruits of knowledge. In Wales, the true remnant of the ancient Britons, as there are good authorities to show the long time they had poets, which they called bards, so through all the conquests of Romans, Saxons, Danes, and Normans, some of whom did seek to ruin all memory of learning from among them, yet do their poets, even to this day, last; so as it is not more notable in the soon beginning, than in long continuing.

But since the authors of most of our sciences were

the Romans, and, before them, the Greeks, let us, a little, stand upon their authorities; but even so far, as to see what names they have given unto this now scorned skill. Among the Romans, a poet was called "vates," which is as much as a diviner, foreseer, or prophet, as by his conjoined words "vaticinium," and "vaticinari," is manifest; so heavenly a title did that excellent people bestow upon this heart-ravishing knowledge! And so far were they carried into the admiration thereof, that they thought in the changeable hitting upon any such verses, great foretokens of their following fortunes were placed. Whereupon grew the word of *sortes Virgilianæ*; when, by sudden opening Virgil's book, they lighted upon some verse, as it is reported by many, whereof the histories of the emperors' lives are full. As of Albinus, the governor of our island, who, in his childhood, met with this verse,

> Arma amens capio, nec sat rationis in armis;

and in his age performed it. Although it were a very vain and godless superstition; as also it was, to think spirits were commanded by such verses; whereupon this word charms, derived of "carmina," cometh, so yet serveth it to show the great reverence those wits were held in; and altogether not without ground, since both the oracles of Delphi and the Sibyl's prophecies were wholly delivered in verses; for that same exquisite observing of number and measure in the words, and that high-flying liberty of conceit proper to the poet, did seem to have some divine force in it.

And may not I presume a little farther, to show the reasonableness of this word "vates," and say, that the holy David's Psalms are a divine Poem? If I do, I shall not do it without the testimony of great learned men, both ancient and modern. But even the name of Psalms will speak for me, which, being interpreted, is nothing but Songs; then, that it is fully written in metre, as all learned Hebricians agree, although the rules be not yet fully found. Lastly, and principally, his handling his prophecy, which is merely poetical. For what else is the awaking his musical instruments; the often and free changing of persons; his notable prosopopœias, when he maketh you, as it were, see God coming in his majesty; his telling of the beasts' joyfulness, and hills leaping, but a heavenly poesy; wherein, almost, he showeth himself a passionate lover of that unspeakable and everlasting beauty, to be seen by the eyes of the mind, only cleared by faith? But, truly, now, having named him, I fear I seem to profane that holy name, applying it to poetry, which is, among us, thrown down to so ridiculous an estimation. But they that, with quiet judgments, will look a little deeper into it, shall find the end and working of it such, as, being rightly applied, deserveth not to be scourged out of the church of God.

But now let us see how the Greeks have named it, and how they deemed of it. The Greeks named him ποιητήν, which name hath, as the most excellent, gone through other languages; it cometh of this word ποιεῖν, which is *to make*; wherein, I know not whether by luck or wisdom, we Englishmen have met with the Greeks in calling him "a maker," which name, how high and incomparable a title it is, I had rather were known by marking the scope of other sciences, than by any partial allegation. There is no art delivered unto mankind, that hath not the works of nature for his principal ob-

ject, without which they could not consist, and on
which they so depend, as they become actors and play-
ers, as it were, of what nature will have set forth. So
doth the astronomer look upon the stars, and by that he
seeth set down what order nature hath taken therein.
So doth the geometrician and arithmetician, in their
diverse sorts of quantities. So doth the musician, in
times, tell you, which by nature agree, which not. The
natural philosopher thereon hath his name; and the
moral philosopher standeth upon the natural virtues,
vices, or passions of man; and follow nature, saith he,
therein, and thou shalt not err. The lawyer saith what
men have determined. The historian, what men have
done. The grammarian speaketh only of the rules of
speech; and the rhetorician and logician, considering
what in nature will soonest prove and persuade, thereon
give artificial rules, which still are compassed within the
circle of a question, according to the proposed matter.
The physician weigheth the nature of man's body, and
the nature of things helpful and hurtful unto it. And
the metaphysic, though it be in the second and abstract
notions, and therefore be counted supernatural, yet doth
he, indeed, build upon the depth of nature. Only the
poet, disdaining to be tied to any such subjection, lifted
up with the vigour of his own invention, doth grow, in
effect, into another nature; in making things either
better than nature bringeth forth, or quite anew; forms
such as never were in nature, as the heroes, demi-gods,
Cyclops, chimeras, furies, and such like; so as he goeth
hand in hand with nature, not enclosed within the nar-
row warrant of her gifts, but freely ranging within the
zodiac of his own wit. Nature never set forth the
earth in so rich tapestry as divers poets have done;

neither with so pleasant rivers, fruitful trees, sweet-smelling flowers, nor whatsoever else may make the too-much-loved earth more lovely; her world is brazen, the poets only deliver a golden.

But let those things alone, and go to man; for whom as the other things are, so it seemeth in him her uttermost cunning is employed; and know, whether she have brought forth so true a lover as Theagenes; so constant a friend as Pylades; so valiant a man as Orlando; so right a prince as Xenophon's Cyrus; and so excellent a man every way as Virgil's Æneas? Neither let this be jestingly conceived, because the works of the one be essential, the other in imitation or fiction; for every understanding knoweth the skill of each artificer standeth in that idea, or fore-conceit of the work, and not in the work itself. And that the poet hath that idea, is manifest, by the delivering them forth in such excellency as he had imagined them; which delivering forth, also, is not wholly imaginative, as we are wont to say by them that build castles in the air; but so far substantially it worketh, not only to make a Cyrus, which had been but a particular excellency, as nature might have done; but to bestow a Cyrus upon the world to make many Cyruses; if they will learn aright, why, and how, that maker made him. Neither let it be deemed too saucy a comparison, to balance the highest point of man's wit with the efficacy of nature; but rather give right honour to the heavenly Maker of that maker, who having made man to his own likeness, set him beyond and over all the works of that second nature; which in nothing he showeth so much as in poetry; when, with the force of a divine breath, he bringeth things forth surpassing her doings, with no small arguments to the incredulous of that first accursed fall of Adam; since our erected wit maketh us know what perfection is, and yet our infected will keepeth us from reaching unto it. But these arguments will by few be understood, and by fewer granted; thus much I hope will be given me, that the Greeks, with some probability of reason, gave him the name above all names of learning.

Now let us go to a more ordinary opening of him, that the truth may be the more palpable; and so, I hope, though we get not so unmatched a praise as the etymology of his names will grant, yet his very description, which no man will deny, shall not justly be barred from a principal commendation.

Poesy, therefore, is an art of imitation; for so Aristotle termeth it in the word μίμησις; that is to say, a representing, counterfeiting, or figuring forth: to speak metaphorically, a speaking picture; with this end, to teach and delight.

Of this have been three general kinds: the *chief*, both in antiquity and excellency, were they that did imitate the inconceivable excellences of God; such were David in his Psalms; Solomon in his Song of Songs, in his Ecclesiastes, and Proverbs; Moses and Deborah in their hymns; and the writer of Job; which, beside others, the learned Emanuel Tremellius and Fr. Junius do entitle the poetical part of the scripture; against these none will speak that hath the Holy Ghost in due holy reverence. In this kind, though in a wrong divinity, were Orpheus, Amphion, Homer in his Hymns, and many others, both Greeks and Romans. And this poesy must be used by whosoever will follow St. Paul's counsel, in singing psalms when they are merry; and I know is used with the fruit of comfort by some, when, in sorrowful pangs of their death-bringing sins, they find the consolation of the never-leaving goodness.

The *second* kind is of them that deal with matter philosophical; either moral, as Tyrtæus, Phocylides, Cato; or natural, as Lucretius, Virgil's Georgics; or astronomical, as Manilius and Pontanus; or historical, as Lucan; which who mislike, the fault is in their judgment, quite out of taste, and not in the sweet food of sweetly uttered knowledge.

But because this second sort is wrapped within the fold of the proposed subject, and takes not the free course of his own invention; whether they properly be poets, or no, let grammarians dispute, and go to the *third*, indeed right poets, of whom chiefly this question ariseth; betwixt whom and these second is such a kind of difference, as betwixt the meaner sort of painters, who counterfeit only such faces as are set before them; and the more excellent, who having no law but wit, bestow that in colours upon you which is fittest for the eye to see; as the constant, though lamenting look of Lucretia, when she punished in herself another's fault; wherein he painteth not Lucretia, whom he never saw, but painteth the outward beauty of such a virtue. For these three be they which most properly do imitate to teach and delight; and to imitate, borrow nothing of what is, hath been, or shall be; but range only, reined with learned discretion, into the divine consideration of what may be, and should be. These be they, that, as the first and most noble sort, may justly be termed "vates;" so these are waited on in the excellentest languages and best understandings, with the fore-described name of poets. For these, indeed, do merely make to imitate, and imitate both to delight and teach, and delight to move men to take that goodness in hand, which, without delight, they would fly as from a stranger; and teach to make them know that goodness whereunto they are moved; which being the noblest scope to which ever any learning was directed, yet want there not idle tongues to bark at them.

These be subdivided into sundry more special denominations; the most notable be the heroic, lyric, tragic, comic, satyric, iambic, elegiac, pastoral, and certain others; some of these being termed according to the matter they deal with; some by the sort of verse they liked best to write in; for indeed the greatest part of poets have apparelled their poetical inventions in that numerous kind of writing which is called verse. Indeed but apparelled verse, being but an ornament, and no cause to poetry, since there have been many most excellent poets that never versified, and now swarm many versifiers that need never answer to the name of poets. For Xenophon, who did imitate so excellently as to give us *effigiem justi imperii*, the portraiture of a just empire, under the name of Cyrus, as Cicero saith of him, made therein an absolute heroical poem. So did Heliodorus, in his sugared invention of that picture of love in Theagenes and Chariclea; and yet both these wrote in prose; which I speak to show, that it is not rhyming and versing that maketh a poet; (no more than a long gown maketh an advocate, who, though he pleaded in armour, should be an advocate and no soldier;) but it is, that feigning notable images of virtues, vices, or what else, with that delightful teaching, which must be the right describing note to know a poet by. Although indeed the senate of poets have chosen verse as their fittest raiment; meaning, as in matter they passed all in all, so in manner to go beyond them; not speaking, table-talk fashion, or like men in a dream, words as they chanceably fall from the mouth, but piecing each syllable of each word by just proportion, according to the dignity of the subject.

Now, therefore, it shall not be amiss, first, to weigh this latter sort of poetry by his *works*, and then, by his *parts*; and if in neither of these anatomies he be commendable, I hope we shall receive a more favourable sentence. This purifying of wit, this enriching of memory, enabling of judgment, and enlarging of conceit, which commonly we call learning, under what name soever it come forth, or to what immediate end soever it be directed; the final end is, to lead and draw us to as high a perfection as our degenerate souls, made worse by their clay lodgings, can be capable of; this, according to the inclination of man, bred many formed impressions; for some that thought this felicity principally to be gotten by knowledge, and no knowledge to be so high or heavenly as to be acquainted with the stars, gave themselves to astronomy; others, persuading themselves to be demi-gods, if they knew the causes of things, became natural and supernatural philosophers. Some an admirable delight drew to music; and some the certainty of demonstrations to the mathematics; but all, one and other, having this scope, to know, and by knowledge to lift up the mind from the dungeon of the body to the enjoying his own divine essence. But when, by the balance of experience, it was found that the astronomer, looking to the stars, might fall in a ditch; that the enquiring philosopher might be blind in himself; and the mathematician might draw forth a straight line with a crooked heart; then lo! did proof, the overruler of opinions, make manifest, that all these are but serving sciences, which, as they have a private end in themselves, so yet are they all directed to the highest end of the mistress knowledge, by the Greeks called ἀρχιτεκτονική, which stands, as I think, in the knowledge of a man's self; in the ethic and politic consideration, with the end of well doing, and not of well knowing only; even as the saddler's next end is to make a good saddle, but his farther end, to serve a nobler faculty, which is horsemanship; so the horseman's to soldiery; and the soldier not only to have the skill, but to perform the practice of a soldier. So that the ending end of all earthly learning being virtuous action, those skills that most serve to bring forth that, have a most just title to be princes over all the rest; wherein, if we can show it rightly, the poet is worthy to have it before any other competitors.

Among whom principally to challenge it, step forth the moral philosophers; whom, methinks, I see coming toward me with a sullen gravity, (as though they could not abide vice by daylight,) rudely clothed, for to witness outwardly their contempt of outward things, with books in their hands against glory, whereto they set their names; sophistically speaking against subtlety, and angry with any man in whom they see the foul fault of anger. These men, casting largesses as they go, of definitions, divisions, and distinctions, with a scornful interrogative do soberly ask: Whether it be possible to find any path so ready to lead a man to virtue, as that which teacheth what virtue is; and teacheth it not only by delivering forth his very being, his causes and effects; but also by making known his enemy, vice, which must be destroyed; and his cumbersome servant, passion, which must be mastered, by showing the generalities that contain it, and the specialities that are derived from it: lastly, by plain setting down how it extends itself out of the limits of a man's own little world, to the government of families, and maintaining of public societies?

The historian scarcely gives leisure to the moralist to say so much, but that he, (ladened with old mouse-eaten records, authorizing himself, for the most part, upon other histories, whose greatest authorities are built upon the notable foundation of hearsay, having much ado to accord differing writers, and to pick truth out of partiality; better acquainted with a thousand years ago than with the present age, and yet better knowing how this world goes than how his own wit runs; curious for antiquities, and inquisitive of novelties, a wonder to young folks, and a tyrant in table-talk,) denieth, in a great chafe, that any man for teaching of virtue and virtuous actions, is comparable to him. I am "Testis temporum, lux veritatis, vita memoriæ, magistra vitæ, nuncia vetustatis." The philosopher, saith he, teacheth a disputative virtue, but I do an active; his virtue is excellent in the dangerless academy of Plato, but mine showeth forth her honourable face in the battles of Marathon, Pharsalia, Poictiers, and Agincourt: he teacheth virtue by certain abstract considerations; but I only bid you follow the footing of them that have gone before you; old-aged experience goeth beyond the fine-witted philosopher; but I give the experience of many ages: lastly, if he make the song book, I put the learner's hand to the lute; and if he be the guide, I am the light. Then would he allege you innumerable examples, confirming story by stories, how much the wisest senators and princes have been directed by the credit of history, as Brutus, Alphonsus of Aragon, (and who not? if need be.) At length, the long line of their disputation makes a point in this, that the one giveth the precept, and the other the example.

Now whom shall we find, since the question standeth for the highest form in the school of learning, to be moderator? Truly, as me seemeth, the poet; and if not a moderator, even the man that ought to carry the title from them both, and much more from all other serving sciences. Therefore compare we the poet with the historian, and with the moral philosopher; and if he go beyond them both, no other human skill can match him: for as for the Divine, with all reverence, he is ever to be excepted, not only for having his scope as far beyond any of these, as eternity exceedeth a moment, but even for passing each of these in themselves: and for the lawyer, though "Jus" be the daughter of Justice, the chief of virtues, yet because he seeks to make men good rather "formidine pœnæ" than "virtutis amore," or, to say righter, doth not endeavour to make men good, but that their evil hurt not others, having no care, so he be a good citizen, how bad a man he be: therefore, as our wickedness maketh him necessary, and necessity maketh him honourable, so is he not in the deepest truth to stand in rank with these, who all endeavour to take naughtiness away, and plant goodness even in the secretest cabinet of our souls. And these four are all that any way deal in the consideration of men's manners, which being the supreme knowledge, they that best breed it deserve the best commendation.

The philosopher, therefore, and the historian are they which would win the goal, the one by precept, the other by example; but both, not having both, do both halt. For the philosopher, setting down with thorny arguments the bare rule, is so hard of utterance, and so misty to be conceived, that one that hath no other guide but him shall wade in him until he be old, before he shall find sufficient cause to be honest. For his knowledge standeth so upon the abstract and general, that happy is that man who may understand him, and more happy, that can apply what he doth understand. On the other side the historian, wanting the precept, is so tied, not to what should be, but to what is; to the particular truth of things, and not to the general reason of things; that his example draweth no necessary consequence, and therefore a less fruitful doctrine.

Now doth the peerless poet perform both; for whatsoever the philosopher saith should be done, he giveth a perfect picture of it, by some one by whom he presupposeth it was done, so as he coupleth the general notion with the particular example. A perfect picture, I say; for he yieldeth to the powers of the mind an image of that whereof the philosopher bestoweth but a wordish description, which doth neither strike, pierce, nor possess the sight of the soul, so much as that other doth. For as, in outward things, to a man that had never seen an elephant, or a rhinoceros, who should tell him most exquisitely all their shape, colour, bigness, and particular marks? or of a gorgeous palace, an architect, who, declaring the full beauties, might well make the hearer able to repeat, as it were, by rote, all he had heard, yet should never satisfy his inward conceit, with being witness to itself of a true living knowledge; but the same man, as soon as he might see those beasts well painted, or that house well in model, should straightway grow, without need of any description, to a judicial comprehending of them; so, no doubt, the philosopher, with his learned definitions, be it of virtues or vices, matters of public policy or private government, replenisheth the memory with many infallible grounds of wisdom, which, notwithstanding, lie dark before the imaginative and judging power, if they be not illuminated or figured forth by the speaking picture of poesy.

Tully taketh much pains, and many times not without poetical helps, to make us know the force love of our country hath in us. Let us but hear old Anchises, speaking in the midst of Troy's flames, or see Ulysses, in the fulness of all Calypso's delights, bewail his absence from barren and beggarly Ithaca. Anger, the Stoics said, was a short madness; let but Sophocles bring you Ajax on a stage, killing or whipping sheep and oxen, thinking them the army of Greeks, with their chieftains Agamemnon and Menelaus; and tell me, if you have not a more familiar insight into anger, than finding in the schoolmen his genus and difference? See whether wisdom and temperance in Ulysses and Diomedes, valour in Achilles, friendship in Nisus and Euryalus, even to an ignorant man, carry not an apparent shining; and, contrarily, the remorse of conscience in Œdipus; the soon-repenting pride in Agamemnon; the self-devouring cruelty in his father Atreus; the violence of ambition in the two Theban brothers; the sour sweetness of revenge in Medea; and, to fall lower, the Terentian Gnatho, and our Chaucer's Pandar, so expressed, that we now use their names to signify their trades; and finally, all virtues, vices, and passions so in their own natural states laid to the view, that we seem not to hear of them, but clearly to see through them?

But even in the most excellent determination of goodness, what philosopher's counsel can so readily direct a prince as the feigned Cyrus in Xenophon? Or a virtuous man in all fortunes, as Æneas in Virgil? Or a whole commonwealth, as the way of Sir Thomas More's Utopia? I say the way, because where Sir Thomas More erred, it was the fault of the man, and not of the poet; for that way of patterning a commonwealth was most absolute, though he, perchance, hath not so absolutely performed it. For the question is, whether the feigned image of poetry, or the regular instruction of philosophy, hath the more force in teaching. Wherein, if the philosophers have more rightly showed themselves philosophers, than the poets have attained to the high top of their profession, (as in truth,

> Mediocribus esse poetis
> Non Dii, non homines, non concessere columnæ,)

it is, I say again, not the fault of the art, but that by few men that art can be accomplished. Certainly, even our Saviour Christ could as well have given the moral common-places of uncharitableness and humbleness, as the divine narration of Dives and Lazarus; or of disobedience and mercy, as the heavenly discourse of the lost child and the gracious father; but that his thorough searching wisdom knew the estate of Dives burning in hell, and of Lazarus in Abraham's bosom, would more constantly, as it were, inhabit both the memory and judgment. Truly, for myself, (me seems,) I see before mine eyes the lost child's disdainful prodigality turned to envy a swine's dinner; which, by the learned divines, are thought not historical acts, but instructing parables.

For conclusion, I say the philosopher teacheth, but

he teacheth obscurely, so as the learned only can understand him; that is to say, he teacheth them that are already taught. But the poet is the food for the tenderest stomachs; the poet is, indeed, the right popular philosopher. Whereof Æsop's tales give good proof; whose pretty allegories, stealing under the formal tales of beasts, make many, more beastly than beasts, begin to hear the sound of virtue from those dumb speakers.

But now may it be alleged, that if this managing of matters be so fit for the imagination, then must the historian needs surpass, who brings you images of true matters, such as, indeed, were done, and not such as fantastically or falsely may be suggested to have been done. Truly, Aristotle himself, in his Discourse of Poesy, plainly determineth this question, saying, that poetry is φιλοσοφώτερον καὶ σπουδαιότερον, that is to say, it is more philosophical and more ingenious than history. His reason is, because poesy dealeth with καθόλου, that is to say, with the universal consideration, and the history καθ' ἕκαστον, the particular. "Now," saith he, "the universal weighs what is fit to be said or done, either in likelihood or necessity; which the poesy considereth in his imposed names; and the particular only marks, whether Alcibiades did, or suffered, this or that:" thus far Aristotle. Which reason of his, as all his, is most full of reason. For, indeed, if the question were, whether it were better to have a particular act truly or falsely set down? there is no doubt which is to be chosen, no more than whether you had rather have Vespasian's picture right as he was, or, at the painter's pleasure, nothing resembling? But if the question be, for your own use and learning, whether it be better to have it set down as it should be, or as it was? then, certainly, is more doctrinable the feigned Cyrus in Xenophon, than the true Cyrus in Justin; and the feigned Æneas in Virgil, than the right Æneas in Dares Phrygius; as to a lady that desired to fashion her countenance to the best grace, a painter should more benefit her, to portrait a most sweet face, writing Canidia upon it, than to paint Canidia as she was, who, Horace sweareth, was full ill favoured. If the poet do his part aright, he will show you in Tantalus, Atreus, and such like, nothing that is not to be shunned; in Cyrus, Æneas, Ulysses, each thing to be followed; where the historian, bound to tell things as things were, cannot be liberal, without he will be poetical, of a perfect pattern; but, as in Alexander, or Scipio himself, show doings, some to be liked, some to be misliked; and then how will you discern what to follow, but by your own discretion, which you had, without reading Q. Curtius? And whereas, a man may say, though in universal consideration of doctrine, the poet prevaileth, yet that the history, in his saying such a thing was done, doth warrant a man more in that he shall follow; the answer is manifest: that if he stand upon that *was*, as if he should argue, because it rained yesterday therefore it should rain to-day; then, indeed, hath it some advantage to a gross conceit. But if he know an example only enforms a conjectured likelihood, and so go by reason, the poet doth so far exceed him, as he is to frame his example to that which is most reasonable, be it in warlike, politic, or private matters; where the historian in his bare *was* hath many times that which we call fortune to overrule the best wisdom. Many times he must tell events whereof he can yield no cause; or if he do, it must be poetically.

For, that a feigned example hath as much force to teach as a true example, (for as for to move, it is clear, since the feigned may be tuned to the highest key of passion,) let us take one example wherein an historian and a poet did concur. Herodotus and Justin do both testify, that Zopyrus, King Darius's faithful servant, seeing his master long resisted by the rebellious Babylonians, feigned himself in extreme disgrace of his King; for verifying of which, he caused his own nose and ears to be cut off, and so flying to the Babylonians, was received; and, for his known valour, so far credited, that he did find means to deliver them over to Darius. Much-like matters doth Livy record of Tarquinius and his son. Xenophon excellently feigned such another stratagem, performed by Abradatus in Cyrus's behalf. Now would I fain know, if occasion be presented unto you, to serve your prince by such an honest dissimulation, why do you not as well learn it of Xenophon's fiction as of the other's verity? and, truly, so much the better, as you shall save your nose by the bargain; for Abradatus did not counterfeit so far. So, then, the best of the historians is subject to the poet; for, whatsoever action or faction, whatsoever counsel, policy, or war-stratagem the historian is bound to recite, that may the poet, if he list, with his imitation, make his own, beautifying it both for farther teaching, and more delighting, as it please him; having all, from Dante's heaven to his hell, under the authority of his pen. Which if I be asked, What poets have done so? as I might well name some, so yet, say I, and say again, I speak of the art, and not of the artificer.

Now, to that which commonly is attributed to the praise of history, in respect of the notable learning which is got by marking the success, as though therein a man should see virtue exalted, and vice punished: truly, that commendation is peculiar to poetry, and far off from history; for, indeed, poetry ever sets virtue so out in her best colours, making fortune her well-waiting handmaid, that one must needs be enamoured of her. Well may you see Ulysses in a storm, and in other hard plights; but they are but exercises of patience and magnanimity, to make them shine the more in the near following prosperity. And, on the contrary part, if evil men come to the stage, they ever go out (as the tragedy writer answered to one that misliked the show of such persons) so manacled, as they little animate folks to follow them. But history being captived to the truth of a foolish world, is many times a terror from well-doing, and an encouragement to unbridled wickedness. For see we not valiant Miltiades rot in his fetters? The just Phocion and the accomplished Socrates put to death like traitors? The cruel Severus live prosperously? The excellent Severus miserably murdered? Sylla and Marius dying in their beds? Pompey and Cicero slain then when they would have thought exile a happiness? See we not virtuous Cato driven to kill himself, and rebel Cæsar so advanced, that his name yet, after sixteen hundred years, lasteth in the highest honour? And mark but even Cæsar's own words of the forenamed Sylla, (who in that only did honestly, to put down his dishonest tyranny,) "literas nescivit:" as if want of learning caused him to do well. He meant it not by poetry, which, not content with earthly plagues, deviseth new punishments in hell for tyrants: nor yet by philosophy, which teacheth "occidentes esse:" but, no doubt, by skill in history; for that, indeed, can afford you Cypselus, Periander, Phalaris, Dionysius, and I know not how many more of the same kennel, that speed well enough in their abominable injustice of usurpation.

I conclude, therefore, that he excelleth history, not only in furnishing the mind with knowledge, but in setting it forward to that which deserves to be called and accounted good: which setting forward, and moving to well-doing, indeed, setteth the laurel crown upon the poets as victorious; not only of the historian, but over the philosopher, howsoever, in teaching, it may be questionable. For suppose it be granted, that which I suppose, with great reason, may be denied, that the philosopher, in respect of his methodical proceeding, teach more perfectly than the poet, yet do I think, that no man is so much φιλοφιλόσοφος, as to compare the philosopher in moving with the poet. And that moving is of a higher degree than teaching, it may by this appear, that it is well nigh both the cause and effect of teaching; for who will be taught, if he be not moved with desire to be taught? And what so much good doth that teaching bring forth (I speak still of moral doctrine) as that it moveth one to do that which it doth teach. For, as Aristotle saith, it is not γνῶσις but πράξις must be the fruit: and how πράξις can be, without being moved to practise, it is no hard matter to consider. The philosopher showeth you the way, he informeth you of the particularities, as well of the tediousness of the way and of the pleasant lodging you shall have when your journey is ended, as of the many by-turnings that may divert you from your way; but this is to no man, but to him that will read him, and read him with attentive, studious painfulness; which constant desire whosoever hath in him, hath already passed half the hardness of the way, and therefore is beholden to the philsopher but for the other half. Nay, truly, learned men have learnedly thought, that where once reason hath so much overmastered passion, as that the mind hath a free desire to do well, the inward light each mind hath in itself is as good as a philosopher's book: since in nature we know it is well to do well, and what is well and what is evil, although not in the words of art which philosophers bestow upon us; for out of natural conceit the philosophers drew it; but to be moved to do that which we know, or to be moved with desire to know, "hoc opus, hic labor est."

Now, therein, of all sciences, (I speak still of human, and according to the human conceit,) is our poet the monarch. For he doth not only show the way, but giveth so sweet a prospect into the way, as will entice any man to enter into it; nay he doth, as if your journey should lie through a fair vineyard, at the very first give you a cluster of grapes, that full of that taste you may long to pass farther. He beginneth not with obscure definitions, which must blur the margin with interpretations, and load the memory with doubtfulness, but he cometh to you with words set in delightful proportion, either accompanied with, or prepared for, the well-enchanting skill of music; and with a tale, forsooth, he cometh unto you with a tale which holdeth children from play, and old men from the chimney-corner;*

* This is conceived to have suggested Shakespeare's exquisite description,—

>That elder ears played truant at his tale,
>And younger hearings were quite ravished,—
>So sweet and voluble was his discourse, etc.

and, pretending no more, doth intend the winning of the mind from wickedness to virtue; even as the child is often brought to take most wholesome things, by hiding them in such other as have a pleasant taste; which, if one should begin to tell them the nature of the aloes or rhubarbarum they should receive, would sooner take their physic at their ears than at their mouth; so it is in men; (most of whom are childish in the best things, till they be cradled in their graves;) glad they will be to hear the tales of Hercules, Achilles, Cyrus, Æneas; and hearing them, must needs hear the right description of wisdom, valour, and justice; which, if they had been barely (that is to say, philosophically) set out, they would swear they be brought to school again. That imitation whereof poetry is, hath the most conveniency to nature of all other; insomuch that, as Aristotle saith, those things which in themselves are horrible, as cruel battles, unnatural monsters, are made, in poetical imitation, delightful. Truly, I have known men, that even with reading Amadis de Gaule, which, God knoweth, wanteth much of a perfect poesy, have found their hearts moved to the exercise of courtesy, liberality, and especially courage. Who readeth Æneas carrying old Anchises on his back, that wisheth not it were his fortune to perform so excellent an act? Whom doth not those words of Turnus move (the tale of Turnus having planted his image in the imagination)

fugientem hæc terra videbit?
Usque adeone mori miserum est? — VIRGIL.

Where the philosophers (as they think) scorn to delight, so much they be content little to move, saving wrangling whether "virtus" be the chief or the only good;

whether the contemplative or the active life do excel; which Plato and Boetius well knew; and therefore made mistress Philosophy very often borrow the masking raiment of poesy. For even those hard-hearted evil men, who think virtue a school-name, and know no other good but "indulgere genio," and therefore despise the austere admonitions of the philosopher, and feel not the inward reason they stand upon; yet will be content to be delighted, which is all the good-fellow poet seems to promise; and so steal to see the form of goodness, which seen, they cannot but love, ere themselves be aware, as if they took a medicine of cherries.

Infinite proofs of the strange effects of this poetical invention might be alleged; only two shall serve, which are so often remembered, as, I think, all men know them. The one of Menenius Agrippa, who, when the whole people of Rome had resolutely divided themselves from the senate, with apparent show of utter ruin, though he were, for that time, an excellent orator, came not among them upon trust, either of figurative speeches, or cunning insinuations, and much less with far-fetched maxims of philosophy, which, especially if they were Platonic, they must have learned geometry before they could have conceived; but, forsooth, he behaveth himself like a homely and familiar poet. He telleth them a tale, that there was a time, when all the parts of the body made a mutinous conspiracy against the belly, which they thought devoured the fruits of each other's labour; they concluded, they would let so unprofitable a spender starve. In the end, to be short, (for the tale is notorious, and as notorious that it was a tale,) with punishing the belly they plagued themselves. This, applied by him, wrought such effect in the people, as I never read that only words brought forth; but then so sudden, and so good an alteration, for upon reasonable conditions a perfect reconcilement ensued.

The other is of Nathan the prophet, who, when the holy David had so far forsaken God, as to confirm adultery with murder, when he was to do the tenderest office of a friend, in laying his own shame before his eyes, being sent by God to call again so chosen a servant, how doth he it? but by telling of a man whose beloved lamb was ungratefully taken from his bosom. The application most divinely true, but the discourse itself feigned; which made David (I speak of the second and instrumental cause) as in a glass see his own filthiness, as that heavenly psalm of mercy well testifieth.

By these, therefore, examples and reasons, I think it may be manifest, that the poet, with that same hand of delight, doth draw the mind more effectually than any other art doth. And so a conclusion not unfitly ensues; that as virtue is the most excellent resting-place for all worldly learning to make his end of, so poetry, being the most familiar to teach it, and most princely to move towards it, in the most excellent work is the most excellent workman.

But I am content not only to decipher him by his works, (although works in commendation and dispraise must ever hold a high authority,) but more narrowly will examine his parts; so that (as in a man) though all together may carry a presence full of majesty and beauty, perchance in some one defectuous piece we may find blemish.

Now, in his parts, kinds, or species, as you list to term them, it is to be noted, that some poesies have coupled together two or three kinds; as the tragical and comical, whereupon is risen, the tragi-comical; some, in the manner, have mingled prose and verse, as Sannazaro and Boetius; some have mingled matters heroical and pastoral; but that cometh all to one in this question; for, if severed they be good, the conjunction cannot be hurtful. Therefore, perchance, forgetting some, and leaving some as needless to be remembered, it shall not be amiss, in a word, to cite the special kinds, to see what faults may be found in the right use of them.

Is it then the pastoral poem which is misliked? (For, perchance, where the hedge is lowest, they will soonest leap over.) Is the poor pipe disdained, which sometimes, out of Mælibeus's mouth, can show the misery of people under hard lords and ravening soldiers? And again, by Tityrus, what blessedness is derived to them that lie lowest from the goodness of them that sit highest? Sometimes under the pretty tales of wolves and sheep, can include the whole considerations of wrong doing and patience; sometimes show, that contentions for trifles can get but a trifling victory; where, perchance, a man may see, that even Alexander and Darius, when they strove who should be cock of this world's dunghill, the benefit they got was, that the after-livers may say,

> Hæc memini et victum frustra contendere Thyrsim;
> Ex illo Corydon, Corydon est tempore nobis. — VIRGIL.

Or is it the lamenting elegiac, which, in a kind heart, would move rather pity than blame; who bewaileth, with the great philosopher Heraclitus, the weakness of mankind, and the wretchedness of the world; who, surely, is to be praised, either for compassionately accompanying just causes of lamentations, or for rightly painting out how weak be the passions of wofulness?

Is it the bitter, but wholesome iambick, who rubs the galled mind, making shame the trumpet of villany, with bold and open crying out against naughtiness?

Or, the satiric? who,

<blockquote>Omne vafer vitium ridenti tangit Amico;</blockquote>

who sportingly never leaveth, until he make a man laugh at folly, and, at length, ashamed to laugh at himself, which he cannot avoid without avoiding the folly; who, while " circum præcordia ludit," giveth us to feel how many headaches a passionate life bringeth us to; who when all is done,

<blockquote>Est Ulubris, animus si nos non deficit æquus.</blockquote>

No, perchance it is the comic; whom naughty playmakers and stage-keepers have justly made odious. To the arguments of abuse I will after answer; only thus much now is to be said, that the comedy is an imitation of the common errors of our life, which he representeth in the most ridiculous and scornful sort that may be; so as it is impossible that any beholder can be content to be such a one. Now, as in geometry, the oblique must be known as well as the right, and in arithmetic, the odd as well as the even; so in the actions of our life, who seeth not the filthiness of evil, wanteth a great foil to perceive the beauty of virtue. This doth the comedy handle so, in our private and domestical matters, as, with hearing it, we get, as it were, an experience of what is to be looked for, of a niggardly Demea, of a crafty Davus, of a flattering Gnatho, of a vain-glorious Thraso; and not only to know what effects are to be expected, but to know who be such, by the signifying badge given them by the comedian. And little reason hath any man to say, that men learn the evil by seeing it so set out; since, as I said before, there is no man living, but by the force truth hath in nature, no sooner seeth these men play their parts, but wisheth them in "pistrinum;" although perchance the sack of his own faults lie so behind his back, that he seeth not himself to dance the same measure, whereto yet nothing can more open his eyes than to see his own actions contemptibly set forth; so that the right use of comedy will, I think, by nobody be blamed.

And much less of the high and excellent tragedy, that openeth the greatest wounds, and showeth forth the ulcers that are covered with tissue; that maketh kings fear to be tyrants, and tyrants to manifest their tyrannical humours; that with stirring the effects of admiration and commiseration, teacheth the uncertainty of this world, and upon how weak foundations gilded roofs are builded; that maketh us know, "qui sceptra sævus duro imperio regit, timet timentes, metus in authorem redit." But how much it can move, Plutarch yieldeth a notable testimony of the abominable tyrant Alexander Pheræus; from whose eyes a tragedy, well made and represented, drew abundance of tears, who without all pity had murdered infinite numbers, and some of his own blood; so as he that was not ashamed to make matters for tragedies, yet could not resist the sweet violence of a tragedy. And if it wrought no farther good in him, it was that he, in despite of himself, withdrew himself from hearkening to that which might mollify his hardened heart. But it is not the tragedy they do mislike, for it were too absurd to cast out so excellent a representation of whatsoever is most worthy to be learned.

Is it the lyric that most displeaseth, who with his tuned lyre and well accorded voice, giveth praise, the reward of virtue, to virtuous acts? who giveth moral precepts and natural problems? who sometimes raiseth up his voice to the height of the heavens, in singing the lauds of the immortal God? Certainly, I must confess mine own barbarousness; I never heard the old song of Percy and Douglas,* that I found not my heart moved more than with a trumpet; and yet it is sung but by some blind crowder, with no rougher voice than rude style; which being so evil apparelled in the dust and cobweb of that uncivil age, what would it work, trimmed in the gorgeous eloquence of Pindar? In Hungary I have seen it the manner at all feasts, and all other such-like meetings, to have songs of their ancestors' valour, which that right soldier-like nation think one of the chiefest kindlers of brave courage. The incomparable Lacedæmonians did not only carry that kind of music ever with them to the field, but even at home, as such songs were made, so were they all content to be singers of them; when the lusty men were to tell what they did, the old men what they had done, and the

---

* Ben Jonson, charmed with the beauties of this old song of Chevy Chace, in which the battle of Otterburn, in 1388, is supposed to have been celebrated, was wont to say, that he would rather have been the author of that little poem, than of all his own works. The ballad, on which there is a beautiful critique in The Spectator, Nos. 70 and 74, is conjectured to have been written after this eulogium of Mr. Sidney, who probably had in contemplation a poem of an older date, which is inserted in Percy's Reliques of Ancient English Poetry. — DR. ZOUCH.

young what they would do. And where a man may say, that Pindar many times praiseth highly victories of small moment, rather matters of sport than virtue; as it may be answered, it was the fault of the poet, and not of the poetry, so, indeed, the chief fault was in the time and custom of the Greeks, who set those toys at so high a price, that Philip of Macedon reckoned a horse-race won at Olympus among his three fearful felicities. But as the inimitable Pindar often did, so is that kind most capable, and most fit, to awake the thoughts from the sleep of idleness, to embrace honourable enterprises.

There rests the heroical, whose very name, I think, should daunt all backbiters. For by what conceit can a tongue be directed to speak evil of that which draweth with him no less champions than Achilles, Cyrus, Æneas, Turnus, Tydeus, Rinaldo? who doth not only teach and move to truth, but teacheth and moveth to the most high and excellent truth: who maketh magnanimity and justice shine through all misty fearfulness and foggy desires? who, if the saying of Plato and Tully be true, that who could see virtue, would be wonderfully ravished with the love of her beauty; this man setteth her out to make her more lovely, in her holiday apparel, to the eye of any that will deign not to disdain until they understand. But if any thing be already said in the defence of sweet poetry, all concurreth to the maintaining the heroical, which is not only a kind, but the best and most accomplished kind, of poetry. For, as the image of each action stirreth and instructeth the mind, so the lofty image of such worthies most inflameth the mind with desire to be worthy, and informs with counsel how to be worthy. Only let Æneas be worn in the tablet of your memory, how he governeth himself in the ruin of his country; in the preserving his old father, and carrying away his religious ceremonies; in obeying God's commandments, to leave Dido, though not only passionate kindness, but even the human consideration of virtuous gratefulness, would have craved other of him; how in storms, how in sports, how in war, how in peace, how a fugitive, how victorious, how besieged, how besieging, how to strangers, how to allies, how to enemies; how to his own, lastly, how in his inward self, and how in his outward government; and I think, in a mind most prejudiced with a prejudicating humour, he will be found in excellency fruitful. Yea, as Horace saith, "melius, Chrysippo, et Crantore:" but, truly, I imagine it falleth out with these poet-whippers as with some good women who often are sick, but in faith they cannot tell where. So the name of poetry is odious to them, but neither his cause nor effects, neither the sum that contains him, nor the particularities descending from him, give any fast handle to their carping dispraise.

Since, then, poetry is of all human learnings the most ancient, and of most fatherly antiquity, as from whence other learnings have taken their beginnings; since it is so universal that no learned nation doth despise it, nor barbarous nation is without it; since both Roman and Greek gave such divine names unto it, the one of prophesying, the other of making, and that indeed that name of making is fit for him, considering, that where all other arts retain themselves within their subject, and receive, as it were, their being from it, the poet only, only bringeth his own stuff, and doth not learn a conceit out of a matter, but maketh matter for a conceit; since neither his description nor end containeth any evil, the thing described cannot be evil; since his effects be so good as to teach goodness, and delight the learners of it; since therein (namely, in moral doctrine, the chief of all knowledges) he doth not only far pass the historian, but, for instructing, is well nigh comparable to the philosopher; for moving, leaveth him behind him; since the Holy Scripture (wherein there is no uncleanness) hath whole parts in it poetical, and that even our Saviour Christ vouchsafed to use the flowers of it; since all his kinds are not only in their united forms, but in their severed dissections fully commendable; I think, and think I think rightly, the laurel crown appointed for triumphant captains, doth worthily, of all other learnings, honour the poet's triumph.

But because we have ears as well as tongues, and that the lightest reasons that may be, will seem to weigh greatly, if nothing be put in the counter-balance, let us hear, and, as well as we can, ponder what objections be made against this art, which may be worthy either of yielding or answering.

First, truly, I note, not only in these μισομούσοι, poet-haters, but in all that kind of people who seek a praise by dispraising others, that they do prodigally spend a great many wandering words in quips and scoffs, carping and taunting at each thing, which, by stirring the spleen, may stay the brain from a thorough beholding the worthiness of the subject. Those kind of objections, as they are full of a very idle easiness, (since there is nothing of so sacred a majesty, but that an itching tongue may rub itself upon it,) so deserve they no other answer, but, instead of laughing at the jest, to laugh at the jester. We know a playing wit can praise the discretion of an ass, the comfortableness of being in debt, and the jolly commodities of being sick of the plague; so, of the contrary side, if we will turn Ovid's verse,

> Ut lateat virtus proximitate mali,

"That good lies hid in nearness of the evil," Agrippa will be as merry in the showing the vanity of science, as Erasmus was in the commending of folly; neither shall any man or matter escape some touch of these smiling railers. But for Erasmus and Agrippa, they had another foundation than the superficial part would promise. Marry, these other pleasant fault-finders, who will correct the verb before they understand the noun, and confute others' knowledge before they confirm their own; I would have them only remember, that scoffing cometh not of wisdom; so as the best title in true English they get with their merriments, is to be called good fools; for so have our grave forefathers ever termed that humorous kind of jesters.

But that which giveth greatest scope to their scorning humour, is rhyming and versing. It is already said, and, as I think, truly said, it is not rhyming and versing that maketh poesy; one may be a poet without versing, and a versifier without poetry. But yet, presuppose it were inseparable, as, indeed, it seemeth Scaliger judgeth truly, it were an inseparable commendation; for if "oratio" next to "ratio," speech next to reason, be the greatest gift bestowed upon mortality, that cannot be praiseless which doth most polish that blessing of speech; which considereth each word, not only as a man may say by his forcible quality, but by his best measured quantity; carrying even in themselves a harmony; without, perchance, number, measure, order, proportion be in our time grown odious.

But lay aside the just praise it hath, by being the only fit speech for music—music, I say, the most divine striker of the senses: thus much is undoubtedly true, that if reading be foolish without remembering, memory being the only treasure of knowledge, those words which are fittest for memory, are likewise most convenient for knowledge. Now, that verse far exceedeth prose in the knitting up of the memory, the reason is manifest: the words, besides their delight, which hath a great affinity to memory, being so set, as one cannot be lost, but the whole work fails: which accusing itself, calleth the remembrance back to itself, and so most strongly confirmeth it. Besides, one word so, as it were, begetting another, as, be it in rhyme or measured verse, by the former a man shall have a near guess to the follower. Lastly, even they that have taught the art of memory, have showed nothing so apt for it as a certain room divided into many places, well and thoroughly known: now that hath the verse in effect perfectly, every word having his natural seat, which seat must needs make the word remembered. But what needs more in a thing so known to all men? Who is it, that ever was a scholar that doth not carry away some verses of Virgil, Horace, or Cato, which in his youth he learned; and even to his old age serve him for hourly lessons? as,

> Percontatorem fugito: nam garrulus idem est.
> Dum sibi quisque placet credula turba sumus.

But the fitness it hath for memory is notably proved by all delivery of arts, wherein, for the most part, from grammar to logic, mathematics, physic, and the rest, the rules chiefly necessary to be borne away, are compiled in verses. So that verse being in itself sweet and orderly, and being best for memory, the only handle of knowledge, it must be in jest that any man can speak against it.

Now then go we to the most important imputations laid to the poor poets; for aught I can yet learn, they are these.

First, that there being many other more fruitful knowledges, a man might better spend his time in them, than in this.

Secondly, that it is the mother of lies.

Thirdly, that it is the nurse of abuse, infecting us with many pestilent desires, with a syren sweetness, drawing the mind to the serpent's tail of sinful fancies; and herein especially, comedies give the largest field to ear,* as Chaucer saith; how, both in other nations and ours, before poets did soften us, we were full of courage, given to martial exercises, the pillars of manlike liberty, and not lulled asleep in shady idleness with poets' pastimes.

And lastly, and chiefly, they cry out with open mouth, as if they had overshot Robin Hood, that Plato banished them out of his commonwealth. Truly, this is much, if there be much truth in it.

First, to the first, that a man might better spend his time, is a reason indeed; but it doth, as they say, but

---

* "To ear" or "ere," is "to till" or "plow," and is a verb sometimes used by Shakespeare, Fletcher, and many others of our old writers. In the present case, the expression "comedies give the largest field to ear," probably means, that they afford the largest matter for discourse. It is in this sense, according to Urry, that the phrase is employed by Chaucer in the passage referred to. Ch. Prol. v. 888.

"petere principium." For if it be, as I affirm, that no learning is so good as that which teacheth and moveth to virtue, and that none can both teach and move thereto so much as poesy, then is the conclusion manifest, that ink and paper cannot be to a more profitable purpose employed. And certainly, though a man should grant their first assumption, it should follow, methinks, very unwillingly, that good is not good, because better is better. But I still and utterly deny, that there is sprung out of earth a more fruitful knowledge.

To the second, therefore, that they should be the principal liars, I answer paradoxically, but truly, I think truly, that of all writers under the sun, the poet is the least liar; and though he would, as a poet, can scarcely be a liar. The astronomer, with his cousin the geometrician, can hardly escape when they take upon them to measure the height of the stars. How often, think you, do the physicians lie, when they aver things good for sicknesses, which afterwards send Charon a great number of souls drowned in a potion before they come to his ferry. And no less of the rest which take upon them to affirm. Now for the poet, he nothing affirmeth, and therefore never lieth; for, as I take it, to lie is to affirm that to be true which is false: so as the other artists, and especially the historian, affirming many things, can, in the cloudy knowledge of mankind, hardly escape from many lies: but the poet, as I said before, never affirmeth; the poet never maketh any circles about your imagination, to conjure you to believe for true what he writeth: he citeth not authorities of other histories, but even for his entry, calleth the sweet Muses to inspire into him a good invention; in troth, not labouring to tell you what is, or is not, but what should, or should not be. And, therefore, though he recount things not true, yet because he telleth them not for true, he lieth not; without we will say, that Nathan lied in his speech, before alleged, to David; which, as a wicked man durst scarce say, so think I none so simple would say, that Æsop lied in the tales of his beasts; for who thinketh that Æsop wrote it for actually true, were well worthy to have his name chronicled among the beasts he writeth of. What child is there, that cometh to a play, and seeing Thebes written in great letters upon an old door, doth believe that it is Thebes? If then a man can arrive to the child's age, to know that the poets' persons and doings are but pictures what should be, and not stories what have been, they will never give the lie to things not affirmatively, but allegorically and figuratively written; and therefore, as in history, looking for truth, they may go away full fraught with falsehood, so in poesy, looking but for fiction, they shall use the narration but as an imaginative ground-plot of a profitable invention.

But hereto is replied, that the poets give names to men they write of, which argueth a conceit of an actual truth, and so, not being true, proveth a falsehood. And doth the lawyer lie then, when, under the names of John of the Stile, and John of the Nokes, he putteth his case? But that is easily answered, their naming of men is but to make their picture the more lively, and not to build any history. Painting men, they cannot leave men nameless: we see we cannot play at chess, but that we must give names to our chess-men; and yet, methinks, he were a very partial champion of truth, that would say we lied for giving a piece of wood the reverend title of a bishop. The poet nameth Cyrus and Æneas no other way than to show what men of their fames, fortunes, and estates should do.

Their third is, how much it abuseth men's wit, training it to a wanton sinfulness, and lustful love. For, indeed, that is the principal if not only abuse I can hear alleged. They say the comedies rather teach, than reprehend, amorous conceits; they say the lyric is larded with passionate sonnets; the elegiac weeps the want of his mistress; and that even to the heroical, Cupid hath ambitiously climbed. Alas! Love, I would thou couldst as well defend thyself, as thou canst offend others! I would those on whom thou dost attend, could either put thee away, or yield good reason why they keep thee! But grant love of beauty to be a beastly fault, although it be very hard, since only man, and no beast, hath that gift to discern beauty; grant that lovely name of love to deserve all hateful reproaches, although even some of my masters the philosophers spent a good deal of their lamp oil in setting forth the excellency of it; grant, I say, what they will have granted, that not only love, but lust, but vanity, but, if they list, scurrility, possess many leaves of the poets' books; yet, think I, when this is granted, they will find their sentence may, with good manners, put the last words foremost; and not say that poetry abuseth man's wit, but that man's wit abuseth poetry. For I will not deny, but that man's wit may make poesy, which should be φραστική, which some learned have defined, figuring forth good things, to be φανταστική; which doth contrariwise infect the fancy with unworthy objects; as the painter, who should give to the eye either some excellent perspective, or some fine picture fit for building or fortification, or containing in it some notable example, as Abraham sacrificing his son Isaac, Judith killing Holofernes, David fighting with Goliath, may leave those, and please an ill-pleased eye with wanton shows of better-hidden matters.

But, what! shall the abuse of a thing make the right use odious? Nay, truly, though I yield that poesy may not only be abused, but that being abused, by the reason of his sweet charming force, it can do more hurt than any other army of words, yet shall it be so far from concluding, that the abuse shall give reproach to the abused, that, contrariwise, it is a good reason, that whatsoever being abused, doth most harm, being rightly used (and upon the right use, each thing receives his title) doth most good. Do we not see skill of physic, the best rampire to our often-assaulted bodies, being abused, teach poison, the most violent destroyer? Doth not knowledge of law, whose end is to even and right all things, being abused, grow the crooked fosterer of horrible injuries? Doth not (to go in the highest) God's word abused, breed heresy, and his name abused, become blasphemy? Truly, a needle cannot do much hurt, and as truly (with leave of ladies be it spoken) it cannot do much good. With a sword thou mayest kill thy father, and with a sword thou mayest defend thy prince and country; so that, as in their calling poets fathers of lies, they said nothing, so in this their argument of abuse, they prove the commendation.

They allege herewith, that before poets began to be in price, our nation had set their heart's delight upon action, and not imagination; rather doing things worthy to be written, than writing things fit to be done. What that before time was, I think scarcely Sphynx can tell; since no memory is so ancient that gives not the precedence to poetry. And certain it is, that, in our plainest homeliness, yet never was the Albion nation without poetry. Marry, this argument, though it be levelled against poetry, yet is it indeed a chain-shot against all learning or bookishness, as they commonly term it. Of such mind were certain Goths, of whom it is written, that having in the spoil of a famous city taken a fair library, one hangman, belike fit to execute the fruits of their wits, who had murdered a great number of bodies, would have set fire in it. "No," said another, very gravely, "take heed what you do, for while they are busy about those toys, we shall with more leisure conquer their countries." This, indeed, is the ordinary doctrine of ignorance, and many words sometimes I have heard spent in it; but because this reason is generally against all learning, as well as poetry, or rather all learning but poetry; because it were too large a digression to handle it, or at least too superfluous, since it is manifest that all government of action is to be gotten by knowledge, and knowledge best by gathering many knowledges, which is reading; I only say with Horace, to him that is of that opinion,

> Jubeo stultum esse libenter———

for as for poetry itself, it is the freest from this objection, for poetry is the companion of camps. I dare undertake, Orlando Furioso, or honest King Arthur, will never displease a soldier: but the quiddity of "ens" and "prima materia," will hardly agree with a corselet. And, therefore, as I said in the beginning, even Turks and Tartars are delighted with poets. Homer, a Greek, flourished before Greece flourished; and if to a slight conjecture a conjecture may be opposed, truly it may seem, that as by him their learned men took almost their first light of knowledge, so their active men receive their first motions of courage. Only Alexander's example may serve, who by Plutarch is accounted of such virtue, that fortune was not his guide, but his footstool; whose acts speak for him, though Plutarch did not: indeed the phœnix of warlike princes. This Alexander left his schoolmaster, living Aristotle, behind him, but took dead Homer with him. He put the philosopher Callisthenes to death, for his seeming philosophical, indeed mutinous, stubbornness; but the chief thing he was ever heard to wish for, was, that Homer had been alive. He well found he received more bravery of mind by the pattern of Achilles, than by hearing the definition of fortitude. And, therefore, if Cato misliked Fulvius for carrying Ennius with him to the field, it may be answered, that if Cato misliked it, the noble Fulvius liked it, or else he had not done it; for it was not the excellent Cato Uticensis, whose authority I would much more have reverenced; but it was the former, in truth a bitter punisher of faults, but else a man that had never sacrificed to the Graces. He misliked and cried out against all Greek learning; and yet, being fourscore years old, began to learn it, belike fearing that Pluto understood not Latin. Indeed, the Roman laws allowed no person to be carried to the wars, but he that was in the soldiers' roll. And, therefore, though Cato misliked his unmustered person, he misliked not his work. And if he had, Scipio Nasica (judged by common consent the best Roman) loved him: both the other Scipio brothers, who had by their virtues no less surnames than of Asia and Afric, so loved him, that they caused his body to be buried in their sepulture.

So, as Cato's authority being but against his person, and that answered with so far greater than himself, is herein of no validity.

But now, indeed, my burthen is great, that Plato's name is laid upon me, whom I must confess of all philosophers, I have ever esteemed most worthy of reverence; and with good reason, since of all philosophers he is the most poetical; yet if he will defile the fountain out of which his flowing streams have proceeded, let us boldly examine with what reason he did it.

First, truly, a man might maliciously object, that Plato, being a philosopher, was a natural enemy of poets. For, indeed, after the philosophers had picked out of the sweet mysteries of poetry, the right discerning true points of knowledge, they forthwith, putting it in method, and making a school art of that which the poets did only teach by a divine delightfulness, beginning to spurn at their guides, like ungrateful apprentices, were not content to set up shop for themselves, but sought by all means to discredit their masters; which, by the force of delight being barred them, the less they could overthrow them, the more they hated them. For, indeed, they found for Homer seven cities strove who should have him for their citizen, where many cities banished philosophers, as not fit members to live among them. For only repeating certain of Euripides' verses, many Athenians had their lives saved of the Syracusans, where the Athenians themselves thought many philosophers unworthy to live. Certain poets, as Simonides and Pindar, had so prevailed with Hiero the first, that of a tyrant they made him a just king: where Plato could do so little with Dionysius, that he himself, of a philosopher, was made a slave.

But who should do thus, I confess, should requite the objections made against poets, with like cavillations against philosophers; as likewise one should do, that should bid one read Phædrus or Symposium in Plato, or the discourse of love in Plutarch, and see whether any poet do authorise abominable filthiness as they do.

Again, a man might ask, out of what commonwealth Plato doth banish them? In sooth, thence where he himself alloweth community of women. So, as belike this banishment grew not for effeminate wantonness, since little should poetical sonnets be hurtful, when a man might have what woman he listed. But I honour philosophical instructions, and bless the wits which bred them, so as they be not abused, which is likewise stretched to poetry. Saint Paul himself sets a watchword upon philosophy, indeed upon the abuse. So doth Plato upon the abuse, not upon poetry. Plato found fault that the poets of his time filled the world with wrong opinions of the gods, making light tales of that unspotted essence, and, therefore, would not have the youth depraved with such opinions. Herein may much be said, let this suffice: the poets did not induce such opinions, but did imitate those opinions already induced. For all the Greek stories can well testify, that the very religion of that time stood upon many and many-fashioned gods; not taught so by poets, but followed according to their nature of imitation. Who list may read in Plutarch, the discourses of Isis and Osiris, of the cause why oracles ceased, of the Divine providence, and see whether the theology of that nation stood not upon such dreams, which the poets indeed superstitiously observed. And truly, since they had not the light of Christ, did much better in it than the philosophers, who, shaking off superstition, brought in atheism.

Plato, therefore, whose authority I had much rather justly construe, than unjustly resist, meant not in general of poets, in those words of which Julius Scaliger saith, "qua authoritate, barbari quidam atque insipidi, abuti velint ad poetas e republicâ exigendos:" but only meant to drive out those wrong opinions of the Deity, whereof now, without farther law, Christianity hath taken away all the hurtful belief, perchance as he thought, nourished by then esteemed poets. And a man need go no farther than to Plato himself to know his meaning; who, in his dialogue called Ion, giveth high, and rightly, divine commendation unto poetry. So as Plato, banishing the abuse, not the thing, not banishing it, but giving due honour to it, shall be our patron, and not our adversary. For, indeed, I had much rather, since truly I may do it, show their mistaking of Plato, under whose lion's skin they would make an ass-like braying against poesy, than go about to overthrow his authority; whom, the wiser a man is, the more just cause he shall find to have in admiration; especially since he attributeth unto poesy more than myself do, namely, to be a very inspiring of a divine force, far above man's wit, as in the forenamed dialogue is apparent.

Of the other side, who would show the honours have been by the best sort of judgments granted them, a whole sea of examples would present themselves; Alexanders, Cæsars, Scipios, all favourers of poets; Lælius, called the Roman Socrates, himself a poet; so as part of Heautontimeroumenos, in Terence, was supposed to be made by him. And even the Greek

Socrates, whom Apollo confirmed to be the only wise man, is said to have spent part of his old time in putting Æsop's Fables into verse: and, therefore, full evil should it become his scholar Plato, to put such words in his master's mouth against poets. But what needs more? Aristotle writes the Art of Poesy; and why, if it should not be written? Plutarch teacheth the use to be gathered of them; and how, if they should not be read? And who reads Plutarch's either history or philosophy, shall find he trimmeth both their garments with gards of poesy.

But I list not to defend poesy with the help of his underling historiographer. Let it suffice to have showed, it is a fit soil for praise to dwell upon; and what dispraise may be set upon it, is either easily overcome, or transformed into just commendation. So, that since the excellencies of it may be so easily and so justly confirmed, and the low creeping objections so soon trodden down; it not being an art of lies, but of true doctrine; not of effeminateness, but of notable stirring of courage; not of abusing man's wit, but of strengthening man's wit; not banished, but honoured by Plato; let us rather plant more laurels for to ingarland the poets' heads (which honour of being laureate, as besides them only triumphant captains were, is a sufficient authority to show the price they ought to be held in) than suffer the ill-favoured breath of such wrong speakers once to blow upon the clear springs of poesy.

But since I have run so long a career in this matter, methinks, before I give my pen a full stop, it shall be but a little more lost time to enquire, why England, the mother of excellent minds, should be grown so hard a step-mother to poets; who, certainly, in wit ought to pass all others, since all only proceeds from their wit, being, indeed, makers of themselves, not takers of others. How can I but exclaim,

> Musa mihi causas memora quo numine læso!

Sweet poesy! that hath anciently had kings, emperors, senators, great captains, such as, besides a thousand others, David, Adrian, Sophocles, Germanicus, not only to favour poets, but to be poets: and of our nearer times, can present for her patrons, a Robert, King of Sicily; the great King Francis of France; King James of Scotland; such cardinals as Bembus and Bibiena; such famous preachers and teachers as Beza and Melancthon; so learned philosophers as Fracastorius and Scaliger; so great orators as Pontanus and Muretus; so piercing wits as George Buchanan; so grave counsellors as, besides many, but before all, that Hospital of France; than whom, I think, that realm never brought forth a more accomplished judgment more firmly builded upon virtue; I say, these, with numbers of others, not only to read others' poesies, but to poetise for others' reading: that poesy, thus embraced in all other places, should only find, in our time, a hard welcome in England, I think the very earth laments it, and therefore decks our soil with fewer laurels than it was accustomed. For heretofore poets have in England also flourished; and, which is to be noted, even in those times when the trumpet of Mars did sound loudest. And now, that an over-faint quietness should seem to strew the house for poets, they are almost in as good reputation as the mountebanks at Venice. Truly, even that, as of the one side it giveth great praise to poesy, which, like Venus, (but to better purpose,) had rather be troubled in the net with Mars, than enjoy the homely quiet of Vulcan; so serveth it for a piece of a reason why they are less grateful to idle England, which now can scarce endure the pain of a pen. Upon this necessarily followeth, that base men, with servile wits, undertake it, who think it enough if they can be rewarded of the printer: and so as Epaminondas is said, with the honour of his virtue, to have made an office, by his exercising it, which before was contemptible, to become highly respected; so these men, no more but setting their names to it, by their own disgracefulness, disgrace the most graceful poesy. For now, as if all the Muses were got with child, to bring forth bastard poets, without any commission, they do post over the banks of Helicon, until they make their readers more weary than post-horses; while, in the mean time, they,

>   Queis meliore luto finxit præcordia Titan,

are better content to suppress the outflowings of their wit, than by publishing them to be accounted knights of the same order.

But I that, before ever I durst aspire unto the dignity, am admitted into the company of the paper-blurrers, do find the very true cause of our wanting estimation, is want of desert, taking upon us to be poets in despite of Pallas. Now, wherein we want desert, were a thankworthy labour to express. But if I knew, I should have mended myself; but as I never desired the title, so have I neglected the means to come by it; only, overmastered by some thoughts, I yielded an inky tribute unto them. Marry, they that delight in poesy itself, should seek to know what they do; and how they do, especially, look themselves in an unflattering glass of reason, if they be inclinable unto it.

For poesy must not be drawn by the ears, it must be gently led, or rather it must lead; which was partly the cause that made the ancient learned affirm, it was a divine, and no human skill, since all other knowledges lie ready for any that have strength of wit: a poet no industry can make, if his own genius be not carried into it. And therefore is an old proverb, "Orator fit, poeta nascitur." Yet confess I always, that as the fertilest ground must be manured, so must the highest flying wit have a Dædalus to guide him. That Dædalus, they say, both in this and in other, hath three wings to bear itself up into the air of due commendation; that is, art, imitation, and exercise. But these, neither artificial rules, nor imitative patterns, we much cumber ourselves withal. Exercise, indeed, we do, but that very fore-backwardly; for where we should exercise to know, we exercise as having known; and so is our brain delivered of much matter, which never was begotten by knowledge. For there being two principal parts, matter to be expressed by words, and words to express the matter, in neither we use art or imitation rightly. Our matter is "quodlibet," indeed, although wrongly, performing Ovid's verse,

> Quicquid conabor dicere, versus erit;

never marshalling it into any assured rank, that almost the readers cannot tell where to find themselves.

Chaucer, undoubtedly, did excellently in his Troilus and Cressida; of whom, truly, I know not whether to marvel more, either that he, in that misty time, could see so clearly, or that we, in this clear age, go so stumblingly after him. Yet had he great wants, fit to be forgiven in so reverend antiquity. I account the Mirror of Magistrates,* meetly furnished of beautiful parts. And in the Earl of Surrey's Lyrics,† many things tasting of a noble birth, and worthy of a noble mind. The Shepherds' Kalendar,‡ hath much poesy in his eclogues, indeed, worthy the reading, if I be not deceived. That same framing of his style to an old rustic language, I dare not allow; since neither Theocritus in Greek, Virgil in Latin, nor Sannazaro in Italian, did affect it. Besides these, I do not remember to have seen but few (to speak boldly) printed that have poetical sinews in them. For proof whereof, let but most of the verses be put in prose, and then ask the meaning, and it will be found, that one verse did but beget another, without ordering, at the first, what should be at the last; which becomes a confused mass of words, with a tinkling sound of rhyme, barely accompanied with reason.

Our tragedies and comedies, not without cause, are cried out against, observing rules neither of honest civil-

---

* The Mirror for Magistrates was the joint production of Thomas Sackville, Lord Buckhurst and Earl of Dorset, and other ingenious persons of less note, his contemporaries and friends. It first appeared in print in 1559. Buckhurst contributed the induction, which has ever been esteemed one of the most vigorous remnants of our ancient poetry. Walpole styles him " the patriarch of a race of genius and wit."

† Henry Howard, Earl of Surrey, was the son of Thomas, Duke of Norfolk. He was the author of several minor poems, of much elegance and spirit; and he afforded the earliest specimen of blank verse in our language, in his translation of the fourth book of the Æneid. The jealousy of Henry the Eighth brought him to the scaffold in 1546–7.

‡ By Spenser, and dedicated to Mr. P. Sidney.

ity nor skilful poetry. Excepting Gorboduc* (again I say of those that I have seen) which notwithstanding, as it is full of stately speeches, and well-sounding phrases, climbing to the height of Seneca his style, and as full of notable morality, which it doth most delightfully teach, and so obtain the very end of poesy; yet, in truth, it is very defectuous in the circumstances, which grieves me, because it might not remain as an exact model of all tragedies. For it is faulty both in place and time, the two necessary companions of all corporal actions. For where the stage should alway represent but one place; and the uttermost time presupposed in it, should be, both by Aristotle's precept, and common reason, but one day; there is both many days and many places inartificially imagined.

But if it be so in Gorboduc, how much more in all the rest? where you shall have Asia of the one side, and Afric of the other, and so many other under kingdoms, that the player, when he comes in, must ever begin with telling where he is, or else the tale will not be conceived. Now shall you have three ladies walk to gather flowers, and then we must believe the stage to be a garden. By and by, we hear news of shipwreck in the same place, then we are to blame if we accept it not for a rock. Upon the back of that comes out a hideous monster with fire and smoke, and then the miserable

---

* This play was written by Lord Buckhurst and Mr. Thomas Norton. It was first printed in the year 1565, under the title of Ferrex and Porrex; but in 1590, its name was changed to that of the "Tragedy of Gorboduc." It was represented before Queen Elizabeth by the gentlemen of the Inner Temple. The first three acts were the composition of Norton; and the fourth and fifth of Lord Buckhurst.

beholders are bound to take it for a cave; while, in the mean time, two armies fly in, represented with four swords and bucklers, and then, what hard heart will not receive it for a pitched field?

Now of time they are much more liberal; for ordinary it is, that two young princes fall in love; after many traverses she is got with child; delivered of a fair boy; he is lost, groweth a man, falleth in love, and is ready to get another child; and all this in two hours' space; which, how absurd it is in sense, even sense may imagine; and art hath taught and all ancient examples justified, and at this day the ordinary players in Italy will not err in. Yet will some bring in an example of the Eunuch in Terence, that containeth matter of two days, yet far short of twenty years. True it is, and so was it to be played in two days, and so fitted to the time it set forth. And though Plautus have in one place done amiss, let us hit it with him, and not miss with him. But they will say, How then shall we set forth a story which contains both many places and many times? And do they not know, that a tragedy is tied to the laws of poesy, and not of history; not bound to follow the story, but having liberty either to feign a quite new matter, or to frame the history to the most tragical convenience? Again, many things may be told, which cannot be showed; if they know the difference betwixt reporting and representing. As for example, I may speak, though I am here, of Peru, and in speech digress from that to the description of Calicut; but in action I cannot represent it without Pacolet's horse. And so was the manner the ancients took by some "Nuntius," to recount things done in former time, or other place.

Lastly, if they will represent an history, they must not, as Horace saith, begin "ab ovo," but they must come to the principal point of that one action which they will represent. By example this will be best expressed; I have a story of young Polydorus, delivered, for safety's sake, with great riches, by his father Priamus to Polymnestor, King of Thrace, in the Trojan war time. He, after some years, hearing of the overthrow of Priamus, for to make the treasure his own, murdereth the child; the body of the child is taken up; Hecuba, she, the same day, findeth a sleight to be revenged most cruelly of the tyrant. Where, now, would one of our tragedy-writers begin, but with the delivery of the child? Then should he sail over into Thrace, and so spend I know not how many years, and travel numbers of places. But where doth Euripides? Even with the finding of the body; leaving the rest to be told by the spirit of Polydorus. This needs no farther to be enlarged; the dullest wit may conceive it.

But, besides these gross absurdities, how all their plays be neither right tragedies nor right comedies, mingling kings and clowns, not because the matter so carrieth it, but thrust in the clown by head and shoulders to play a part in majestical matters, with neither decency nor discretion; so as neither the admiration and commiseration, nor the right sportfulness, is by their mongrel tragi-comedy obtained. I know Apuleius did somewhat so, but that is a thing recounted with space of time, not represented in one moment: and I know the ancients have one or two examples of tragi-comedies as Plautus hath Amphytrio. But, if we mark them well, we shall find, that they never, or very daintily, match hornpipes and funerals. So falleth it out, that having indeed no right comedy in that comical part of our tragedy, we have nothing but scurrility, unworthy of any chaste ears; or some extreme show of doltishness, indeed fit to lift up a loud laughter, and nothing else: where the whole tract of a comedy should be full of delight; as the tragedy should be still maintained in a well-raised admiration.

But our comedians think there is no delight without laughter, which is very wrong; for though laughter may come with delight, yet cometh it not of delight, as though delight should be the cause of laughter; but well may one thing breed both together. Nay, in themselves, they have, as it were, a kind of contrariety. For delight we scarcely do, but in things that have a conveniency to ourselves, or to the general nature. Laughter almost ever cometh of things most disproportioned to ourselves and nature: delight hath a joy in it either permanent or present; laughter hath only a scornful tickling. For example; we are ravished with delight to see a fair woman, and yet are far from being moved to laughter: we laugh at deformed creatures, wherein certainly we cannot delight: we delight in good chances: we laugh at mischances: we delight to hear the happiness of our friends and country, at which he were worthy to be laughed at that would laugh: we shall, contrarily, sometimes laugh to find a matter quite mistaken, and go down the hill against the bias, in the mouth of some such men, as for the respect of them, one shall be heartily sorry he cannot choose but laugh, and so is rather pained than delighted with laughter. Yet deny I not, but that they may go well together; for, as in Alexander's picture well set out, we delight without laughter, and in twenty mad antics we laugh without delight: so in Hercules, painted with his great beard and furious countenance, in a woman's attire, spinning at Omphale's commandment, it breeds both delight and laughter; for the representing of so strange a power in love, procures delight, and the scornfulness of the action stirreth laughter.

But I speak to this purpose, that all the end of the comical part be not upon such scornful matters as stir laughter only, but mix with it that delightful teaching which is the end of poesy. And the great fault, even in that point of laughter, and forbidden plainly by Aristotle, is, that they stir laughter in sinful things, which are rather execrable than ridiculous; or in miserable, which are rather to be pitied than scorned. For what is it to make folks gape at a wretched beggar, and a beggarly clown; or against the law of hospitality, to jest at strangers, because they speak not English so well as we do? what do we learn, since it is certain,

> Nil habet infelix paupertas durius in se,
> Quam quod ridiculos homines facit?

But rather a busy loving courtier, and a heartless threatening Thraso; a self-wise seeming schoolmaster; a wry-transformed traveller: these, if we saw walk in stage names, which we play naturally, therein were delightful laughter, and teaching delightfulness: as in the other, the tragedies of Buchanan do justly bring forth a divine admiration.

But I have lavished out too many words of this play matter; I do it, because, as they are excelling parts of poesy, so is there none so much used in England, and none can be more pitifully abused; which, like an unmannerly daughter, showing a bad education, causeth her mother Poesy's honesty to be called in question.

Other sorts of poetry, almost, have we none, but that lyrical kind of songs and sonnets,* which, if the Lord gave us so good minds, how well it might be employed, and with how heavenly fruits, both private and public, in singing the praises of the immortal beauty, the immortal goodness of that God, who giveth us hands to write, and wits to conceive; of which we might well want words, but never matter; of which we could turn our eyes to nothing, but we should ever have new budding occasions.

But, truly, many of such writings as come under the banner of unresistible love, if I were a mistress, would never persuade me they were in love; so coldly they apply fiery speeches, as men that had rather read lover's writings, and so caught up certain swelling phrases, which hang together like a man that once told me, "the wind was at north-west and by south;" because he would be sure to name winds enough; than that, in truth, they feel those passions, which easily, as I think, may be bewrayed by that same forcibleness, or "energia," (as the Greeks call it) of the writer. But let this be a sufficient, though short note, that we miss the right use of the material point of poesy.

Now for the outside of it, which is words, or (as I may term it) diction, it is even well worse; so is that honey-flowing matron eloquence, apparelled, or rather disguised, in a courtezan-like painted affectation. One time with so far-fetched words, that many seem monsters, but most seem strangers to any poor Englishman:

* The Psalms of David.

another time with coursing of a letter, as if they were bound to follow the method of a dictionary: another time with figures and flowers, extremely winter-starved.

But I would this fault were only peculiar to versifiers, and had not as large possession among prose-printers: and, which is to be marvelled, among many scholars, and, which is to be pitied, among some preachers. Truly, I could wish (if at least I might be so bold to wish, in a thing beyond the reach of my capacity) the diligent imitators of Tully and Demosthenes, most worthy to be imitated, did not so much keep Nizolian paper-books of their figures and phrases, as by attentive translation, as it were, devour them whole, and make them wholly theirs. For now they cast sugar and spice upon every dish that is served at the table: like those Indians, not content to wear ear-rings at the fit and natural place of the ears, but they will thrust jewels through their nose and lips, because they will be sure to be fine. Tully, when he was to drive out Cataline, as it were with a thunderbolt of eloquence, often useth the figure of repetition, as "vivit et vincit, imo in senatum venit, imo in senatum venit," etc. Indeed, inflamed with a well-grounded rage, he would have his words, as it were, double out of his mouth; and so do that artificially, which we see men in choler do naturally. And we, having noted the grace of those words, hale them in sometimes to a familiar epistle, when it were too much choler to be choleric.

How well, store of "similiter cadences" doth sound with the gravity of the pulpit, I would but invoke Demosthenes' soul to tell, who with a rare daintiness useth them. Truly, they have made me think of the sophister, that with too much subtlety would prove two eggs three, and though he might be counted a sophister, had none for his labour. So these men bringing in such a kind of eloquence, well may they obtain an opinion of a seeming fineness, but persuade few, which should be the end of their fineness.

Now for similitudes in certain printed discourses, I think all herbalists, all stories of beasts, fowls, and fishes are rifled up, that they may come in multitudes to wait upon any of our conceits, which certainly is as absurd a surfeit to the ears as is possible. For the force of a similitude not being to prove any thing to a contrary disputer, but only to explain to a willing hearer; when that is done, the rest is a most tedious prattling, rather overswaying the memory from the purpose whereto they were applied, than any whit informing the judgment, already either satisfied, or by similitudes not to be satisfied.

For my part, I do not doubt, when Antonius and Crassus, the great forefathers of Cicero in eloquence, the one (as Cicero testifieth of them) pretended not to know art, the other not to set by it, because with a plain sensibleness they might win credit of popular ears, which credit is the nearest step to persuasion (which persuasion is the chief mark of oratory) I do not doubt, I say, but that they used these knacks very sparingly; which who doth generally use, any man may see, doth dance to his own music; and so to be noted by the audience, more careful to speak curiously than truly. Undoubtedly (at least to my opinion undoubtedly) I have found in divers small-learned courtiers a more sound style, than in some professors of learning; of which I can guess no other cause, but that the courtier following that which by practice he findeth fittest to nature, therein (though he know it not) doth according to art, though not by art: where the other, using art to show art, and not hide art (as in these cases he should do) flieth from nature, and indeed abuseth art.

But what! methinks I deserve to be pounded for straying from poetry to oratory: but both have such an affinity in the wordish considerations, that I think this digression will make my meaning receive the fuller understanding: which is not to take upon me to teach poets how they should do, but only finding myself sick among the rest, to show some one or two spots of the common infection grown among the most part of writers; that, acknowledging ourselves somewhat awry, we may bend to the right use both of matter and manner: whereto our language giveth us great occasion, being, indeed, capable of any excellent exercising of it. I know some will say, it is a mingled language: and why not so much the better, taking the best of both the other? Another will say, it wanteth grammar. Nay, truly, it hath that praise, that it wants not grammar; for grammar it might have, but needs it not; being so easy in itself, and so void of those cumbersome differences of cases, genders, moods, and tenses; which, I think, was a piece of the tower of Babylon's curse, that a man should be put to school to learn his mother tongue. But for the uttering sweetly and properly the conceit of the mind, which is the end of speech, that hath it equally with any other tongue in the world, and is particularly happy in compositions of two or three words together, near the Greek, far beyond the Latin; which is one of the greatest beauties can be in a language.

Now, of versifying there are two sorts, the one ancient, the other modern; the ancient marked the quantity of each syllable, and according to that framed his verse; the modern, observing only number, with some regard of the accent, the chief life of it standeth in that like sounding of the words, which we call rhyme. Whether of these be the more excellent, would bear many speeches; the ancient, no doubt, more fit for music, both words and time observing quantity; and more fit lively to express divers passions, by the low or lofty sound of the well-weighed syllable. The latter, likewise, with his rhyme striketh a certain music to the ear; and, in fine, since it doth delight, though by another way, it obtaineth the same purpose; there being in either, sweetness, and wanting in neither, majesty. Truly the English, before any vulgar language I know, is fit for both sorts; for, for the ancient, the Italian is so full of vowels, that it must ever be cumbered with elisions. The Dutch so, of the other side, with consonants, that they cannot yield the sweet sliding fit for a verse. The French, in his whole language, hath not one word that hath his accent in the last syllable, saving two, called antepenultima; and little more hath the Spanish; and therefore very gracelessly may they use dactiles. The English is subject to none of these defects.

Now for rhyme, though we do not observe quantity, we observe the accent very precisely, which other languages either cannot do, or will not do so absolutely. That "cæsura," or breathing-place, in the midst of the verse, neither Italian nor Spanish have, the French and we never almost fail of. Lastly, even the very rhyme itself the Italian cannot put in the last syllable, by the French named the masculine rhyme, but still in the next to the last, which the French call the female; or the next before that, which the Italian calls "sdrucciola;"* the example of the former is, "buono," "suono;" of the sdrucciola is, "femina," "semina." The French, of the other side, hath both the male, as "bon," "son," and the female, as "plaise," "taise;" but the "sdrucciola" he hath not; where the English hath all three, as "due," "true," "father," "rather," "motion," "potion;" with much more which might be said, but that already I find the trifling of this discourse is much too much enlarged.

So that since the ever praiseworthy poesy is full of virtue, breeding delightfulness, and void of no gift that ought to be in the noble name of learning; since the blames laid against it are either false or feeble; since the cause why it is not esteemed in England, is the fault of poet-apes, not poets; since, lastly, our tongue is most fit to honour poesy, and to be honoured by poesy; I conjure you all that have had the evil luck to read this ink-wasting toy of mine, even in the name of the Nine Muses, no more to scorn the sacred mysteries of poesy; no more to laugh at the name of poets, as though they were next inheritors to fools; no more to jest at the reverend title of "a rhymer;" but to believe, with Aristotle, that they were the ancient treasurers of the Grecians' divinity; to believe, with Bembus, that they were the first bringers in of all civility; to believe, with Scaliger, that no philosopher's precepts can sooner make you an honest man, than the reading of Virgil; to believe, with Clauserus, the translator of Cornutus, that it pleased the heavenly deity by Hesiod and Homer, under

---

* That is, the easy sliding of words of three or more syllables.

the veil of fables, to give us all knowledge, logic, rhetoric, philosophy natural and moral, and "quid non?" to believe, with me, that there are many mysteries contained in poetry, which of purpose were written darkly, lest by profane wits it should be abused; to believe, with Landin, that they are so beloved of the gods, that whatsoever they write, proceeds of a divine fury. Lastly, to believe themselves, when they tell you, they will make you immortal by their verses.

Thus doing, your names shall flourish in the printers' shops: thus doing, you shall be of kin to many a poetical preface: thus doing, you shall be most fair, most rich, most wise, most all: you shall dwell upon superlatives: thus doing, though you be "Libertino patre natus," you shall suddenly grow "Herculea proles,"

        Si quid mea Carmina possunt :

thus doing, your soul shall be placed with Dante's Beatrix, or Virgil's Anchises.

But if (fie of such a but!) you be born so near the dull-making cataract of Nilus, that you cannot hear the planet-like music of poetry; if you have so earth-creeping a mind, that it cannot lift itself up to look to the sky of poetry, or rather, by a certain rustical disdain, will become such a Mome, as to be a Momus of poetry; then, though I will not wish unto you the ass's ears of Midas, nor to be driven by a poet's verses, as Bubonax was, to hang himself; nor to be rhymed to death, as is said to be done in Ireland; yet thus much curse I must send you in the behalf of all poets; that while you live, you live in love, and never get favour, for lacking skill of a sonnet; and when you die, your memory die from the earth, for want of an epitaph.

ASTROPHEL AND STELLA.

The succeeding collection of sonnets and songs was originally published under the following title: " Sir P. S. his Astrophel and Stella, wherein the excellence of true poetry is concluded. To the end of which are added sundry other rare sonnets of divers noblemen and gentlemen:" printed for T. Newman, 1591, 4to. It was annexed to the second edition of the Arcadia, in 1593, and to all later editions. Sidney meant to designate himself by the name of Astrophel, and his "load-star of delight," the Lady Rich, by that of Stella. Spenser, in his Elegy on Sir Philip's death, has converted the story of these lovers into a most beautiful and imaginative fiction.

ASTROPHEL AND STELLA.

LOVING in truth, and fain in verse my love to show,
   That she, dear she! might take some pleasure of my pain;
Pleasure might cause her read, reading might make her know,
   Knowledge might pity win, and pity grace obtain:
I sought fit words to paint the blackest face of woe,
   Studying inventions fine, her wits to entertain:
Oft turning others' leaves, to see if thence would flow
   Some fresh and fruitful showers upon my sun-burn'd brain.
But words came halting forth, wanting invention's stay;
   Invention, Nature's child, fled step-dame Study's blows,
And others' feet still seem'd but strangers in my way.
   Thus, great with child to speak, and helpless in my throes,
Biting my truant pen, beating myself for spite,
Fool! said my Muse to me, look in thy heart, and write.

II.

Not at first sight, nor with a dribbed shot,
Love gave the wound, which, while I breathe, will bleed;
But known worth did in mine of time proceed,
   'Till, by degrees, it had full conquest got.
I saw, and lik'd; I lik'd, but loved not;
   I lov'd, but straight did not what Love decreed:
   At length, to Love's decrees, I, forc'd, agreed,
Yet with repining at so partial lot.

   Now, ev'n, that footstep of lost liberty
Is gone, and now, like slave-born Muscovit',
   I call it praise to suffer tyranny;
And now employ the remnant of my wit,
   To make myself believe that all is well,
   While, with a feeling skill, I paint my hell.

III.

Let dainty wits cry on the sisters nine,
That, bravely mask'd, their fancies may be told:
   Or, Pindar's apes, flaunt they in phrases fine,
Enam'ling, with py'd flowers, their thoughts of gold.
   Or else, let them in statelier glory shine,
Ennobling new-found tropes, with problems old:
   Or, with strange similes enrich each line,
Of herbs, or beasts, which Ind' or Afric hold.

For me, in sooth, no Muse but one I know,
Phrases and problems from my reach do grow,
   And strange things cost too dear for my poor sp'rits.
How then? even thus, in Stella's face I read,

What love and beauty be, then all my deed
  But copying is, what in her Nature writes.

IV.

  Virtue, alas! now let me take some rest,
Thou sett'st a bait betwixt my will and wit,
  If vain love have my simple soul oppress'd,
Leave what thou likest not, deal not thou with it.
  Thy sceptre use in some old Cato's breast;
Churches, or schools, are for thy seat more fit:
  I do confess, pardon a fault confess'd,
My mouth too tender is for thy hard bit.

But, if that needs thou wilt usurping be
The little reason that is left in me,
  And still th' effect of thy persuasions prove,
I swear, my heart such one shall show to thee,
That shrines in flesh so true a deity,
  That, Virtue, thou thyself shalt be in love.

V.

  It is most true, that eyes are form'd to serve
The inward light; and, that the heav'nly part
  Ought to be king, from whose rules who do swerve,
Rebels to nature, strive for their own smart.
  It is most true, what we call Cupid's dart,
An image is, which for ourselves we carve;
  And, fools, adore in temple of our heart,
'Till that good god make church and churchmen starve.

True, that true beauty virtue is, indeed,
Whereof this beauty can be but a shade,
 Which, elements, with mortal mixture breed :
True, that, on earth, we are but pilgrims made,
 And should, in soul up to our country move ;
 True, and yet true ! that I must Stella love.

VI.

 Some lovers speak, when they their muses entertain,
Of hopes begot by fear, of wot not what desires,
 Of force of heav'nly beams, infusing hellish pain,
Of living deaths, dear wounds, fair storms, and freezing fires ;
 Some one his song in Jove, and Jove's strange tales attires,
Border'd with bulls and swans, powder'd with golden rain :
 Another, humbler wit, to shepherd's pipe retires,
Yet, hiding royal blood, full oft, in rural vein.

To some, a sweetest plaint, a sweetest style affords,
While tears pour out his ink, and sighs breathe out his words ;
 His paper pale despair, and pain his pen doth move :
I can speak what I feel, and feel as much as they,
But think, that all the map of my state I display,
 When trembling voice brings forth, that I do Stella love.

VII.

When Nature made her chief work, Stella's eyes,
In colour black, why wrapp'd she beams so bright ?

Would she, in beamy black, like painter wise,
Frame daintiest lustre, mix'd of shades and light?
  Or, did she, else, that sober hue devise,
In object best, to knit and strength our sight,
  Lest, if no veil these brave gleams did disguise,
They, sun-like, should more dazzle than delight?

Or, would she her mirac'lous power show,
That, whereas black seems beauty's contrary,
  She! even in black, doth make all beauty flow?
Both so, and thus, she, minding Love should be
  Plac'd ever there, gave him this mourning weed,
  To honour all their deaths, who for her bleed.

VIII.

Love, born in Greece, of late fled from his native
    place,
Forc'd, by a tedious proof, that Turkish harden'd heart
Is no fit mark to pierce with his fine pointed dart;
  And, pleas'd with our soft peace, staid here his flying
    race:
  But, finding these north climes do coldly him embrace,
Not us'd to frozen clips, he strove to find some part,
Where, with most ease and warmth, he might employ
    his dart;
  At length, he perch'd himself in Stella's joyful face;

Whose fair skin, beamy eyes, like morning sun on
    snow,
Deceiv'd the quaking boy, who thought, from so pure
    light,
  Effects of lively heat, must needs in nature grow:

But she! most fair, most cold, made him thence take
    his flight
  To my close heart, where, while some firebrands he
    did lay,
  He burnt un'wares his wings, and cannot fly away.

  Queen Virtue's court, which some call Stella's face,
Prepar'd by Nature's choicest furniture,
Hath his front built of alabaster pure;
  Gold is the covering of that stately place.
The door, by which, sometimes, comes forth her grace,
  Red porphyr is, which lock of pearl makes sure;
    Whose porches rich (which name of cheeks en-
    dure)
Marble, mix'd red, and white, do interlace.

  The windows now, thro' which this heav'nly guest
Looks o'er the world, and can find nothing such,
    Which dare claim from those lights the name of
    best,
Of touch they are, that, without touch, doth touch,
  Which Cupid's self, from Beauty's mind did draw:
  Of touch they are, and, poor I! am their straw.

X.

  Reason! in faith, thou art well serv'd, that still
Would'st brabbling be with sense and love in me;
  I rather wish'd thee climb the Muses' hill;
Or reach the fruit of Nature's choicest tree;

Or seek heav'ns course, or heav'ns inside to see:
Why shouldst thou toil our thorny soil to till?
   Leave sense, and those which senses objects be,
Deal thou with powers of thoughts, leave love to will.

   But thou wouldst needs fight, both with love and sense,
With sword of wit, giving wounds of dispraise,
   'Till downright blows did foil thy cunning fence;
For soon as they struck thee with Stella's rays,
     Reason, thou kneel'dst, and offered'st straight to prove,
     By reason good, good reason her to love.

XI.

In truth, O Love, with what a boyish kind
Thou dost proceed, in thy most serious ways,
That when the heav'n to thee his best displays,
   Yet of that best, thou leav'st the best behind?
   For, like a child, that some fair book doth find,
With gilded leaves, or colour'd vellum plays,
Or, at the most, on some fine picture stays,
   But never heeds the fruit of writer's mind:

So when thou saw'st, in Nature's cabinet,
Stella, thou straight look'dst babies in her eyes,
   In her cheeks' pit, thou did'st thy pitfold set,
And in her breast, bo-peep, or couching, lies,
     Playing, and shining in each outward part;
     But, fool! seek'st not to get into her heart.

XII.

Cupid, because thou shin'st in Stella's eyes,
That from her looks, thy dances none scapes free,
That those lips swell'd, so full of thee they be,
    That her sweet breath, makes oft thy flames to rise,
    That in her breast thy pap well sugar'd lies,
That her grace, gracious makes thy wrongs, that she,
What words soe'er she speak, persuades for thee,
    That her clear voice lifts thy fame to the skies.

Thou countest Stella thine, like those whose powers
    Having got up a breach by fighting well,
Cry, Victory! this fair day all is ours!
    O no, her heart is such a citadel,
So fortified with wit, stor'd with disdain,
That to win it, is all the skill and pain.

XIII.

Phœbus was judge between Jove, Mars, and Love,
Of those three gods, whose arms the fairest were:
Jove's golden shield did eagle sables bear,
    Whose talons held young Ganymede above:
But in *vert* field Mars bore a golden spear,
    Which through a bleeding heart his point did shove.
    Each had his crest, Mars carried Venus' glove,
Jove, on his helm, the thunderbolt did rear.

Cupid then smiles, for on his crest there lies
Stella's fair hair, her face he makes his shield,
Where roses *gules* are borne in silver field.
    Phœbus drew wide the curtains of the skies,

To blaze these last, and sware devoutly then,
The first, thus match'd, were scantly gentlemen.

XIV.

Alas! have I not pain enough, my friend,
Upon whose breast a fiercer gripe doth tire,
Than did on him who first stole down the fire,
   While Love on me doth all his quiver spend;
But with your rhubarb words ye must contend,
   To grieve me worse, in saying, that desire
   Doth plunge my well form'd soul even in the mire
Of sinful thoughts, which do in ruin end.

   If that be sin which doth the manners frame,
Well staid with truth in word, and faith of deed,
   Ready of wit, and fearing nought but shame;
If that be sin, which in fix'd hearts doth breed
   A loathing of all loose unchastity,
   Then love is sin, and let me sinful be.

XV.

You that do search for every purling spring,
Which from the ribs of old Parnassus flows,
And ev'ry flower, not sweet, perhaps, which grows
   Near thereabouts, into your poesy wring.
You that do dictionary's method bring
   Into your rhymes, running in rattling rows;
   You that poor Petrarch's long deceased woes,
With new-born sighs, and denizen'd wit do sing:

You take wrong ways; those far-fetch'd helps be such,
As do bewray a want of inward touch.

And sure, at length, stol'n goods do come to light;
But if (both for your love and skill) your name
You seek to nurse at fullest breasts of fame,
   Stella behold, and then begin t' indite.

XVI.

In Nature, apt to like, when I did see
Beauties, which were of many carats fine,
My boiling sp'rits, did thither soon incline;
   And, Love! I thought, that I was full of thee;
But, finding not those restless flames in me,
   Which others said did make their souls to pine,
   I thought those babes of some pin's hurt did whine,
By my soul judging what love's pain might be:

But while I, fool! thus with this lion play'd,
Mine eyes (shall I say curst, or blest?) beheld
   Stella; now she is nam'd, need more be said?
In her sight, I a lesson new have spell'd;
   I now have learn'd love right, and learn'd ev'n so,
   As who, by being poison'd, doth poison know.

XVII.

His mother dear, Cupid offended late,
Because that Mars, grown slacker in her love,
With pricking shot he did not throughly move,
   To keep the pace of their first loving state.
The boy refus'd for fear of Mars's hate,
   Who threaten'd stripes, if he his wrath did prove;
   But she, in chafe, him from her lap did shove,
Brake bow, brake shafts, while Cupid weeping sat;

'Till that his grandame Nature, pitying it,
Of Stella's brows, made him two better bows,
   And in her eyes of arrows infinite :
O how for joy he leaps ! O how he crows !
   And straight therewith, like wags new got to play,
   Falls to shrewd turns, and I was in his way.

XVIII.

With what sharp checks I in myself am shent,
When into reason's audit I do go :
And by just 'compts myself a bankrupt know
   Of all those goods, which heav'n to me hath lent :
Unable quite to pay even Nature's rent,
   Which unto it by birthright I do owe :
   And, which is worse, no good excuse can show,
But that my wealth I have most idly spent ?

My youth doth waste, my knowledge brings forth toys,
My wit doth strive those passions to defend,
   Which, for reward, spoil it with vain annoys.
I see, my course to lose myself doth bend :
   I see and yet no greater sorrow take,
   Than that I lose no more for Stella's sake.

XIX.

On Cupid's bow how are my heart-strings bent,
That see my wrack, and yet embrace the same !
When most I glory, then I feel most shame ;
   I willing run, yet while I run, repent ;
   My best wits still their own disgrace invent :
My very ink turns straight to Stella's name ;

And yet my words, as them my pen doth frame,
  Avise themselves that they are vainly spent.

  For though she pass all things, yet what is all
That unto me, who fare like him that both
  Looks to the skies, and in a ditch doth fall!
O! let me prop my mind, yet in his growth,
  And not in nature, for best fruits unfit:
  Scholar, saith Love, bend hitherward your wit.

XX.

  Fly, fly, my friends, I have my death's wound! fly,
See there that boy, that murdering boy, I say,
  Who, like a thief, hid in dark bush, doth lie,
Till bloody bullet get him wrongful prey.
  So, tyrant he, no fitter place could spy,
Nor so fair level in so secret stay,
  As that sweet black which veils the heavenly eye;
There himself with his shot he close doth lay.

  Poor passenger! pass now thereby I did;
And staid, pleas'd with the prospect of the place;
  While that black hue from me the bad guest hid:
But straight I saw motions of lightning grace;
  And then descried the glistering of his dart,
  But, ere I could fly thence, it pierc'd my heart.

XXI.

  Your words, my friend, (right healthful caustics,) blame
My young mind marr'd, whom Love doth windlass so

That mine own writings, like bad servants, show
   My wits quick in vain thoughts, in virtue lame;
   That Plato I read for nought; but if he tame
Such coltish years, that to my birth I owe
Nobler desires, lest else that friendly foe,
   Great expectation, were a train of shame.

   For since mad March great promise made of me,
If now the May of my years much decline,
   What can be hop'd my harvest-time will be?
Sure, you say well, your wisdom's golden mine,
   Dig deep with learning's spade, now tell me this,
   Hath this world aught so fair as Stella is?

XXII.

In highest way of heav'n the sun did ride,
Progressing then from fair twins' golden place;
Having no scarf of clouds before his face,
   But shining forth of heat in his chief pride;
   When some fair ladies, by hard promise tied,
On horseback met him in his furious race,
Yet each prepar'd with fan's well-shading grace,
   From that foe's wounds their tender skins to hide:

Stella, alone, with face unarmed, march'd
   Either to do like him which open shone;
   Or, careless of the wealth, because her own;
Yet were the hid and meaner beauties parch'd,
   Her daintiest, bare, went free; the cause was this,
   The sun, which others burn'd, did her but kiss.

XXIII.

The curious wits, seeing dull pensiveness
Bewray itself in my long-settled eyes,
Whence those same fumes of melancholy rise,
   With idle pains, and missing aim, do guess.
   Some that know how my spring I did address,
Deem that my muse some fruit of knowledge plies;
Others, because the prince my service tries,
   Think that I think state errors to redress.

But harder judges judge ambition's rage,
   Scourge of itself, still climbing slipp'ry place,
Holds my young brain captiv'd in golden cage.
   O fools, or over-wise, alas! the race
Of all my thoughts hath neither stop nor start,
But only Stella's eyes, and Stella's heart.

XXIV.

Rich fools there be, whose base and filthy heart,
Lies hatching still the goods wherein they flow:
   And damning their own selves to Tantal's smart,
Wealth breeding want, more blest, more wretched grow;
   Yet to those fools heav'n doth such wit impart,
As what their hands do hold, their heads do know,
   And knowing love, and loving lay apart,
As sacred things, far from all dangers show.

But that Rich fool, who by blind Fortune's lot,
The richest gem of love and life enjoys,
   And can with foul abuse such beauties blot;
   Let him, depriv'd of sweet but unfelt joys,

(Exil'd for aye from those high treasures, which
He knows not) grow in only folly Rich.*

XXV.

The wisest scholar of the wight most wise,
By Phœbus' doom, with sugar'd sentence says,
   That virtue, if it once met with our eyes,
Strange flames of love it in our souls would raise.
   But for that man with pain this truth descries,
Whilst he each thing in sense's balance weighs,
   And so, nor will, nor can, behold those skies,
Which inward sun t' heroic mind displays.

   Virtue of late, with virtuous care to stir
Love of herself, took Stella's shape, that she
   To mortal eyes might sweetly shine in her:
It is most true, for since I her did see,
   Virtue's great beauty in that face I prove,
And find th' effect, for I do burn in love.

XXVI.

Though dusty wits dare scorn astrology,
And fools can think those lamps of purest light,
   Whose numbers weigh greatness, eternity,
Promising wonders, wonder do invite,
   To have, for no cause, birthright in the sky,
But for to spangle the black weeds of night:
   Or for some brawl, which in that chamber high,
They should still dance to please a gazer's sight.

---

* Lord Rich, to whom Sidney very evidently makes allusion in this sonnet, was notoriously a person of a low and brutal character.

For me, I do nature unidle know,
And know, great causes great effects procure;
   And know, those bodies high reign on the low.
And if these rules did fail, proof makes me sure,
   Who oft fore-judge my after-following race,
   By only those two stars in Stella's face.

XXVII.

Because I oft, in dark abstracted guise,
Seem most alone in greatest company;
With dearth of words, or answers quite awry,
   To them that would make speech of speech arise:
   They deem, and of their doom the rumour flies,
That poison foul of bubbling pride doth lie
So in my swelling breast, that only I
   Fawn on myself, and others do despise:

Yet pride, I think, doth not my soul possess,
   Which looks too oft in his unflatt'ring glass:
But one worse fault, ambition, I confess,
   That makes me oft my best friends overpass,
Unseen, unheard, while thought to highest place
   Bends all his power, even unto Stella's grace.

XXVIII.

You that with allegory's curious frame,
Of others' children changelings use to make,
With me those pains, for God's sake, do not take;
   I list not dig so deep for brazen fame.
When I say Stella, I do mean the same
   Princess of beauty, for whose only sake,

The reins of Love I love, though never slack,
And joy therein, though nations count it shame.

I beg no subject to use eloquence,
Nor in hid ways do guide philosophy :
  Look at my hands for no such quintessence ;
But know, that I, in pure simplicity,
  Breathe out the flames which burn within my heart,
  Love only reading unto me this art.

XXIX.

Like some weak lords, neighbour'd by mighty kings,
To keep themselves and their chief cities free,
Do eas'ly yield, that all their coasts may be
  Ready to store their camps of needful things :
So Stella's heart, finding what power Love brings,
  To keep itself in life and liberty,
  Doth willing grant, that in the frontiers he
Use all to help his other conquerings :

  And thus her heart escapes, but thus her eyes,
Serve him with shot, her lips his heralds are ;
Her breasts his tents, legs his triumphal car ;
  Her flesh his food, her skin his armour brave,
  And I, but for because my prospect lies
Upon that coast, am giv'n up for a slave.

XXX.

Whether the Turkish new moon minded be
To fill his horns this year on Christian coast ?
How Poles' right king means, without leave of host,

To warm, with ill-made fire, cold Muscovy?
If French can yet three parts in one agree?
   What now the Dutch in their full diets boast?
   How Holland hearts, now so good towns be lost,
Trust in the shade of pleasant *Orange*-tree?

   How Ulster likes of that same golden bit,
Wherewith my father once made it half tame?
   If in the Scotch court be no welt'ring yet?
These questions busy wits to me do frame;
   I, cumber'd with good manners, answer do,
   But know not how, for still I think of you.

XXXI.

With how sad steps, O moon, thou climb'st the skies!
   How silently, and with how wan a face!
   What! may it be, that ev'n in heav'nly place
That busy archer his sharp arrows tries?
   Sure, if that long-with-love-acquainted eyes
Can judge of love, thou feel'st a lover's case;
   I read it in thy looks, thy languish'd grace
To me, that feel the like, thy state descries.

   Then, ev'n of fellowship, O moon, tell me,
Is constant love deem'd there but want of wit?
   Are beauties there as proud as here they be?
Do they above love to be lov'd, and yet
   Those lovers scorn, whom that love doth possess?
   Do they call virtue there ungratefulness?

XXXII.

Morpheus, the lively son of deadly Sleep,
Witness of life to them that living die;
A prophet oft, and oft an history,
  A poet eke, as humours fly or creep:
Since thou in me so sure a power dost keep,
That never I with close-up sense do lie,
But by thy work, my Stella, I descry,
  Teaching blind eyes both how to smile and weep:

Vouchsafe, of all acquaintance, this to tell,
  Whence hast thou ivory, rubies, pearl, and gold,
To show her skin, lips, teeth, and head so well?
  Fool! answers he, no Inds such treasure hold,
But from thy heart, while my fire charmeth thee,
Sweet Stella's image I do steal to me.

XXXIII.

I might, unhappy word! O me! I might,
And then would not, or could not, see my bliss:
  Till now, wrapt in a most infernal night,
I find, how heav'nly day, wretch! I did miss.
  Heart! rent thyself, thou dost thyself but right,
No lovely Paris made thy Helen his:
  No force, no fraud, robb'd thee of thy delight,
Nor fortune of thy fortune author is:

But to myself, myself did give the blow,
While too much wit, forsooth, so troubled me,
  That I respects for both our sakes must show:
And yet could not, by rising morn, foresee

How fair a day was near. O punish'd eyes!
That I had been more foolish, or more wise!

XXXIV.

Come, let me write, and to what end? to ease
A burthen'd heart; how can words ease, which are
The glasses of the daily vexing care?
 Oft cruel fights, well pictur'd forth, do please;
 "Art not asham'd to publish thy disease"?
Nay, that may breed my fame, it is so rare:
But will not wise men think thy words fond ware?
 Then be they close, and so none shall displease.

What idler thing, than speak, and not be heard?
What harder thing, than smart, and not to speak?
 Peace, foolish wit, with wit my wit is marr'd.
Thus write I, while I doubt to write, and wreak
 My harms on ink's poor loss, perhaps some find
 Stella's great powers, that so confuse my mind.

XXXV.

What may words say, or what may words not say,
 Where truth itself must speak like flattery?
Within what bounds can one his liking stay,
 Where Nature doth with infinite agree?
What Nestor's counsel can my flames allay,
 Since Reason's self doth blow the coal in me?
And, ah! what hope, that hope should once see day,
 Where Cupid is sworn page to chastity?

Honour is honour'd, that thou dost possess
 Him as thy slave, and now long needy fame

Doth even grow rich, naming my Stella's name.
Wit learns in thee perfection to express,
  Not thou by praise, but praise in thee is rais'd :
It is a praise to praise, when thou art prais'd.

XXXVI.

Stella, whence doth this new assault arise,
  A conquer'd golden ransack'd heart to win?
Whereto long since, through my long batter'd eyes,
  Whole armies of thy beauties ent'red in.
  And there, long since, Love, thy lieutenant, lies,
My forces raz'd, thy banners rais'd within :
  Of conquest, do not these effects suffice,
But wilt now war upon thine own begin ?

  With so sweet voice, and by sweet nature so
In sweetest strength, so sweetly skill'd withal,
  In all sweet stratagems, sweet art can show,
That not my soul, which at thy foot did fall,
  Long since, forc'd by thy beams, but stone nor tree,
  By Sense's privilege, can scape from thee.

XXXVII.

My mouth doth water, and my breast doth swell,
My tongue doth itch, my thoughts in labour be ;
Listen then, lordings, with good ear to me,
  For of my life I must a riddle tell :
  Toward Aurora's court a nymph doth dwell,
Rich in all beauties which man's eye can see ;
Beauties so far from reach of words, that we,
  Abase her praise, saying she doth excel :

Rich in the treasure of deserv'd renown ;
  Rich in the riches of a royal heart ;
Rich in those gifts which give th' eternal crown :
  Who, tho' most rich in these and ev'ry part
Which make the patents of true worldly bliss,
Hath no misfortune, but that Rich * she is.

XXXVIII.

This night, while sleep begins, with heavy wings,
To hatch mine eyes, and that unbitted thought
Doth fall to stray, and my chief powers are brought
  To leave the sceptre of all subject things ;
  The first that straight my fancy's error brings
Unto my mind, is Stella's image, wrought
By Love's own self, but, with so curious draught,
  That she, methinks, not only shines, but sings :

I start, look, hark, but what in clos'd-up sense
  Was held, in open'd sense it flies away,
Leaving me nought but wailing eloquence :
  I, seeing better sights in sights decay,
Call'd it anew, and wooed sleep again ;
But him, her host, that unkind guest had slain.

XXXIX.

Come, Sleep : O Sleep ! the certain knot of peace,
The baiting place of wit, the balm of woe,
  The poor man's wealth, the prisoner's release,

---

* A play upon his mistress's name, and an allusion to the source of his misery — her marriage to another. The same conceit has been already remarked in the xxiv. sonnet.

Th' indifferent judge between the high and low;
  With shield of proof, shield me from out the prease
Of those fierce darts, Despair at me doth throw:
    O make in me those civil wars to cease;
I will good tribute pay, if thou do so.

  Take thou of me, smooth pillows, sweetest bed;
A chamber deaf to noise, and blind to light;
  A rosy garland, and a weary head:
And if these things, as being thine by right,
  Move not thy heavy grace, thou shalt, in me,
  Livelier than elsewhere, Stella's image see.

XL.

  As good to write, as for to lie and groan,
O Stella dear! how much thy power hath wrought,
Thou hast my mind, none of the basest, brought
    My still kept course, while others sleep, to moan.
  Alas! if from the height of Virtue's throne,
Thou canst vouchsafe the influence of a thought
Upon a wretch that long thy grace hath sought;
    Weigh then, how I by thee am overthrown:

And then, think thus, although thy beauty be
Made manifest by such a victory,
  Yet noble conquerors do wrecks avoid:
Since then thou hast so far subdued me,
That, in my heart, I offer still to thee,
  O do not let thy temple be destroy'd.

XLI.

Having this day my horse, my hand, my lance,
Guided so well, that I obtain'd the prize,
Both by the judgment of the English eyes,
    And of some sent from that sweet en'my France;
    Horsemen, my skill in horsemanship advance;
Town-folks my strength; a daintier judge applies
His praise to sleight, which from good use doth rise:
    Some lucky wits impute it but to chance:

Others, because of both sides I do take
    My blood from them who did excel in this,
Think Nature me a man of arms did make;
    How far they shot awry! the true cause is,
Stella look'd on, and from her heav'nly face,
Sent forth the beams which made so fair my race.

XLII.

O eyes! which do the spheres of beauty move,
Whose beams be joys, whose joys all virtues be,
    Who, while they make Love conquer, conquer love,
The schools where Venus hath learn'd chastity.
    O eyes! where humble looks most glorious prove,
Only, lov'd tyrants, just in cruelty,
    Do not, O do not, from poor me remove,
Keep still my zenith, ever shine on me:

For though I never see them, but straightways
My life forgets to nourish languish'd sp'rits,
    Yet still on me, O eyes, dart down your rays;
And if, from majesty of sacred lights

Oppressing mortal sense, my death proceed,
Wracks triumphs be, which love, high set, doth breed.

XLIII.

Fair eyes, sweet lips, dear heart, that foolish I,
Could hope, by Cupid's help, on you to prey,
  Since to himself he doth your gifts apply,
As his main force, choice sport, and easeful stay:
  For when he will see who dare him gainsay,
Then with those eyes he looks; lo! by and by,
  Each soul doth at Love's feet his weapon lay,
Glad if for her he give them leave to die.

When he will play, then in her lips he is,
Where blushing red, that Love's self them doth love,
  With either lip he doth the other kiss;
But when he will, for quiet-sake, remove
  From all the world, her heart is then his rome,
Where, well he knows, no man to him can come.

XLIV.

My words, I know, do well set forth my mind,
My mind bemoans his sense of inward smart,
Such smart may pity claim of any heart,
  Her heart, sweet heart! is of no tiger's kind:
  And yet she hears, yet I no pity find;
But more I cry, less grace she doth impart,
Alas! what cause is there so overthwart,
  That nobleness itself makes thus unkind?

I much do guess, yet find no truth, save this,
   That when the breath of my complaints doth touch
   Those dainty doors unto the court of bliss,
The heav'nly nature of that place is such,
   That, once come there, the sobs of mine annoys
   Are metamorphos'd straight to tunes of joys.

XLV.

Stella oft sees the very face of woe
Painted in my beclouded stormy face;
But cannot skill to pity my disgrace,
   Not though thereof the cause herself she know.
   Yet hearing late a fable, which did show,
Of lovers, never known, a grievous case,
Pity thereof, 'gat in her breast such place,
   That, from that sea deriv'd, tears' spring did flow.

Alas! if fancy, drawn by imag'd things,
   Tho' false, yet, with free scope, more grace doth breed
Than servants' wreck, where new doubts honour brings;
   Then think, my dear, that you in me do read,
Of lover's ruin, some sad tragedy:
I am not I; pity the tale of me.

XLVI.

I curst thee oft; I pity now thy case,
Blind-hitting boy, since she, that thee and me
Rules with a beck, so tyranniseth thee,
   That thou must want or food or dwelling-place;
   For she protests to banish thee her face;
Her face? O Love! a rogue thou then shouldst be!

If Love learn not alone to love and see,
  Without desire to feed of farther grace.

Alas! poor wag, that now a scholar art,
  To such a schoolmistress, whose lessons new
Thou needs must miss, and so thou needs must smart.
  Yet, dear, let me his pardon get of you,
So long (tho' he from book to miche * desire)
  Till without fuel you can make hot fire.

XLVII.

What! have I thus betray'd my liberty?
Can those black beams such burning marks engrave
In my free side? or am I born a slave,
  Whose neck becomes such yoke of tyranny?
  Or want I sense to feel my misery?
Or sp'rit, disdain of such disdain to have?
Who for long faith, tho' daily help I crave,
  May get no alms, but scorn of beggary.

Virtue, awake; beauty, but beauty is,
  I may, I must, I can, I will, I do
Leave following that which it is gain to miss.
  Let her go.—Soft! but here she comes! go to;
Unkind! I love you not:—O me! that eye
Doth make my heart to give my tongue the lie.

XLVIII.

Soul's joy, bend not those morning stars from me,
Where virtue is made strong by beauty's might;

* That is, to play truant.

Where love is chasteness, pain doth learn delight,
   And humbleness grows one with majesty :
   Whatever may ensue, O let me be
Copartner of the riches of that sight :
Let not mine eyes be hell-driv'n from that light :
   O look ! O shine ! O let me die, and see !

For though I oft myself of them bemoan,
That through my heart their beamy darts be gone :
   Whose cureless wounds, e'en now, most freshly bleed :
Yet, since my death-wound is already got,
Dear killer, spare not thy sweet cruel shot,
   A kind of grace it is to slay with speed.

XLIX.

I on my horse, and Love on me, doth try
Our horsemanships, while, by strange work, I prove
A horseman to my horse, a horse to Love ;
   And now man's wrongs in me, poor beast, descry.
   The rein wherewith my rider doth me tie,
Are humbled thoughts, which bit of rev'rence move,
Curb'd in with fear, but with gilt boss above
   Of hope, which makes it seem fair to the eye.

The wand is Will ; thou, Fancy, saddle art,
   Girt fast by Memory ; and while I spur
My horse, he spurs, with sharp desire, my heart :
   He sits me fast, however I do stir,
And now hath made me to his hand so right,
That in the menage myself takes delight.

L.

Stella! the fulness of my thoughts of thee
Cannot be stay'd within my panting breast;
   But they do swell and struggle forth of me,
Till that in words thy figure be exprest:
   And yet, as soon as they so formed be,
According to my lord Love's own behest,
   With sad eyes I their weak proportion see,
To portrait that which in this world is best;

   So that I cannot choose but write my mind,
And cannot choose but put out what I write,
   While these poor babes their death in birth do find;
And now my pen these lines had dashed quite;
   But that they stopp'd his fury from the same,
   Because their fore-front bare sweet Stella's name.

LI.

Pardon mine ears, both I and they do pray,
So may your tongue still fluently proceed,
To them that do such entertainment need;
   So may you still have somewhat new to say.
   On silly me do not the burthen lay
Of all the grave conceits your brain doth breed,
But find some Hercules to bear, instead
   Of Atlas tir'd, your wisdom's heav'nly sway.

For me, while you discourse of courtly tides,
   Of cunning fishers in most troubled streams,
Of straying ways, when valiant error guides;
   Meanwhile my heart confers with Stella's beams,

And is e'en irk'd that so sweet comedy,
By such unsuited speech should hinder'd be.

LII.

A strife is grown between Virtue and Love,
While each pretends that Stella must be his:
Her eyes, her lips, her all, saith Love, do this
   (Since they do wear his badge) most firmly prove;
   But Virtue thus that title doth disprove,
That Stella, O dear name! that Stella is
That virtuous soul, sure heir of heav'nly bliss:
   Not this fair outside, which our hearts doth move;

And, therefore, tho' her beauty and her grace
   Be Love's, indeed, in Stella's self he may,
By no pretence, claim any manner place.
   Well, Love, since this demur our suit doth stay,
Let Virtue have that Stella's self; yet thus,
That Virtue but that body grant to us.

LIII.

In martial sports I had my cunning tried,
And yet to break more staves did me address,
While, with the people's shouts, I must confess,
   Youth, luck, and praise e'en fill'd my veins with pride;
   When Cupid, having me, his slave, descried
In Mars's livery, prancing in the press:
What now, Sir Fool? said he, I would no less:
   Look here, I say;—I look'd, and Stella spied;

Who, hard by, made a window send forth light:
　My heart then quak'd, then dazzled were mine eyes,
One hand forgot to rule, th' other to fight.
　Nor trumpet's sound I heard, nor friendly cries;
My foe came on, and beat the air for me,
Till that her blush taught me my shame to see.

LIV.

Because I breathe not love to ev'ry one,
Nor do hot use set colours for to wear;
Nor nourish special locks of vowed hair;
　Nor give each speech a full point of a groan;
　The courtly nymphs, acquainted with the moan
Of them, who, in their lips, Love's standard bear;
What he? say they of me, now dare I swear,
　He cannot love: no, no; let him alone.

And think so still, so Stella know my mind,
　Profess, indeed, I do not, Cupid's art;
But you, fair maids, at length this true shall find,
　That his right badge is but worn in the heart:
Dumb swans, not chatt'ring pies, do lovers prove,
They love indeed who quake to say they love.

LV.

Muses, I oft invok'd your holy aid,
With choicest flowers, my speech t' engarland so,
That it, despis'd in true but naked show,
　Might win some grace in your sweet grace array'd;
　And oft whole troops of saddest words I stay'd,
Striving abroad a foraging to go,

Until, by your inspiring, I might know,
   How their black banner might be best display'd ;

But now I mean no more your help to try,
   Nor other sug'ring of my speech to prove,
But on her name incessantly to cry ;
   For let me but name her whom I do love,
So sweet sounds straight mine ear and heart do hit,
That I well find no eloquence like it.

LVI.

Fie, school of Patience, fie, your lesson is
Far, far too long to learn it without book :
What! a whole week without one piece of look,
   And think I should not your large precepts miss?
   When I might read those letters fair of bliss,
Which in her face teach virtue, I could brook
Somewhat thy leaden counsels, which I took,
   As of a friend that meant not much amiss ;

But now, that I, alas! do want her sight,
   What! dost thou think that I can ever take
In thy cold stuff a phlegmatic delight?
   No, Patience, if thou wilt my good, then make
Her come and hear with patience my desire,
And then with patience bid me bear my fire.

LVII.

Woe having made, with many fights, his own,
Each sense of mine, each gift, each power of mind,
Grown now his slaves, he forc'd them out to find

The thoroughest words, fit for Woe's self to groan,
    Hoping, that when they might find Stella alone,
Before she could prepare to be unkind,
Her soul, arm'd but with such a dainty rind,
    Should soon be pierc'd with sharpness of the moan :

She heard my plaints, and did not only hear,
    But them (so sweet is she) most sweetly sing,
With that fair breast, making Woe's darkness clear :
    A pretty case ; I hoped her to bring
To feel my griefs, and she, with face and voice,
So sweets my pains, that my pains me rejoice.

LVIII.

Doubt there hath been, when, with his golden chain,
The orator so far men's hearts doth bind,
That no pace else their guided steps can find,
    But as he them more short or slack doth rein ;
    Whether with words this sovereignty he gain,
Cloth'd with fine tropes, with strongest reasons lin'd ?
Or else, pronouncing grace, wherewith his mind
    Prints his own lively form in rudest brain ?

Now judge by this, in piercing phrases late,
Th' anatomy of all my woes I wrate :
    Stella's sweet breath the same to me did read :
O voice ! O face ! maugre my speech's might,
Which wooed woe, most ravishing delight
    Ev'n those sad words, ev'n in sad me did breed.

LIX.

Dear! why make you more of a dog than me?
If he do love, I burn, I burn in love;
If he wait well, I never thence would move:
   If he be fair, yet but a dog can be:
   Little he is, so little worth is he;
He barks, my songs thine own voice oft doth prove:
Bidden, perhaps, he fetcheth thee a glove,
   But I, unbid, fetch ev'n my soul to thee.

Yet, while I languish, him that bosom clips,
   That lap doth lap, nay lets, in spite of spite,
This sour-breath'd mate taste of those sugar'd lips:
   Alas! if you grant only such delight
To witless things, then Love, I hope, (since wit
Becomes a clog,) will soon ease me of it.

LX.

When my good angel guides me to the place
Where all my good I do in Stella see,
That heav'n of joys throws only down on me,
   Thund'ring disdains, and lightnings of disgrace;
   But when the rugged'st step of Fortune's race
Makes me fall from her sight, then, sweetly, she
With words, wherein the Muse's treasures be,
   Shows love and pity to my absent case.

Now I, wit-beaten long by hardest fate,
   So dull am, that I cannot look into
The ground of this fierce love, and lovely hate;
   Then, some good body, tell me how I do,

Whose presence absence, absence presence is;
Bliss'd in my curse, and cursed in my bliss?

LXI.

Oft with true sighs, oft with uncalled tears,
Now with slow words, now with dumb eloquence,
   I Stella's eyes assay'd, invade her ears;
But this, at last, is her sweet-breath'd defence:
   That who, indeed, in-felt affection bears,
So captives to his saint both soul and sense;
   That, wholly her's, all selfness he forbears,
Then his desires he learns his life's course thence.

   Now, since her chaste mind hates this love in me,
   With chasten'd mind, I straight must show, that she
Shall quickly me, from what she hates, remove.
   O Doctor Cupid! thou for me reply,
   Driv'n, else, to grant, by angels' sophistry,
That I love not, without I leave to love.

LXII.

Late, tir'd with woe, ev'n ready for to pine
With rage of love, I call'd my love unkind;
   She in whose eyes love, tho' unfelt, doth shine,
Sweet said, that I true love in her should find;
   I joy'd, but straight thus water'd was my wine,
That love she did, but lov'd a love not blind,
   Which would not let me, whom she lov'd, decline
From nobler course, fit for my birth and mind:

And therefore, by her love's authority,
Will'd me these tempests of vain love to fly,
And anchor fast myself on Virtue's shore.
    Alas! if this the only metal be
    Of love, new coin'd to help my beggary,
Dear! love me not, that you may love me more.

LXIII.

    O grammar rules! O now your virtues show!
So children still read you with awful eyes,
As my young dove may, in your precepts wise,
    Her grant to me by her own virtue know;
    For late, with heart most high, with eyes most low,
I crav'd the thing which ever she denies:
She, light'ning Love, displaying Venus' skies,
    Lest once should not be heard, twice said, No, no.

Sing then, my Muse, now Io Pæan sing;
Heav'ns, envy not at my high triumphing;
    But grammar's force with sweet success confirm:
For grammar says, (O this, dear Stella, say!)
For grammar says, (to grammar who says nay?)
    That in one speech two negatives affirm.

FIRST SONG.

Doubt you to whom my Muse these notes intendeth,
Which now my breast, o'ercharg'd, to music lendeth?
    To you, to you, all song of praise is due,
Only in you my song begins and endeth.

Who hath the eyes which marry state with pleasure?
Who keeps the key of Nature's chiefest treasure?
  To you, to you, all song of praise is due,
Only for you the heav'n forgot all measure.

Who hath the lips, where wit in fairness reigneth?
Who womankind at once both decks and staineth?
  To you, to you, all song of praise is due,
Only by you Cupid his crown maintaineth.

Who hath the feet, whose step of sweetness planteth?
Who else, for whom Fame worthy trumpets wanteth?
  To you, to you, all song of praise is due,
Only to you her sceptre Venus granteth.

Who hath the breast, whose milk doth passions nourish?
Whose grace is such, that when it chides doth cherish?
  To you, to you, all song of praise is due,
Only through you the tree of life doth flourish.

Who hath the hand which, without stroke, subdueth?
Who long-dead beauty with increase reneweth?
  To you, to you, all song of praise is due,
Only at you all envy hopeless rueth.

Who hath the hair, which loosest, fasteth tieth?
Who makes a man live, then glad when he dieth?
  To you, to you, all song of praise is due,
Only of you the flatterer never lieth.

Who hath the voice, which soul from senses sunders?
Whose force, but yours, the bolts of beauty thunders?
  To you, to you, all song of praise is due,
Only with you not miracles are wonders.

Doubt you, to whom my Muse these notes intendeth,
Which now my breast, o'ercharged, to music lendeth?
  To you, to you, all song of praise is due:
Only in you my song begins and endeth.

LXIV.

No more, my dear, no more these counsels try,
O give my passions leave to run their race:
Let Fortune lay on me her worst disgrace,
  Let folk o'ercharged with brain against me cry.
  Let clouds bedim my face, break in mine eye;
Let me no steps but of lost labour trace;
Let all the earth with scorn recount my case:
  But do not will me from my love to fly.

I do not envy Aristotle's wit,
Nor do aspire to Cæsar's bleeding fame;
  Nor aught do care, though some above me sit:
Nor hope, nor with another course to frame,
  But that which once may win thy cruel heart:
  Thou art my wit, and thou my virtue art.

LXV.

Love, by sure proof, I may call thee unkind,
That giv'st no better ear to my just cries:
  Thou whom to me such my good turns should bind,
As I may well recount, but none can prize:
  For when, nak'd boy, thou couldst no harbour find
In this old world, grown now so too too wise:
  I lodg'd thee in my heart, and being blind
By nature born, I gave to thee mine eyes.

Mine eyes, my light, my heart, my life, alas !
If so great services may scorned be :
  Yet let this thought thy tig'rish courage pass,
That I perhaps am somewhat kin to thee ;
  Since in thine arms, if learn'd fame truth had spread,
  Thou bear'st the arrow, I the arrow head.

LXVI.

And do I see some cause a hope to feed,
Or doth the tedious burthen of long woe
  In weaken'd minds, quick apprehending breed,
Of every image which may comfort show ?
  I cannot brag of word, much less of deed,
Fortune's wheels still with me in one sort slow,
  My wealth no more, and no whit less my need,
Desire still on the stilts of Fear doth go.

  And yet amid all fears as hope there is,
Stol'n to my heart since last fair night, nay day,
  Stella's eyes sent to me the beams of bliss,
Looking on me, while I look'd other way :
  But when mine eyes back to their heav'n did move,
  They fled with blush, which guilty seem'd of love.

LXVII.

Hope ! art thou true, or dost thou flatter me ?
Doth Stella now begin with piteous eye,
  The ruins of her conquest to espy ?
  Will she take time before all wrack'd he be ?
  Her eyes' speech is translated thus by thee :
But fail'st thou not in phrase so heav'nly high ?

Look on again, the fair text better try:
    What blushing notes dost thou in margin see?

    What sighs stol'n out, or kill'd before full born?
  Hast thou found such and such like arguments?
    Or art thou else to comfort me forsworn?
  Well, how-so thou interpret the contents,
    I am resolv'd thy error to maintain,
    Rather than by more truth to get more pain.

LXVIII.

  Stella, the only planet of my light,
Light of my life, and life of my desire,
Chief good, whereto my hope doth only aspire,
  World of my wealth, and heav'n of my delight;
  Why dost thou spend the treasures of thy sprite,
With voice more fit to wed Amphion's lyre,
Seeking to quench in me the noble fire,
  Fed by thy worth, and blinded by thy sight?

  And all in vain, for while thy breath most sweet,
With choicest words, thy words with reasons rare,
  Thy reasons firmly set on Virtue's feet,
Labour to kill in me this killing care:
  O think I then, what paradise of joy
  It is, so fair a virtue to enjoy.

LXIX.

  O joy! too high for my low style to show;
O bliss! fit for a nobler state than me:
Envy, put out thine eyes, lest thou do see

What oceans of delight in me do flow.
My friend, that oft saw through all masks my woe,
Come, come and let me pour myself on thee ;
Gone is the winter of my misery :
My spring appears, O see what here doth grow.

For Stella hath with words where faith doth shine,
  Of her high heart giv'n me the monarchy ;
I, I, O I may say that she is mine :
  And though she give but thus conditionly
This realm of bliss, while virtuous course I take,
No kings be crown'd, but they some cov'nants make.

LXX.

My Muse may well grudge at my heav'nly joy,
If still I force her in sad rhymes to creep :
  She oft hath drunk my tears, now hopes t' enjoy
Nectar of mirth, since I Love's cup do keep.
  Sonnets be not bound prentice to annoy :
Trebles sing high, as well as bases deep :
  Grief but Love's winter-livery is, the boy
Hath cheeks to smile, as well as eyes to weep.

Come then, my Muse, show thou height of delight
In well-raised notes ; my pen, the best it may,
  Shall paint out joy, though but in black and white.
Cease, eager Muse ; peace, pen, for my sake stay,
  I give you here my hand for truth of this,
  Wise silence is best music unto bliss.

LXXI.

Who will in fairest book of Nature know
How virtue may best lodg'd in beauty be,
Let him but learn of Love to read in thee,
    Stella, those fair lines which true goodness show:
    There shall he find all vices overthrow,
Not by rude force, but sweetest sovereignty
Of reason, from whose light those night-birds fly;
    That inward sun in thine eyes shineth so.

And not content to be Perfection's heir
    Thyself, dost strive all minds that way to move:
Who mark in thee what is in thee most fair:
    So while thy beauty draws the heart to love,
As fast thy virtue bends that love to good:
But, ah! Desire still cries, Give me some food.

LXXII.

Desire, though thou my old companion art,
And oft so clings to my pure love, that I
One from the other scarcely can descry,
    While each doth blow the fire of my heart;
    Now from thy fellowship I needs must part;
Venus is taught with Dian's wings to fly,
I must no more in thy sweet passions lie,
    Virtue's gold now must head my Cupid's dart.

Service and honour, wonder with delight,
    Fear to offend, well worthy to appear,
Care shining in mine eyes, faith in my sprite:
    These things are left me by my only dear;

But thou, Desire, because thou wouldst have all,
Now banish'd art; but yet, alas! how shall?

SECOND SONG.

Have I caught my heav'nly jewel,
   Teaching Sleep most fair to be?
   Now will I teach her that she,
When she wakes, is too, too cruel.

Since sweet Sleep her eyes hath charm'd,
   The two only darts of Love;
   Now will I, with that boy, prove
Some play, while he 's disarm'd.

Her tongue, waking, still refuseth,
   Giving frankly niggard *no*;
   Now will I attempt to know,
What *no* her tongue, sleeping, useth.

See the hand which, waking, guardeth,
   Sleeping, grants a free resort:
   Now will I invade the fort;
Cowards Love with loss rewardeth.

But, O fool! think of the danger
   Of her just and high disdain:
   Now will I, alas! refrain;
Love fears nothing else but anger.

Yet those lips, so sweetly swelling,
   Do invite a stealing kiss:

Now will I but venture this,
   Who will read, must first learn spelling.

   Oh! sweet kiss! but ah! she's waking;
      Low'ring beauty chastens me:
      Now will I away hence flee:
   Fool! more fool! for no more taking.

LXXIII.

Love, still a boy, and oft a wanton is,
School'd only by his mother's tender eye:
   What wonder then, if he his lesson miss,
When for so soft a rod, dear play he try?
   And yet my Star, because a sugar'd kiss
In sport I suck'd, while she asleep did lie,
   Doth low'r, nay chide, nay threat for only this:
Sweet, it was saucy Love, not humble I.

   But no 'scuse serves, she makes her wrath appear
   In beauty's throne; see now, who dares come near
Those scarlet judges, threat'ning bloody pain?
   O heav'nly fool! thy most kiss-worthy face,
   Anger invests with such a lovely grace,
That Anger's self I needs must kiss again.

LXXIV.

   I never drank of Aganippe well,
Nor ever did in shade of Tempe sit:
   And Muses scorn with vulgar brains to dwell:

Poor layman I, for sacred rites unfit.
  Some do I hear of poets' fury tell,
But (God wot) wot not what they mean by it;
  And this I swear, by blackest brook of hell,
I am no pickpurse of another's wit.

  How falls it then, that with so smooth an ease
My thoughts I speak, and what I speak doth flow
  In verse, and that my verse best wits doth please?
Guess we the cause? What, is it thus? Fie, no:
  Or so? Much less: How then? Sure thus it is,
  My lips are sweet, inspir'd with Stella's kiss.

LXXV.

Of all the kings that ever here did reign,
  Edward, nam'd fourth, as first in praise, I name,
Not for his fair outside, nor well-lin'd brain;
Although less gifts imp feathers oft on fame:
  Nor that he could, young-wise, wise-valiant, frame
  His sire's revenge, join'd with a kingdom's gain:
And gain'd by Mars, could yet mad Mars so tame,
That balance weigh'd what sword did late obtain.

  Nor that he made the flower-de-luce so 'fraid,
Though strongly hedg'd of bloody lions' paws,
  That witty Lewis to him a tribute paid:
Nor this, nor that, nor any such small cause,
  But only for this worthy knight durst prove
  To lose his crown, rather than fail his love.

LXXVI.

She comes, and straight therewith her shining twins do move
Their rays to me, who in her tedious absence lay
Benighted in cold woe; but now appears my day,
   The only light of joy, the only warmth of love.
   She comes with light and warmth, which, like Aurora, prove
Of gentle force, so that mine eyes dare gladly play
With such a rosy morn, whose beams, most freshly gay,
   Scorch not, but only do dark chilling sp'rits remove.

But, lo! while I do speak, it groweth noon with me;
   Her flamy glist'ring lights increase with time and place;
My heart cries ah! it burns, mine eyes now dazzled be:
   No wind, no shade can cool; what help then in my case?
But with short breath, long looks, staid feet, and walking head,
Pray that my sun go down, with meeker beams, to bed.

LXXVII.

Those looks, whose beams be joy, whose motion is delight;
That face, whose lecture shows what perfect beauty is;
   That presence, which doth give dark hearts a living light;
That grace, which Venus weeps that she herself doth miss;

That hand, which without touch holds more than
      Atlas might;
Those lips, which make death's pay a mean price for a
      kiss;
   That skin, whose pass-praise hue scorns this poor
      term of white;
Those words, which do sublime the quintessence of bliss;

   That voice, which makes the soul plant himself in
      the ears;
That conversation sweet, where such high comforts be,
   As constru'd in true speech, the name of heav'n it
      bears;
Makes me in my best thoughts, and quiet'st judgment,
      see
   That in no more but these I might be fully blest;
   Yet, ah! my maiden Muse doth blush to tell the best.

LXXVIII.

   O how the pleasant airs of true love be
Infected by those vapours, which arise
From out that noisome gulf, which gaping lies
   Between the jaws of hellish jealousy!
   A monster, others' harm, self-misery,
Beauty's plague, virtue's scourge, succour of lies;
Who his own joy to his own hurt applies,
   And only cherish doth with injury.

Who since he hath, by Nature's special grace,
So piercing paws as spoil when they embrace;
   So nimble feet as stir still, though on thorns;
So many eyes, aye seeking their own woe;

So ample ears as never good news know:
Is it not evil that such a devil wants horns?

LXXIX.

Sweet kiss, thy sweets I fain would sweetly indite,
Which, ev'n of sweetness, sweetest sweet'ner art;
Pleasing'st consort, where each sense holds a part;
   Which coupling doves guides Venus' chariot right:
   Best charge, and brav'st retreat in Cupid's fight;
A double key, which opens to the heart,
Most rich, when most his riches is impart:
   Nest of young joys, schoolmaster of delight;

Teaching the mean, at once to take and give;
   The friendly fray, where blows both wound and heal:
The pretty death, while each in other live:
   Poor hope's first wealth, hostage of promis'd weal,
Breakfast of love:—But lo! lo! where she is,
Cease we to praise, now pray we for a kiss.

LXXX.

Sweet swelling lip, well may'st thou swell in pride,
Since best wits think it wit thee to admire:
Nature's praise, Virtue's stall, Cupid's cold fire;
   Whence words, not words, but heav'nly graces slide.
   The new Parnassus, where the Muses bide;
Sweet'ner of music, wisdom's beautifier:
Breather of life, and fast'ner of desire,
   Where beauty's blush in honour's grain is dy'd.

Thus much my heart compell'd my mouth to say,
But now, spite of my heart, my mouth will stay,
   Loathing all lies, doubting this flatt'ry is;
   And no spur can his resty race renew,
Without, how far this praise is short of you,
   Sweet lip, you teach my mouth with one sweet kiss.

LXXXI.

O kiss! which dost those ruddy gems impart,
Or gems, or fruits, of new-found Paradise:
   Breathing all bliss and sweet'ning to the heart;
Teaching dumb lips a nobler exercise.
   O kiss! which souls, ev'n souls, together ties
By links of love, and only Nature's art:
   How fain would I paint thee to all men's eyes,
Or of thy gifts, at least, shade out some part!

   But she forbids, with blushing words, she says,
   She builds her fame on higher-seated praise:
But my heart burns, I cannot silent be.
   Then since, dear life, you fain would have me peace,
   And I, mad with delight, want wit to cease,
Stop you my mouth with still, still kissing me.

LXXXII.

Nymph of the garden, where all beauties be:
Beauties, which do in excellency pass
His, who, till death, look'd in a wat'ry glass;
   Or her's, whom nak'd the Trojan boy did see:
Sweet garden nymph, which keeps the cherry-tree,
   Whose fruit doth far the Hesperian taste surpass:

Most sweet-fair, most fair-sweet, do not alas!
From coming near those cherries banish me:

For though, full of desire, empty of wit,
Admitted late by your best-graced grace,
  I caught, at one of them, a hungry bit;
Pardon that fault, once more grant me the place,
  And I do swear, ev'n by the same delight,
  I will but kiss, I never more will bite.

LXXXIII.

Good brother Philip, I have borne you long,
I was content you should in favour creep,
While craftily you seem'd your cut to keep,
  As though that fair soft hand did you great wrong:
  I bare (with envy) yet I bare your song,
When in her neck, you did love ditties peep;
Nay, more fool, I oft suffer'd you to sleep,
  In lily's nest, where Love's self lies along.

  What, doth high place ambitious thoughts augment?
Is sauciness reward of courtesy?
  Cannot such grace your silly self content,
But you must needs with those lips billing be?
  And through those lips drink nectar from that tongue;
  Leave that, Sir Phip, lest off your neck be wrung.

THIRD SONG.

If Orpheus' voice had force to breathe such music's love
Through pores of senseless trees, as it could make them move:

If stones good measure danc'd, the Theban walls to build,
To cadence of the tunes, which Amphion's lyre did yield;
More cause, a like effect, at least-wise bringeth :
O stones! O trees! learn hearing, Stella singeth.

If love might sweeten so a boy of shepherd brood,
To make a lizard dull, to taste love's dainty food:
If eagle fierce could so in Grecian maid delight,
As his light was her eyes, her death his endless night:
Earth give that love; heaven, I trow, love refineth:
O beasts! O birds! look, Love! lo! Stella shineth.

The birds, beasts, stones, and trees feel this, and, feeling, love :
And if the trees, nor stones, stir not the same to prove,
Nor beasts, nor birds, do come unto this blessed gaze,
Know, that small love is quick, and great love doth amaze :
They are amaz'd, but you with reason arm'd,
O eyes, O ears of men, how are you charm'd!

LXXXIV.

Highway, since you my chief Parnassus be;
And that my Muse, to some ears not unsweet,
Tempers her words to trampling horses' feet,
More oft than to a chamber melody.
Now blessed you, bear onward blessed me,
To her, where I my heart, safe left, shall meet;
My Muse and I must you of duty greet
With thanks and wishes, wishing thankfully.

Be you still fair, honour'd by public heed;
By no encroachment wrong'd, nor time forgot:
  Nor blam'd for blood, nor sham'd for sinful deed;
And that you know, I envy you no lot
    Of highest wish, I wish you so much bliss,
    Hundreds of years you Stella's feet may kiss.

LXXXV.

I see the house, my heart thyself contain;
Beware full sails drown not thy tott'ring barge;
Lest joy by nature apt sp'rits to enlarge,
  Thee to thy wreck, beyond thy limits strain.
  Nor do like lords, whose weak confused brain,
Not pointing to fit folks, each undercharge,
While ev'ry office themselves will discharge;
  With doing all, leave nothing done but pain.

But give apt servants their due place, let eyes
  See beauty's total sum, summ'd in her face;
Let ears hear speech, which wit to wonder ties;
  Let breath suck up those sweets, let arms embrace
The globe of weal, lips Love's indentures make;
Thou, but of all the kingly tribute take.

FOURTH SONG.

Only joy, now here you are,
Fit to hear and ease my care;
  Let my whisp'ring voice obtain,
  Sweet reward for sharpest pain:
Take me to thee, and thee to me.
No, no, no, no, my dear, let be.

Night hath clos'd all in her cloke,
  Twinkling stars love-thoughts provoke :
Danger hence good care doth keep,
Jealousy itself doth sleep :
   Take me to thee, and thee to me.
   No, no, no, no, my dear, let be.

Better place no wit can find,
Cupid's yoke to loose or bind :
   These sweet flowers on fine bed too,
   Us in their best language woo :
Take me to thee, and thee to me.
No, no, no, no, my dear, let be.

  This small light the moon bestows,
  Serves thy beams but to disclose ;
So to raise my hap more high ;
Fear not else, none can us spy :
   Take me to thee, and thee to me.
   No, no, no, no, my dear, let be.

That you heard was but a mouse,
Dumb sleep holdeth all the house :
   Yet asleep, methinks they say,
   Young folks, take time while you may :
Take me to thee, and thee to me.
No, no, no, no, my dear, let be.

  Niggard time threats, if we miss
  This large offer of our bliss,
Long stay, ere he grant the same.
Sweet, then, while each thing doth frame,

Take me to thee, and thee to me.
No, no, no, no, my dear, let be.

Your fair mother is abed,
Candles out, and curtains spread;
　She thinks you do letters write;
　Write, but let me first indite:
Take me to thee, and thee to me.
No, no, no, no, my dear, let be.

　Sweet, alas! why strive you thus?
　Concord better fitteth us;
Leave to Mars the force of hands,
Your power in your beauty stands:
　Take thee to me, and me to thee.
　No, no, no, no, my dear, let be.

Woe to me, and do you swear
Me to hate? but I forbear;
　Cursed be my dest'nies all,
　That brought me so high to fall:
Soon with my death I will please thee,
No, no, no, no, my dear, let be.

LXXXVI.

Alas! whence came this change of looks? If I
Have chang'd desert, let mine own conscience be
　A still-felt plague, to self-condemning me:
Let woe gripe on my heart, shame load mine eye.
But if all faith, like spotless ermine, lie
　Safe in my soul, which only doth to thee,

(As his sole object of felicity)
With wings of love in air of wonder fly.

O ease your hand, treat not so hard your slave :
  In justice pains come not till faults do call ;
Or, if I needs, sweet judge, must torments have,
  Use something else to chasten me withal,
Than those blest eyes, where all my hopes do dwell ;
No doom should make once heav'n become his hell.

FIFTH SONG.

While favour fed my hope, delight with hope is brought ;
Thought waited on delight, and speech did follow thought ;
  Then grew my tongue and pen records unto thy glory :
I thought all words were lost, that were not spent of thee ;
I thought each place was dark, but where thy lights would be,
  And all ears worse than deaf, that heard not out thy story.

I said thou wert most fair, and so, indeed, thou art ;
I said thou art most sweet, sweet poison to my heart ;
  I said my soul was thine, O that I then had lied !
I said thine eyes were stars, thy breasts the milken way,
Thy fingers Cupid's shafts, thy voice the angels' lay :
  And all I said so well, as no man it denied.

But now that hope is lost, unkindness kills delight,
Yet thought and speech do live, though metamorphos'd
   quite ;
   For rage now rules the reins, which guided were by
      pleasure ;
I think now of thy faults, who late thought of thy
   praise ;
That speech falls now to blame, which did thy honour
   raise ;
   The same key open can, which can lock up a treasure.

Thou then, whom partial heav'ns conspir'd in one to
   frame
The proof of beauty's worth, th' inheritrix of fame ;
   The mansion seat of bliss, and just excuse of lovers ;
See now those feathers pluck'd, wherewith thou flew
   most high ;
See what clouds of reproach shall dark thy honour's
   sky :
   Whose own faults cast him down, hardly high seat
      recovers.

And, O my Muse ! though oft you lull'd her in your
   lap,
And then, a heav'nly child, gave her ambrosian pap,
   And to that brain of hers your kindest gifts infused,
Since she, disdaining me, doth you in me disdain,
Suffer not her to laugh, while both we suffer pain :
   Princes, in subjects wrong'd, must deem themselves
      abused.

Your client, poor myself, shall Stella handle so ?
Revenge, revenge, my Muse ! defiance trumpet blow ;

'Threaten what may be done, yet do no more than
    threaten :
Ah, my suit granted is, I feel my breast doth swell ;
Now, child, a lesson new you shall begin to spell :
    Sweet babes must babies have, but shrewd girls must
    be beaten.

'Think now no more to hear of warm fine odour'd snow,
Nor blushing lilies, nor pearls' ruby-hidden row,
    Nor of that golden sea, whose waves in curls are
    broken ;
But of thy soul, so fraught with such ungratefulness
As where thou soon might'st help, most faith dost most
    oppress :
    Ungrateful who is call'd, the worst of evils is spoken.

Yet worse than worst, I say thou art a thief.—A
    thief!
Now God forbid : a thief, and of worst thieves, the
    chief!
    Thieves steal for need, and steal but goods which pain
    recovers ;
But thou, rich in all joys, dost rob my joys from me,
Which cannot be restor'd by time nor industry :
    Of foes the spoil is evil, far worse of constant lovers.

Yet, gentle English thieves do rob, but will not slay ;
Thou English murd'ring thief, wilt have hearts for thy
    prey ?
    The name of murd'rer now on thy fair forehead
    sitteth :
And ev'n while I do speak, my death-wounds bleeding
    be ;

Which, I protest, proceed from only cruel thee :
  Who may, and will not save, murder, in truth, com‑
    mitteth.

But, murder, private fault ! seems but a toy to thee,
I lay then to thy charge unjustest tyranny,
  If rule, by force, without all claim, a tyrant showeth;
For thou dost lord my heart, who am not born thy
    slave,
And, which is worse, makes me most guiltless torments
    have :
  A rightful prince by unright deeds a tyrant groweth.

Lo ! you grow proud with this, for tyrants make folk
    bow :
Of foul rebellion then I do appeach thee now ;
  Rebel by Nature's law, rebel by law of Reason,
Thou, sweetest subject, wert born in the realm of Love,
And yet, against the prince thy force dost daily prove :
  No virtue merits praise, once touch'd with blot of
    treason.

But valiant rebels oft, in fools' mouths, purchase fame :
I now then stain thy white with vagabonding shame,
  Both rebel to the son, and vagrant from the mother ;
For wearing Venus' badge in every part of thee,
Unto Diana's train thou, runaway, didst flee :
  Who faileth one is false, though trusty to another.

What ! is not this enough ? nay, far worse cometh here;
A witch, I say, thou art, though thou so fair appear ;
  For, I protest, my sight never thy face enjoyeth,
But I in me am chang'd ; I am alive and dead :

My feet are turn'd to roots, my heart becometh lead :
  No witchcraft is so evil, as which man's mind destroyeth.

Yet witches may repent ; thou art far worse than they :
Alas ! that I am forc'd such evil of thee to say :
  I say, thou art a devil, though cloth'd in angel's shining ;
For thy face tempts my soul to leave the heav'n for thee,
And thy words of refuse, do pour even hell on me :
  Who tempt, and tempting plague, are devils in true defining.

You, then, ungrateful thief, you murd'ring tyrant, you,
You rebel runaway, to lord and lady untrue,
  You witch, you devil,'(alas !) you still of me beloved,
You see what I can say ; mend yet your froward mind,
And such skill in my muse, you, reconcil'd, shall find,
  That all these cruel words your praises shall be proved.

SIXTH SONG.

O you that hear this voice,
  O you that see this face,
Say, whether, of the choice,
  Deserves the former place ?
Fear not to judge this bate,
For it is void of hate.

  This side doth Beauty take,
For that doth Music speak ;
  Fit orators to make

  The strongest judgments weak :
   The bar to plead their right,
   Is only true delight.

  Thus doth the voice and face,
These gentle lawyers, wage,
  Like loving brothers' case,
For father's heritage ;
  That each, while each contends,
  Itself to other lends.

  For Beauty beautifies,
With heav'nly hue and grace,
  The heav'nly harmonies ;
And in this faultless face,
  The perfect beauties be
  A perfect harmony.

  Music more lofty swells
In speeches nobly placed ;
  Beauty as far excels,
In action aptly graced ;
  A friend each party draws
  To countenance his cause.

  Love more affected seems
To Beauty's lovely light,
  And Wonder more esteems
Of Music's wond'rous might ;
  But both to both so bent,
  As both in both are spent.

  Music doth witness call
The ear, his truth to try ;

Beauty brings to the hall
Eye-judgment of the eye;
  Both in their objects such,
  As no exceptions touch.

The common sense, which might
Be arbiter of this,
  To be, forsooth, upright,
To both sides partial is:
  He lays on this chief praise,
  Chief praise on that he lays.

Then Reason, princess high,
Whose throne is in the mind,
  Which Music can in sky
And hidden beauties find;
  Say, whether thou wilt crown,
  With limitless renown?

SEVENTH SONG.

Whose senses in so evil consort their step-dame Nature
    lays,
That ravishing delight in them most sweet tunes do not
    raise;
Or if they do delight therein, yet are so clos'd with
    wit,
As with sententious lips to set a title vain on it:
O let them hear these sacred tunes, and learn in won-
    ders' schools,
To be, in things past bounds of wit, fools—if they be
    not fools.

Who have so leaden eyes, as not to see sweet beauty's
    show;
Or, seeing, have so wooden wits, as not that worth to
    know;
Or, knowing, have so muddy minds, as not to be in
    love;
Or, loving, have so frothy thoughts, as eas'ly thence to
    move:
O let them see these heav'nly beams, and in fair letters
    read
A lesson fit, both sight and skill, love and firm love to
    breed.

Hear then, but then with wonder hear; see, but adoring,
    see,
No mortal gifts, no earthly fruits, now here descended
    be:
See! do you see this face? a face! nay, image of the
    skies,
Of which, the two life-giving lights are figur'd in her
    eyes:
Hear you this soul-invading voice, and count it but a
    voice?
The very essence of their tunes, when angels do
    rejoice.

EIGHTH SONG.

In a grove most rich of shade,
Where birds wanton music made,
May, then young, his pied weeds showing,
New perfum'd, with flowers fresh growing:

Astrophel with Stella sweet,
Did for mutual comfort meet,
Both within themselves oppressed,
But each in the other blessed.

Him great harms had taught much care;
Her fair neck a foul yoke bare;
But her sight his cares did banish;
In his sight her yoke did vanish.

Wept they had, alas! the while,
But now tears themselves did smile,
While their eyes, by love directed,
Interchangeably reflected.

Sigh they did, but now, betwixt
Sighs of woes, were glad sighs mix'd;
With arms crost, yet testifying
Restless rest, and living dying.

Their ears hungry of each word,
Which the dear tongue would afford;
But their tongues restrain'd from walking,
'Till their hearts had ended talking.

But when their tongues could not speak,
Love itself did silence break;
Love did set his lips asunder,
Thus to speak in love and wonder.

Stella! sovereign of my joy,
Fair triumpher of annoy:
Stella! star of heav'nly fire:
Stella! loadstar of desire:

Stella! in whose shining eyes
Are the lights of Cupid's skies,
Whose beams, where they once are darted,
Love therewith is straight imparted:

Stella! whose voice, when it speaks,
Senses all asunder breaks:
Stella! whose voice, when it singeth,
Angels to acquaintance bringeth.

Stella! in whose body is
Writ each character of bliss;
Whose face all, all beauty passeth,
Save thy mind, which yet surpasseth.

Grant! O grant! but speech, alas!
Fails me, fearing on to pass:
Grant! —— O me! what am I saying?
But no fault there is in praying.

Grant —— O dear! on knees I pray,
(Knees on ground he then did stay)
That, not I, but since I love you,
Time and place for me may move you.

Never season was more fit;
Never room more apt for it;
Smiling air allows my reason;
These birds sing, "Now use the season."

This small wind, which so sweet is,
See how it the leaves doth kiss,
Each tree in his best attiring,
Sense of love to love inspiring.

Love makes earth the water drink;
Love to earth makes water sink;
And, if dumb things be so witty,
Shall a heav'nly grace want pity?

There his hands, in their speech, fain
Would have made tongue's language plain;
But her hands, his hands repelling,
Gave repulse all grace excelling.

Then she spake; her speech was such,
As not ear, but heart did touch:
While such-wise she love denied,
As yet love she signified.

Astrophel, said she, my love,
Cease, in these effects, to prove;
Now be still, yet still believe me,
Thy grief more than death would grieve me.

If that any thought in me
Can taste comfort but of thee,
Let me, fed with hellish anguish,
Joyless, hopeless, endless languish.

If those eyes you praised, be
Half so dear as you to me,
Let me home return, stark blinded
Of those eyes, and blinder minded;

If to secret of my heart,
I do any wish impart,
Where thou art not foremost placed,
Be both wish and I defaced.

If more may be said, I say,
All my bliss in thee I lay;
If thou love, my love, content thee,
For all love, all faith is meant thee.

Trust me, while I thee deny,
In myself the smart I try;
Tyrant Honour doth thus use thee,
Stella's self might not refuse thee.

Therefore, dear! this no more move,
Lest, though I leave not thy love,
Which too deep in me is framed,
I should blush when thou art named.

Therewithal away she went,
Leaving him so·passion rent,
With what she had done and spoken,
That therewith my song is broken.

NINTH SONG.

Go, my flock, go, get you hence,
Seek a better place of feeding,
  Where you may have some defence
For the storms in my breast breeding,
And showers from mine eyes proceeding.

  Leave a wretch, in whom all woe
Can abide to keep no measure;
  Merry flock, such one forego,
Unto whom mirth is displeasure,
Only rich in mischief's treasure.

Yet, alas! before you go,
Hear your woeful master's story,
  Which to stones I else would show:
Sorrow only then hath glory,
When 'tis excellently sorry.

  Stella! fiercest shepherdess,
Fiercest, but yet fairest ever;
  Stella! whom, O heav'ns, do bless!
Though against me she persever,
Though I bliss inherit never.

  Stella hath refused me;
Stella! who more love hath proved,
  In this caitiff heart to be,
Than can in good ewes be moved
Toward lambkins best beloved.

  Stella hath refused me!
Astrophel, that so well served
  In this pleasant spring, must see,
While in pride flowers be preserved,
Himself only winter-starved.

  Why, alas! doth she then swear,
That she loveth me so dearly,
  Seeing me so long to bear
Coals of love that burn so clearly;
And yet leave me helpless merely?

  Is that love? forsooth, I trow,
If I saw my good dog grieved,
  And a help for him did know,

My love should not be believed,
But he were by me relieved.

No, she hates me; wel-away!
Feigning love, somewhat to please me;
  For she knows, if she display
All her hate, death soon would seize me,
And of hideous torments ease me.

  Then adieu! dear flock, adieu;
But, alas! if in your straying
  Heav'nly Stella meet with you,
Tell her, in your piteous blaying,
Her poor slave's unjust decaying.

LXXXVII.

When I was forc'd from Stella, ever dear,
Stella! food of my thoughts, heart of my heart,
  Stella! whose eyes make all my tempests clear,
By iron laws of duty to depart:
Alas! I found that she, with me, did smart;
  I saw that tears did in her eyes appear;
I saw that sighs her sweetest lips did part,
  And her sad words my saddest sense did hear:

For me, I wept to see pearls scatter'd so,
I sigh'd her sighs, and wailed for her woe,
  Yet swam in joy, such love in her was seen:
Thus, while th' effect most bitter was to me,
And nothing than the cause more sweet could be,
  I had been vex'd, if vex'd I had not been.

LXXXVIII.

Out, traitor Absence! dar'st thou counsel me,
From my dear captainess to run away,
  Because, in brave array, here marcheth she,
That, to win me, oft shows a present pay?
  Is faith so weak? or is such force in thee?
When sun is hid, can stars such beams display?
  Cannot heav'ns food, once felt, keep stomachs free
From base desire on earthly cates to prey?

  Tush, Absence, while thy mists eclipse that light,
  My orphan sense flies to the inward sight,
Where memory sets forth the beams of love,
  That where before heart lov'd, and eyes did see,
  In heart both sight and love now coupled be;
United powers make each the stronger prove.

LXXXIX.

Now, that of absence, the most irksome night,
With darkest shade, doth overcome my day;
Since Stella's eyes, wont to give me my day,
  Leaving my hemisphere, leave me in night:
  Each day seems long, and longs for long-stay'd night;
The night, as tedious, woos th' approach of day;
Tir'd with the dusty toils of busy day,
  Languish'd with horrors of the silent night;

  Suff'ring the evils both of day and night,
While no night is more dark than is my day,
  Nor no day hath less quiet than my night:
With such bad mixture of my night and day,

That living thus in blackest winter night,
I feel the flames of hottest summer day.

XC.

Stella! think not that I by verse seek fame,
Who seek, who hope, who love, who live but thee?
Thine eyes my pride, thy lips mine history:
   If thou praise not, all other praise is shame.
   Nor so ambitious am I, as to frame
A nest for my young praise in laurel tree:
In truth I swear, I wish not there should be
   Grav'd in my epitaph a Poet's name:

Ne, if I would, I could just title make,
   That any laud to me thereof should grow;
Without my plumes from others' wings I take:
   For nothing from my wit, or will, doth flow;
Since all my words thy beauty doth indite,
And Love doth hold my hand, and makes me write.

XCI.

Stella, while now, by honour's cruel might,
I am from you, light of my life, misled,
And that fair you, my sun, thus overspread
   With absence veil, I live in sorrow's night.
   If this dark place yet show like candle-light,
Some beauty's piece, as amber-colour'd head,
Milk hands, rose cheeks, or lips more sweet, more red;
   Or seeing jet's black, but in blackness, bright;

They please, I do confess, they please mine eyes;
  But why? because of you they models be:
Models! such be wood-globes of glist'ring skies.
  Dear, therefore be not jealous over me,
If you hear that they seem my heart to move;
Not them, O no, but you in them I love.

XCII.

Be your words made, good Sir, of Indian ware,
That you allow me them by so small rate?
Or do you curted Spartans imitate?
  Or do you mean my tender ears to spare,
  That to my questions you so total are?
When I demand of Phœnix-Stella's state,
You say, forsooth, you left her well of late:
  O God! think you that satisfies my care?

I would know whether she do sit or walk?
  How cloth'd? How waited on? Sigh'd she, or smil'd?
Whereof? With whom? How often did she talk?
  With what pastime, Time's journey she beguil'd?
If her lips deign'd to sweeten my poor name?
Say all; and all well said, still say the same.

TENTH SONG.

O dear life, when shall it be,
  That mine eyes thine eyes may see;
  And in them thy mind discover,
Whether absence have had force,

Thy remembrance to divorce,
  From the image of thy lover?

Or if I myself find not,
After parting, aught forgot:
  Nor debarr'd from beauty's treasure,
Let not tongue aspire to tell
In what high joys I shall dwell;
  Only thought aims at the pleasure.

Thought, therefore, I will send thee
To take up the place for me:
  Long I will not after tarry:
There, unseen, thou may'st be bold,
Those fair wonders to behold,
  Which in them my hopes do carry.

Thought, see thou no place forbear,
Enter bravely everywhere;
  Seize on all to her belonging:
But, if thou wouldst guarded be,
Fearing her beams, take with thee
  Strength of liking, rage of longing.

Think of that most grateful time,
When thy leaping heart will climb,
  In my lips to have his biding;
There those roses for to kiss,
Which do breathe a sugar'd bliss,
  Opening rubies, pearls dividing.

Think of my most princely power,
Which I, blessed, shall devour

With my greedy lick'rous senses,
Beauty, music, sweetness, love,
While she doth against me prove
    Her strong darts but weak defences.

Think, think of those dallyings,
When with dove-like murmurings,
    With glad moaning passed anguish,
We change eyes; and heart for heart,
Each to other do depart,
    Joying till joy makes us languish.

O my thought! my thoughts surcease,
Thy delights my woes increase;
    My life melts with too much thinking:
Think no more, but die in me,
Till thou shalt revived be,
    At her lips my nectar drinking.

XCIII.

O fate! O fault! O curse! child of my bliss,
What sobs can give words grace my grief to show?
What ink is black enough to paint my woe?
    Through me, wretch me! even Stella vexed is.
Yet, truth (if caitiff's breath may call thee) this
    Witness with me, that my foul stumbling so,
    From carelessness did in no manner grow;
But wit, confus'd with too much care, did miss.

And do I then myself this vain scuse give?
I have (live I, and know this?) harmed thee,
    Though words quit me, shall I myself forgive!

Only with pains, my pains thus eased be,
  That all thy hurts, in my heart's wreck I read;
I cry thy sighs, my dear, thy tears I bleed.

XCIV.

Grief, find the words, for thou hast made my brain
So dark with misty vapours, which arise
From out thy heavy mould, that inbent eyes
  Can scarce discern the shape of mine own pain.
  Do thou then (for thou canst) do thou complain
For my poor soul, which now that sickness tries,
Which ev'n to sense, sense of itself denies,
  Though harbinger of death lodge there his train.

Or, if thy love of plaint yet mine forbears,
  As of a caitiff worthy so to die,
Yet wail thyself, and wail, with causeful tears,
  That though in wretchedness thy life doth lie,
Yet grow'st more wretched than thy nature bears,
  By being plac'd in such a wretch as I.

XCV.

  Yet sighs, dear sighs! indeed true friends you are,
That do not leave your left friend at the worst;
But as you with my breast I oft have nurst,
  So, grateful now, you wait upon my care.
  Faint coward Joy no longer tarry dare,
Seeing Hope yield, when this woe strake him first:
Delight protests he is not for th' accurst,
  Though oft himself my mate in arms he sware.

Nay, Sorrow comes with such main rage, that he
  Kills his own children, tears, finding that they
By love were made apt to consort with me.
  Only, true sighs, you do not go away;
Thank may you have for such a thankful part;
Thank-worthiest yet, when you shall break my heart.

XCVI.

  Thought, with good cause, thou lik'st so well the
      night,
Since kin or chance gives both one livery;
Both sadly black, both blackly darken'd be;
  Night barr'd from sun, thou from thy own sun's light;
Silence in both displays his sullen might,
  Low heaviness in both holds one degree;
  That full of doubts, thou of perplexity:
Thy tears express Night's native moisture right.

  In both amazeful solitariness:
In night of sp'rits, the ghastly powers to stir;
  In thee, or sp'rits, or sp'rited ghastliness:
But, but (alas!) Night's side the odds hath far;
  For that, at length, yet doth invite some rest,
  Thou, though still tir'd, yet still dost it detest.

XCVII.

  Dian, that fain would cheer her friend the Night,
Shows her oft, at the full, her fairest face,
Bringing with her those starry nymphs, whose chase
  From heav'nly standing hits each mortal wight.
But ah! poor Night, in love with Phœbus' light,

And endlessly despairing of his grace,
  Herself (to show no other joy hath place)
Silent and sad, in mourning weeds doth dight:

  Even so, alas! a lady, Dian's peer,
With choice delights, and rarest company,
  Would fain drive clouds from out my heavy cheer:
But, woe is me! though joy itself were she,
  She could not show my blind brain ways of joy,
  While I despair my sun's sight to enjoy.

XCVIII.

  Ah, bed! the field where joy's peace some do see;
The field where all my thoughts to war be train'd;
How is thy grace by my strange fortune stain'd!
  How thy lee-shores by my sighs stormed be!
  With sweet soft shades, thou oft invitest me
To steal some rest; but, wretch! I am constrain'd,
(Spurr'd with Love's spur, though gold, and shortly rein'd
  With Care's hard hand) to turn and toss in thee.

While the black horrors of the silent night
Paint Woe's black face so lively to my sight,
  That tedious leisure marks each wrinkled line:
But when Aurora leads out Phœbus' dance,
Mine eyes then only wink, for spite perchance,
  That worms should have their sun, and I want mine.

XCIX.

When far-spent Night persuades each mortal eye,
  To whom nor Art nor Nature granteth light,

To lay his then mark-wanting shafts of sight,
Clos'd with their quivers, in Sleep's armory;
With windows ope, then most my mind doth lie,
   Viewing the shape of darkness and delight;
   Takes in that sad hue, which, with th' inward night
Of his maz'd powers, keeps perfect harmony:

But when birds charm, and that sweet air, which is
Morn's messenger, with rose-enamell'd skies,
   Calls each wight to salute the flower of bliss;
In tomb of lids then buried are mine eyes,
   Forc'd by their lord, who is asham'd to find
   Such light in sense, with such a darken'd mind.

C.

O tears! no tears, but rain, from Beauty's skies,
Making those lilies and those roses grow,
Which aye most fair, now more than most fair show,
   While graceful Pity beauty beautifies.
   O honey'd sighs! which from that breast do rise,
Whose pants do make unspilling cream to flow;
Wing'd with whose breath, so pleasing zephyrs blow,
   As can refresh the hell where my soul fries.

   O plaints! conserv'd in such a sugar'd phrase,
   That eloquence itself envies your praise;
While sobb'd out words a perfect music give.
   Such tears, sighs, plaints, no sorrow is, but joy:
   Or, if such heav'nly sighs must prove annoy,
All mirth farewell, let me in sorrow live.

CI.

Stella is sick, and in that sick bed lies
Sweetness, which breathes and pants as oft as she:
    And Grace, sick too, such fine conclusions tries,
That Sickness brags itself best grace to be.
    Beauty is sick, but sick in so fair guise,
That in that paleness Beauty's white we see,
    And joy, which is unsever'd from those eyes,
Stella, now learns (strange case!) to weep in thee.

    Love moves thy pain, and like a faithful page,
As thy looks stir, comes up and down, to make
    All folks press'd at thy will, thy pain t' assuage;
Nature with care sweats for her darling's sake,
    Knowing worlds pass, ere she enough can find,
    Of such heav'n-stuff to clothe so heav'nly mind.

CII.

    Where be those roses gone, which sweeten'd so our eyes?
Where those red cheeks, which oft, with fair increase, doth frame
The height of honour in the kindly badge of shame?
    Who hath the crimson weeds stol'n from my morning skies?
    How doth the colour vade of those vermilion dies,
Which Nature's self did make, and self-ingrain'd the same?
I would know by what right this paleness overcame
    That hue, whose force my heart still unto thraldom ties?

Galen's adoptive sons, who by a beaten way
Their judgments hackney on, the fault on sickness lay;
   But feeling pulse makes me (say they) mistake it far.
It is but love which makes this paper perfect white,
To write therein more fresh the story of delight,
   While Beauty's reddest ink Venus for him doth stir.

CIII.

O happy Thames, that didst my Stella bear,
I saw thee with full many a smiling line,
   Upon thy cheerful face joy's livery wear:
While those fair planets on thy streams did shine,
   The boat for joy could not to dance forbear,
While wanton winds, with beauties so divine
   Ravish'd, staid not, till in her golden hair
They did themselves (O sweetest prison!) twine.

And fain those Æol's youth there would their stay
Have made, but forc'd by nature still to fly,
   First did with puffing kiss those locks display:
She, so dishevell'd blush'd; from window I
   With sight thereof cried out, "O fair disgrace,
   Let Honour's self to thee grant highest place."

CIV.

Envious wits, what hath been mine offence,
That with such pois'nous care my looks you mark,
That to each word, nay sigh, of mine, you hark,
   As grudging me my sorrow's eloquence?
   Ah! is it not enough, that I am thence,
Thence, so far thence, that scarcely any spark

Of comfort dare come to this dungeon dark,
  Where rig'rous exile locks up all my sense?

But if I by a happy window pass,
  If I but stars upon mine armour bear;
Sick, thirsty, glad (though but of empty glass):
  Your mortal notes straight my hid meaning tear
From out my ribs, and, puffing, prove that I
Do Stella love: fools! who doth it deny?

ELEVENTH SONG.

Who is it that this dark night,
  Underneath my window plaineth?
It is one, who from thy sight
  Being (ah!) exil'd, disdaineth
Ev'ry other vulgar light.

Why, alas! and are you he?
  Be not yet those fancies chang'd?
Dear, when you find change in me,
  Though from me you be estrang'd,
Let my change to ruin be.

Well, in absence this will die;
  Leave to see, and leave to wonder.
Absence sure will help, if I
  Can learn, how myself to sunder
From what in my heart doth lie.

But time will these thoughts remove:
  Time doth work what no man knoweth;
Time doth as the subject prove;

With time still affection groweth
In the faithful turtle-dove.

What if ye new beauties see,
　Will not they stir new affection?
I will think they pictures be,
　(Image-like, of saint-perfection)
Poorly counterfeiting thee.

But your reason's purest light,
　Bids you leave such minds to nourish.
Dear, do reason no such spite;
　Never doth thy beauty flourish
More than in thy reason's sight.

But the wrongs love bears, will make
　Love at length leave undertaking.
No, the more fools it doth shake,
　In a ground of so firm making,
Deeper still they drive the stake.

Peace! I think that some give ear;
　Come no more, lest I get anger.
Bliss, I will my bliss forbear;
　Fearing (sweet) you to endanger;
But my soul shall harbour there.

Well, begone; begone, I say,
　Lest that Argus' eyes perceive you.
O unjust is Fortune's sway!
　Which can make me thus to leave you;
And from louts to run away.

CV.

Unhappy sight, and hath she vanish'd by
So near, in so good time, so free a place?
Dead glass, dost though thy object so embrace,
    As what my heart still sees thou canst not spy?
    I swear by her I love and lack, that I
Was not in fault, who bent thy dazzling race
Only unto the heav'n of Stella's face;
    Counting but dust what in the way did lie.

But cease, mine eyes, your tears do witness well,
    That you, guiltless thereof, your nectar miss'd:
Curs'd be the page from whom the bad torch fell:
    Curs'd be the night which did your will resist:
Curs'd be the coachman which did drive so fast,
    Which no less curse than absence makes me taste.

CVI.

O absent presence, Stella is not here;
False flatt'ring hope, that with so fair a face
Bare me in hand, that in this orphan place,
    Stella, I say my Stella, should appear?
    What say'st thou now! where is that dainty cheer
Thou told'st mine eyes should help their famish'd case?
But thou art gone, now that self-felt disgrace,
    Doth make me most to wish thy comfort near.

But here I do store of fair ladies meet,
Who may with charm of conversation sweet,
    Make in my heavy mould new thoughts to grow.
Sure they prevail as much with me, as he

That bade his friend, but then new maim'd, to be
  Merry with him, and not think of his woe.

CVII.

Stella, since thou so right a princess art
Of all the pow'rs which life bestows on me,
That e'er by them aught undertaken be,
  They first resort unto that sov'reign part;
  Sweet, for a while give respite to my heart,
Which pants as though it still should leap to thee:
And on my thoughts give thy lieutenancy
  To this great cause, which needs both use and art.

And as a queen, who from her presence sends
  Whom she employs, dismiss from thee my wit,
Till it hath wrought what thy own will attends.
  On servants' shame oft master's blame doth sit;
O! let not fools in me thy works reprove,
And scorning say, "See what it is to love!"

CVIII.

When Sorrow (using mine own fire's might)
Melts down his lead into my boiling breast,
Through that dark furnace to my heart opprest,
  There shines a joy from thee my only light:
  But soon as thought of thee breeds my delight,
And my young soul flutters to thee his nest,
Most rude Despair, my daily unbidden guest,
  Clips straight my wings, straight wraps me in his night,

And makes me then bow down my head, and say,
   Ah! what doth Phœbus' gold that wretch avail,
Whom iron doors do keep from use of day?
   So strangely, alas! thy works in me prevail,
That in my woes for thee, thou art my joy,
And in my joys for thee, my sole annoy.

MISCELLANEOUS POEMS.

Under the title of "Miscellaneous Poems" we have reprinted the whole productions of Sir Philip Sidney's Muse, as far at least as we have been able to discover them, which are not contained in the Arcadia, the Astrophel and Stella, the Lady of May, or his Translation, conjointly with his sister, the Countess of Pembroke, of the Psalms of David. The six compositions here inserted last in order, are now for the first time collected.

MISCELLANEOUS POEMS.

A REMEDY FOR LOVE.

PHILOCLEA and Pamela sweet,
By chance, in one great house did meet ;
And meeting, did so join in heart,
That th' one from th' other could not part :
And who indeed (not made of stones)
Would separate such lovely ones ?
The one is beautiful, and fair
As orient pearls and rubies are ;
And sweet as, after gentle showers,
The breath is of some thousand flowers :
For due proportion, such an air
Circles the other, and so fair,
That it her brownness beautifies,
And doth enchant the wisest eyes.

Have you not seen, on some great day,
Two goodly horses, white and bay,
Which were so beauteous in their pride,
You knew not which to choose or ride ?

Such are these two; you scarce can tell,
Which is the daintier bonny belle;
And they are such, as, by my troth,
I had been sick with love of both,
And might have sadly said, "Good-night
Discretion and good fortune quite;"
But that young Cupid, my old master,
Presented me a sov'reign plaster:
Mopsa! ev'n Mopsa! (precious peat)
Whose lips of marble, teeth of jet,
Are spells and charms of strong defence,
To conjure down concupiscence.

How oft have I been reft of sense,
By gazing on their excellence,
But meeting Mopsa in my way,
And looking on her face of clay,
Been heal'd, and cur'd, and made as sound,
As though I ne'er had had a wound?
And when in tables of my heart,
Love wrought such things as bred my smart,
Mopsa would come, with face of clout,
And in an instant wipe them out.
And when their faces made me sick,
Mopsa would come, with face of brick,
A little heated in the fire,
And break the neck of my desire.
Now from their face I turn mine eyes,
But (cruel panthers!) they surprise
Me with their breath, that incense sweet,
Which only for the gods is meet;
And jointly from them doth respire,
Like both the Indies set on fire:

Which so o'ercomes man's ravish'd sense,
That souls, to follow it, fly hence.
No such-like smell you if you range
By th' Stocks, or Cornhill's square Exchange;
There stood I still as any stock,
Till Mopsa (with her puddle dock)
Her compound or electuary,
Made of old ling and young canary;
Bloat-herring, cheese, and voided physic,
Being somewhat troubled with a phthisic,
Did cough, and fetch a sigh so deep,
As did her very bottom sweep:
Whereby to all she did impart,
How love lay rankling at her heart:
Which, when I smelt, desire was slain,
And they breath'd forth perfumes in vain.
Their angel voice surpris'd me now;
But Mopsa, her Too-whit, To-hoo,
Descending through her oboe nose,
Did that distemper soon compose.

And, therefore, O thou precious owl!
The wise Minerva's only fowl;
What, at thy shrine, shall I devise
To offer up a sacrifice?
Hang Æsculapius, and Apollo,
And Ovid, with his precious shallow.
Mopsa is love's best medicine,
True water to a lover's wine.
Nay, she's the yellow antidote,
Both bred and born to cut Love's throat:
Be but my second, and stand by,
Mopsa, and I'll them both defy;

And all else of those gallant races,
Who wear infection in their faces;
For thy face (that Medusa's shield!)
Will bring me safe out of the field.

SONNET.

SINCE shunning pain, I ease can never find;
    Since bashful dread seeks where he knows me harmed;
    Since will is won, and stopped ears are charmed;
Since force doth faint, and sight doth make me blind;
Since loosing long, the faster still I bind;
    Since naked sense can conquer reason armed;
    Since heart, in chilling fear, with ice is warmed;
In fine, since strife of thought but mars the mind,
    I yield, O Love! unto thy loathed yoke,
Yet craving law of arms, whose rule doth teach,
    That, hardly us'd, who ever prison broke,
In justice quit, of honour made no breach:
    Whereas, if I a grateful guardian have,
    Thou art my lord, and I thy vowed slave.

SONNET.

WHEN Love, puff'd up with rage of high disdain,
    Resolv'd to make me pattern of his might,

Like foe, whose wits inclin'd to deadly spite,
Would often kill, to breed more feeling pain;

  He would not, arm'd with beauty, only reign
    On those affects which easily yield to sight;
    But virtue sets so high, that reason's light,
For all his strife can only bondage gain:

  So that I live to pay a mortal fee,
Dead palsy-sick of all my chiefest parts,
  Like those whom dreams make ugly monsters see,
And can cry help with naught but groans and starts:

  Longing to have, having no wit to wish,
  To starving minds such is god Cupid's dish.

SONG.

To the tune of " Non credo gia che piu infelice amante."

THE nightingale, as soon as April bringeth,
  Unto her rested sense, a perfect waking,
While late bare earth, proud of new clothing, springeth,
  Sings out her woes, a thorn her song-book making;

  And mournfully bewailing,
Her throat in tunes expresseth
What grief her breast oppresseth,
  For Tereus' force on her chaste will prevailing.

O Philomela fair! O take some gladness,
That here is juster cause of plaintful sadness:
Thine earth now springs, mine fadeth;
Thy thorn without, my thorn my heart invadeth.

II.

Alas! she hath no other cause of anguish,
But Tereus' love, on her by strong hand wroken,
  Wherein she suffering, all her spirits languish,
Full womanlike, complains her will was broken.

  But I, who daily craving,
Cannot have to content me,
Have more cause to lament me,
  Since wanting is more woe than too much having.

O Philomela fair! O take some gladness,
That here is juster cause of plaintful sadness:
Thine earth now springs, mine fadeth;
Thy thorn without, my thorn my heart invadeth.

SONG.

To the tune of "Basciami vita mia."

Sleep, baby mine, Desire's nurse, Beauty, singeth;
  Thy cries, O baby! set mine head on aching:
    The babe cries, "'Way, thy love doth keep me waking."

Lully, lully, my babe, Hope cradle bringeth
  Unto my children alway good rest taking :
  The babe cries, " 'Way, thy love doth keep me waking."

Since, baby mine, from me thy watching springeth,
  Sleep then a little, pap Content is making;
  The babe cries, " Nay, for that abide I waking."

VERSES.

To the tune of the Spanish song, " Si tu señnora no dueles de mi."

O FAIR ! O sweet ! when I do look on thee,
  In whom all joys so well agree,
Heart and soul do sing in me.
  This you hear is not my tongue,
Which once said what I conceived ;
For it was of use bereaved,
  With a cruel answer stung.
No ! though tongue to roof be cleaved,
  Fearing lest he chastis'd be,
  Heart and soul do sing in me.

O fair ! O sweet ! when I do look on thee,
  In whom all joys so well agree,
  Just accord all music makes ;
In thee just accord excelleth,
Where each part in such peace dwelleth,
  One of other beauty takes.
Since then truth to all minds telleth,

That in thee lives harmony,
Heart and soul do sing in me.

O fair! O sweet! when I do look on thee,
  In whom all joys so well agree,
  They that heav'n have known do say,
That whoso that grace obtaineth,
To see what fair sight there reigneth,
  Forced are to sing alway:
So then since that heav'n remaineth
  In thy face, I plainly see,
  Heart and soul do sing in me.

O fair! O sweet! when I do look on thee,
  In whom all joys so well agree,
  Sweet! think not I am at ease,
For because my chief part singeth;
This song from death's sorrow springeth:
  As to swan in last disease:
For no dumbness, nor death, bringeth
  Stay to true love's melody:
  Heart and soul do sing in me.

SONNETS.*

I.

THE scourge of life, and death's extreme disgrace;
  The smoke of hell, the monster called Pain:

---

* The four following sonnets, says a MS. in the Bodleian Library, " were made by Sir P. Sidney when his Lady hadd a payne in her face, the small poxe."

Long sham'd to be accurs'd in ev'ry place,
  By them who of his rude resort complain ;

Like crafty wretch, by time and travel taught,
  His ugly evil in others' good to hide ;
Late harbours in her face, whom Nature wrought
  As treasure-house where her best gifts do bide ;

And so by privilege of sacred seat,
  A seat where beauty shines and virtue reigns,
He hopes for some small praise, since she hath great,
  Within her beams wrapping his cruel stains.
Ah ! saucy Pain, let not thy terror last,
More loving eyes she draws, more hate thou hast.

II.

WOE ! woe to me, on me return the smart :
  My burning tongue hath bred my mistress pain ;
For oft in pain, to pain my painful heart,
  With her due praise did of my state complain.

I prais'd her eyes, whom never chance doth move ;
  Her breath, which makes a sour answer sweet ;
Her milken breasts, the nurse of child-like love ;
  Her legs (O legs !) her aye well-stepping feet :

Pain heard her praise, and full of inward fire,
  (First sealing up my heart as prey of his)
He flies to her, and, bolden'd with desire,
  Her face (this age's praise) the thief doth kiss.

O Pain ! I now recant the praise I gave,
And swear she is not worthy thee to have.

III.

Thou Pain, the only guest of loath'd Constraint;
The child of Curse, man's weakness foster-child;
  Brother to Woe, and father of Complaint:
Thou Pain, thou hated Pain, from heav'n exil'd,

  How hold'st thou her whose eyes constraint doth fear,
Whom curs'd, do bless; whose weakness, virtues arm;
  Who others' woes and plaints can chastely bear:
In whose sweet heav'n angels of high thoughts swarm?

  What courage strange hath caught thy caitiff heart?
Fear'st not a face that oft whole hearts devours?
  Or art thou from above bid play this part,
And so no help 'gainst envy of those powers?
  If thus, alas! yet while those parts have woe;
  So stay her tongue, that she no more say, "O."

IV.

And have I heard her say, "O cruel pain!"
And doth she know what mould her beauty bears?
  Mourns she in truth, and thinks that others feign?
Fears she to feel, and feels not others' fears?

  Or doth she think all pain the mind forbears?
That heavy earth, not fiery sp'rits, may plain?
  That eyes weep worse than heart in bloody tears?
That sense feels more than what doth sense contain?

  No, no, she is too wise, she knows her face
Hath not such pain as it makes others have:

She knows the sickness of that perfect place
Hath yet such health, as it my life can save.
   But this, she thinks, our pain high cause excuseth,
Where her, who should rule pain, false pain abuseth.

TRANSLATION.

From HORACE, *Book* II. *Ode* X. *beginning,*
" Rectius vives, Licini," *etc.*

You better sure shall live, not evermore
   Trying high seas ; nor, while sea's rage you flee,
Pressing too much upon ill-harbour'd shore.

   The golden mean who loves, lives safely free
From filth of foreworn house, and quiet lives,
   Releas'd from court, where envy needs must be.

The wind most oft the hugest pine tree grieves :
   The stately towers come down with greater fall :
The highest hills the bolt of thunder cleaves.

   Evil haps do fill with hope, good haps appal
With fear of change, the courage well prepar'd :
   Foul winters, as they come, away they shall.

Though present times, and past, with evils be snar'd,
   They shall not last : with Cithern silent muse,
Apollo wakes, and bow hath sometime spar'd.

In hard estate, with stout shows, valour use,
The same man still, in whom wisdom prevails;
In too full wind draw in thy swelling sails.

IMITATIONS.

From Catullus, Carm. lxx.

I.

Nulli se dicit mulier mea nubere malle,
    Quam mihi; non si se Jupiter ipse petat:
Dicit: sed mulier cupido quod dicit amanti,
    In vento, et rapidâ scribere oportet aquâ.

Englished.

Unto nobody, my woman saith, she had rather a wife be
Than to myself, not though Jove grew a suitor of hers:
These be her words, but a woman's words to a love that is eager,
In wind or water's stream do require to be writ.

II.

Qui sceptra sævus duro imperio regit,
    Timet timentes; metus in authorem redit.

Fair, seek not to be fear'd; most lovely, beloved by thy servants;
For true it is, that they fear many whom many do fear.

SONNET.

Like as the dove, which seeled up doth fly,
  Is neither freed, nor yet to service bound;
But hopes to gain some help by mounting high,
  Till want of force do force her fall to ground:

Right so my mind, caught by his guiding eye,
  And thence cast off, where his sweet hurt he found,
Hath neither leave to live, nor doom to die;
  Nor held in evil, nor suffer'd to be sound.

But with his wings of fancies up he goes,
  To high conceits, whose fruits are oft but small;
Till wounded, blind, and wearied spirit, lose
  Both force to fly, and knowledge where to fall:
O happy dove, if she no bondage tried!
More happy I, might I in bondage bide!

SONNETS.*

I.

Prometheus, when first from heav'n high
  He brought down fire, till then on earth not seen;

---

* This first piece, Anthony Wood informs us, was written by Sir Edward Dyer, chancellor of the most noble Order of the Garter, and the initials E. D. are accordingly prefixed to it in the folio editions of Sidney's Works. The second is a reply to the first from the pen of our author.

Fond of delight, a satyr, standing by,
  Gave it a kiss, as it like sweet had been.

Feeling forthwith the other burning power,
  Wood with the smart, with shouts and shrieking shrill,
He sought his ease in river, field, and bower;
  But, for the time, his grief went with him still.

So silly I, with that unwonted sight,
  In human shape, an angel from above,
Feeding mine eyes, th' impression there did light;
  That since I run and rest as pleaseth love:
The difference is, the satyr's lips, my heart,
He for a while, I evermore, have smart.

II.

  A satyr once did run away for dread,
With sound of horn which he himself did blow:
  Fearing and fear'd, thus from himself he fled,
Deeming strange evil in that he did not know.

  Such causeless fears when coward minds do take,
It makes them fly that which they fain would have;
  As this poor beast, who did his rest forsake,
Thinking not why, but how, himself to save.

  Ev'n thus might I, for doubts which I conceive
Of mine own words, my own good hap betray;
  And thus might I, for fear of may be, leave
The sweet pursuit of my desired prey.
  Better like I thy satyr, dearest Dyer,
  Who burnt his lips to kiss fair shining fire.

SONNET.

My mistress lowers, and saith I do not love:
  I do protest, and seek with service due,
In humble mind, a constant faith to prove;
But for all this, I cannot her remove
  From deep vain thought that I may not be true.

  If oaths might serve, ev'n by the Stygian lake,
Which poets say, the gods themselves do fear;
  I never did my vowed word forsake:
  For why should I, whom free choice slave doth make,
Else-what in face, than in my fancy bear?

  My Muse, therefore, (for only thou canst tell,)
Tell me the cause of this my causeless woe?
  Tell, how ill thought disgrac'd my doing well?
  Tell, how my joys and hopes thus foully fell
To so low ebb that wonted were to flow.

  O this it is, the knotted straw is found;
In tender hearts, small things engender hate:
  A horse's worth laid waste the Trojan ground:
  A three-foot stool in Greece made trumpets sound:
An ass's shade e'er now hath bred debate.

  If Greeks themselves were mov'd with so small cause,
To twist those broils, which hardly would untwine:
  Should ladies fair be tied to such hard laws,
  As in their moods to take a ling'ring pause?
I would it not, their metal is too fine.

My hand doth not bear witness with my heart,
She saith, because I make no woeful lays,
  To paint my living death and endless smart:
  And so for one that felt god Cupid's dart,
She thinks I lead and live too merry days.

Are poets then the only lovers true,
Whose hearts are set on measuring a verse?
  Who think themselves well blest, if they renew
  Some good old dump that Chaucer's mistress knew;
And use but you for matters to rehearse.

Then, good Apollo, do away thy bow;
Take harp and sing in this our versing time:
  And in my brain some sacred humour flow:
  That all the earth my woes, sighs, tears may know;
And see you not that I fall now to rhyme.

As for my mirth, how could I but be glad,
Whilst that me-thought I justly made my boast,
  That only I the only mistress had?
  But now, if e'er my face with joy be clad,
Think Hannibal did laugh when Carthage lost.

Sweet lady, as for those whose sullen cheer,
Compar'd to me, made me in lightness sound;
  Who, stoic-like, in cloudy hue appear;
  Who silence force to make their words more dear;
Whose eyes seem chaste, because they look on ground:

  Believe them not, for physic true doth find,
  Choler adust is joy'd in woman-kind.

SONNET.

In wonted walks, since wonted fancies change,
  Some cause there is, which of strange cause doth rise:
For in each thing whereto mine eye doth range;
  Part of my pain, me-seems, engraved lies.

The rocks, which were of constant mind the mark,
In climbing steep, now hard refusal show:
  The shading woods seem now my sun to dark,
And stately hills disdain to look so low.

The restful caves now restless visions give;
In dales I see each way a hard ascent:
  Like late-mown meads, late cut from joy I live;
Alas! sweet brooks do in my tears augment:

Rocks, woods, hills, caves, dales, meads, brooks, answer me;
Infected minds infect each thing they see.

SONNET.

If I could think how these my thoughts to leave,
  Or thinking still, my thoughts might have good end:
If rebel sense would reason's law receive;
  Or reason foil'd, would not in vain contend:
Then might I think what thoughts were best to think:
Then might I wisely swim, or gladly sink.

If either you would change your cruel heart,
    Or cruel (still) time did your beauties stain :
If from my soul this love would once depart,
    Or for my love some love I might obtain ;
Then might I hope a change, or ease of mind,
By your good help, or in myself, to find.

But since my thoughts in thinking still are spent,
With reason's strife, by senses overthrown ;
    You fairer still, and still more cruel bent,
I loving still a love that loveth none :
    I yield and strive, I kiss and curse the pain,
    Thought, reason, sense, time, You, and I, maintain.

A FAREWELL.

OFT have I mus'd, but now at length I find,
    Why those that die, men say, they do depart :
Depart ! a word so gentle to my mind,
    Weakly did seem to paint Death's ugly dart.

But now the stars, with their strange course, do bind
    Me one to leave, with whom I leave my heart ;
I hear a cry of spirits faint and blind,
    That parting thus, my chiefest part I part.

Part of my life, the loathed part to me,
    Lives to impart my weary clay some breath ;
But that good part, wherein all comforts be,
    Now dead, doth show departure is a death :

Yea, worse than death, death parts both woe and joy,
From joy I part, still living in annoy.

SONNET.

FINDING those beams, which I must ever love,
  To mar my mind, and with my hurt to please,
I deem'd it best, some absence for to prove,
  If farther place might further me to ease.

My eyes thence drawn, where lived all their light,
  Blinded forthwith in dark despair did lie,
Like to the mole, with want of guiding sight,
  Deep plung'd in earth, deprived of the sky.

In absence blind, and wearied with that woe,
  To greater woes, by presence, I return ;
Even as the fly, which to the flame doth go,
  Pleas'd with the light, that his small corse doth burn :

Fair choice I have, either to live or die
A blinded mole, or else a burned fly.

THE SEVEN WONDERS OF ENGLAND.

I.

NEAR Wilton sweet, huge heaps of stones are found,*
  But so confus'd, that neither any eye

    * Stonehenge on Salisbury Plain.

Can count them just, nor Reason reason try,
What force brought them to so unlikely ground.

To stranger weights my mind's waste soil is bound,
   Of passion-hills, reaching to Reason's sky,
From Fancy's earth, passing all number's bound,
   Passing all guess, whence into me should fly
So maz'd a mass ; or, if in me it grows,
A simple soul should breed so mixed woes.

II.

The Bruertons have a lake, which, when the sun
Approaching warms, not else, dead logs up sends
From hideous depth ; which tribute, when it ends,
   Sore sign it is the lord's last thread is spun.

My lake is Sense, whose still streams never run
But when my sun her shining twins there bends ;
   Then from his depth with force in her begun,
Long drowned hopes to watery eyes it lends ;
   But when that fails my dead hopes up to take,
   Their master is fair warn'd his will to make.

III.

We have a fish, by strangers much admir'd,
Which caught, to cruel search yields his chief part :
(With gall cut out) clos'd up again by art,
   Yet lives until his life be new requir'd.

A stranger fish, myself, not yet expir'd,
Tho', rapt with Beauty's hook, I did impart

Myself unto th' anatomy desir'd,
Instead of gall, leaving to her my heart :
  Yet live with thoughts clos'd up, 'till that she will,
  By conquest's right, instead of searching, kill.

IV.

Peak hath a cave, whose narrow entries find
Large rooms within, where drops distil amain :
'Till knit with cold, though there unknown remain,
  Deck that poor place with alabaster lin'd.

Mine eyes the strait, the roomy cave, my mind ;
Whose cloudy thoughts let fall an inward rain
Of sorrow's drops, till colder reason bind
  Their running fall into a constant vein
Of truth, far more than alabaster pure,
Which, though despis'd, yet still doth truth endure.

V.

A field there is, where, if a stake be prest
Deep in the earth, what hath in earth receipt,
Is chang'd to stone in hardness, cold, and weight,
  The wood above doth soon consuming rest.

The earth her ears ; the stake is my request ;
Of which, how much may pierce to that sweet seat,
  To honour turn'd, doth dwell in honour's nest,
Keeping that form, though void of wonted heat ;
  But all the rest, which fear durst not apply,
  Failing themselves, with wither'd conscience die.

VI.

Of ships, by shipwreck cast on Albion's coast,
Which rotting on the rocks, their death do die:
From wooden bones, and blood of pitch, doth fly
   A bird, which gets more life than ship had lost.

My ship, Desire, with wind of Lust long tost,
Brake on fair cliffs of constant Chastity;
Where plagued for rash attempt, gives up his ghost;
   So deep in seas of virtue, beauties lie:
But of this death flies up the purest love,
Which seeming less, yet nobler life doth move.

VII.

These wonders England breeds; the last remains —
A lady, in despite of Nature, chaste,
On whom all love, in whom no love is plac'd,
   Where Fairness yields to Wisdom's shortest reins.

An humble pride, a scorn that favour stains;
A woman's mould, but like an angel grac'd;
An angel's mind, but in a woman cas'd;
   A heav'n on earth, or earth that heav'n contains:
Now thus this wonder to myself I frame;
She is the cause that all the rest I am.

A DIALOGUE BETWEEN TWO SHEPHERDS,

Uttered in a Pastoral Show at Wilton.

WILL. Dick, since we cannot dance, come, let a cheerful voice
 Show that we do not grudge at all when others do rejoice.
DICK. Ah Will! though I grudge not, I count it feeble glee,
 With sight, made dim with daily tears, another's sport to see.
 Whoever lambkins saw, yet lambkins love to play,
 To play when that their loved dams are stol'n, or gone astray?
 If this in them be true, as true in men think I
 A lustless song forsooth thinks he, that hath more lust to cry.
WILL. A time there is for all, my mother often says,
 When she, with skirts tuck'd very high, with girls at football plays.
 When thou hast mind to weep, seek out some smoky room:
 Now let those lightsome sights we see, thy darkness overcome.
DICK. What joy the joyful sun gives unto bleared eyes;
 That comfort in these sports you like, my mind his comfort tries.
WILL. What? Is thy bagpipe broke, or are thy lambs miswent;
 Thy wallet, or thy tar-box, lost; or thy new raiment rent?

DICK. I would it were but thus, for thus it were too
       well.
WILL. Thou see'st my ears do itch at it: good Dick
       thy sorrow tell.
DICK. Hear then, and learn to sigh: a mistress I do
       serve,
    Whose wages make me beg the more, who
       feeds me till I starve;
    Whose livery is such, as most I freeze appar-
       elled most,
    And looks so near unto my cure, that I must
       needs be lost.
WILL. What? These are riddles sure: art thou then
       bound to her?
DICK. Bound as I neither power have, nor would have
       power, to stir.
WILL. Who bound thee?
DICK.   Love, my lord.
WILL.   What witnesses thereto?
DICK. Faith in myself, and worth in her, which no
       proof can undo.
WILL. What seal?
DICK.   My heart deep graven.
WILL.   Who made the band so fast?
DICK. Wonder that, by two so black eyes, the glitt-
       'ring stars be past.
WILL. What keepeth safe thy band?
DICK.   Remembrance is the chest
    Lock'd fast with knowing that she is, of worldly
       things, the best.
WILL. Thou late of wages plain'dst: what wages
       may'st thou have?
DICK. Her heavenly looks, which more and more do
       give me cause to crave.

WILL. If wages make you want, what food is that she
        gives?
DICK. Tear's drink, sorrow's meat, wherewith not I,
        but in me my death lives.
WILL. What living get you then?
DICK.   Disdain; but just disdain:
    So have I cause myself to plain, but no cause to
        complain.
WILL. What care takes she for thee?
DICK.   Her care is to prevent
    My freedom, with show of her beams, with vir-
        tue, my content.
WILL. God shield us from such dames! If so our
        dames be sped,
    The shepherds will grow lean I trow, their
        sheep will be ill-fed.
    But Dick, my counsel mark: run from the
        place of woe:
    The arrow being shot from far, doth give the
        smaller blow.
DICK. Good Will, I cannot take thy good advice; be-
        fore
    That foxes leave to steal, they find they die
        therefore.
WILL. Then, Dick, let us go hence, lest we great folks
        annoy:
    For nothing can more tedious be, than plaint in
        time of joy.
DICK. Oh hence! O cruel word! which even dogs do
        hate:
    But hence, even hence, I must needs go; such
        is my dogged fate.

SONG.

To the tune of " Wilhelmus van Nassau," etc.

Who hath his fancy pleased,
　With fruits of happy sight,
Let here his eyes be raised
　On Nature's sweetest light;
A light which doth dissever,
　And yet unite the eyes;
A light which, dying, never
　Is cause the looker dies.

　She never dies, but lasteth
In life of lover's heart;
　He ever dies that wasteth
In love his chiefest part.
　Thus is her life still guarded,
In never dying faith;
　Thus is his death rewarded,
Since she lives in his death.

　Look then and die, the pleasure
Doth answer well the pain;
　Small loss of mortal treasure,
Who may immortal gain.
　Immortal be her graces,
Immortal is her mind;
　They, fit for heav'nly places,
This heav'n in it doth bind.

But eyes these beauties see not,
Nor sense that grace descries;
　Yet eyes deprived be not
From sight of her fair eyes:
　Which, as of inward glory
They are the outward seal;
　So may they live still sorry,
Which die not in that weal.

But who hath fancies pleased,
With fruits of happy sight,
　Let here his eyes be raised
On Nature's sweetest light.

THE SMOKES OF MELANCHOLY.

I.

Who hath e'er felt the change of love,
And known those pangs that losers prove,
May paint my face without seeing me,
And write the state how my fancies be,
The loathsome buds grown on Sorrow's tree.

But who by hearsay speaks, and hath not fully felt
What kind of fires they be, in which those spirits melt,
Shall guess, and fail, what doth displease,
Feeling my pulse, miss my disease.

II.

O no! O no! trial only shows
The bitter juice of forsaken woes;
Where former bliss, present evils do stain;
Nay, former bliss adds to present pain,
While remembrance doth both states contain.

Come, learners, then to me, the model of mishap,
Ingulphed in despair, slid down from Fortune's lap;
And, as you like my double lot,
Tread in my steps, or follow not.

III.

For me, alas! I am full resolv'd
Those bands, alas! shall not be dissolv'd;
Nor break my word, though reward come late;
Nor fail my faith in my failing fate;
Nor change in change, tho' change change my state:

But always own myself, with eagle-eyed Truth, to fly
Up to the sun, altho' the sun my wings do fry;
For if those flames burn my desire,
Yet shall I die in Phœnix' fire.

ODE.

When, to my deadly pleasure,
When to my lively torment,
Lady, mine eyes remained
Joined, alas! to your beams.

With violence of heav'nly
Beauty, tied to virtue;
Reason abash'd retired;
Gladly my senses yielded.

Gladly my senses yielding,
Thus to betray my heart's fort,
Left me devoid of all life.

They to the beamy suns went,
Where, by the death of all deaths,
Find to what harm they hast'ned.

Like to the silly Sylvan,
Burn'd by the light he best lik'd,
When with a fire he first met.

Yet, yet, a life to their death,
Lady you have reserved;
Lady the life of all love.

For though my sense be from me,
And I be dead, who want sense,
Yet do we both live in you.

Turned anew, by your means,
Unto the flow'r that ay turns,
As you, alas! my sun bends.

Thus do I fall to rise thus;
Thus do I die to live thus;
Chang'd to a change, I change not.

Thus may I not be from you;
Thus be my senses on you;
Thus what I think is of you;
Thus what I seek is in you;
All what I am, it is you.

VERSES.

To the tune of a Neapolitan song, which beginneth,
" No, no, no, no."

No, no, no, no, I cannot hate my foe,
Although with cruel fire,
   First thrown on my desire,
She sacks my render'd sprite;
   For so fair a flame embraces
   All the places,
Where that heat of all heats springeth,
That it bringeth
   To my dying heart some pleasure,
   Since his treasure
Burneth bright in fairest light.   No, no, no, no.

No, no, no, no, I cannot hate my foe,
Although with cruel fire,
  First thrown on my desire,
She sacks my render'd sprite;
  Since our lives be not immortal,
  But to mortal
Fetters tied, do wait the hour
Of death's power,
  They have no cause to be sorry,
  Who with glory
End the way, where all men stay. No, no, no, no.

No, no, no, no, I cannot hate my foe,
Although with cruel fire,
  First thrown on my desire,
She sacks my render'd sprite;
  No man doubts, whom beauty killeth,
  Fair death feeleth,
And in whom fair death proceedeth,
Glory breedeth:
  So that I, in her beams dying,
  Glory trying,
Though in pain, cannot complain. No, no, no, no.

SONG.

To the tune of a Neapolitan Villanel.

ALL my sense thy sweetness gained;
Thy fair hair my heart enchained;

My poor reason thy words moved,
So that thee, like heav'n, I loved.

Fa, la, la, leridan, dan, dan, dan, deridan :
   Dan, dan, dan, deridan, deridan, dei :
While to my mind the outside stood,
For messenger of inward good.

Nor thy sweetness sour is deemed ;
Thy hair not worth a hair esteemed ;
Reason hath thy words removed,
Finding that but words they proved.

Fa, la, la, leridan, dan, dan, dan, deridan,
   Dan, dan, dan, deridan, deridan, dei :
For no fair sign can credit win,
If that the substance fail within.

No more in thy sweetness glory,
For thy knitting hair be sorry ;
Use thy words but to bewail thee,
That no more thy beams avail thee ;
     Dan, dan,
     Dan, dan,
Lay not thy colours more to view,
Without the picture be found true.

Woe to me, alas ! she weepeth !
Fool ! in me what folly creepeth ?
Was I to blaspheme enraged,
Where my soul I have engaged ?
     Dan, dan,
     Dan, dan,

And wretched I must yield to this;
The fault I blame, her chasteness is.

Sweetness! sweetly pardon folly;
Tie me, hair, your captive wholly:
Words! O words of heav'nly knowledge!
Know, my words their faults acknowledge;
   Dan, dan,
   Dan, dan,
And all my life I will confesss,
The less I love, I live the less.

TRANSLATION.

From LA DIANA DE MONTE-MAYOR, in Spanish; where Sireno, a shepherd, whose mistress Diana had utterly forsaken him, pulling out a little of her hair, wrapped about with green silk, to the hair he thus bewailed himself.

WHAT changes here, O hair!
 I see, since I saw you?
How ill fits you this green to wear,
 For hope, the colour due?
Indeed, I well did hope,
 Though hope were mix'd with fear,
No other shepherd should have scope
 Once to approach this hair.

Ah hair! how many days
My Dian made me show,

With thousand pretty childish plays,
If I ware you or no:
  Alas! how oft with tears,
O tears of guileful breast!
  She seemed full of jealous fears.
Whereat I did but jest.

  Tell me, O hair of gold,
If I then faulty be,
  That trust those killing eyes I would,
Since they did warrant me?
  Have you not seen her mood,
What streams of tears she spent,
  'Till that I sware my faith so stood,
As her words had it bent?

  Who hath such beauty seen
In one that changeth so?
  Or where one's love so constant been,
Who ever saw such woe?
  Ah, hair! are you not griev'd
To come from whence you be,
  Seeing how once you saw I liv'd,
To see me as you see?

  On sandy bank of late,
I saw this woman sit;
  Where, "Sooner die than change my state,"
She with her finger writ:
  Thus my belief was staid,
Behold Love's mighty hand
  On things were by a woman said,
And written in the sand.

The same Sireno in MONTE-MAYOR, holding his mistress's glass before her, and looking upon her while she viewed herself, thus sang :—

> OF this high grace, with bliss conjoin'd,
>   No farther debt on me is laid,
> Since that in self-same metal coin'd,
>   Sweet lady, you remain well paid ;
>
> For if my place give me great pleasure,
> Having before my nature's treasure,
>   In face and eyes unmatch'd being,
>   You have the same in my hands, seeing
> What in your face mine eyes do measure.
>
> Nor think the match unev'nly made,
> That of those beams in you do tarry,
>   The glass to you but gives a shade,
>   To me mine eyes the true shape carry ;
>   For such a thought most highly prized,
>   Which ever hath Love's yoke despised,
> Better than one captiv'd perceiveth,
> Though he the lively form receiveth,
>   The other sees it but disguised.

DIRGE.

RING out your bells, let mourning shows be spread,
For Love is dead:
   All Love is dead, infected
With plague of deep disdain:
   Worth, as nought worth, rejected,
And faith fair scorn doth gain.
     From so ungrateful fancy;
     From such a female frenzy;
     From them that use men thus,
     Good Lord, deliver us.

Weep, neighbours, weep, do you not hear it said,
That Love is dead?
   His death-bed, peacock's folly:
His winding-sheet is shame;
   His will, false-seeming holy,
His sole exec'tor, blame.
     From so ungrateful fancy;
     From such a female frenzy;
     From them that use men thus,
     Good Lord, deliver us.

Let dirge be sung, and trentals* rightly read,
For Love is dead:
   Sir Wrong his tomb ordaineth

---

* "Tricennalia," says Bishop Fleetwood, "were called 'trentals' from 'trigintalia,' and in English 'a month's-mind;' because the service lasted a month, or thirty days, in which they said so many masses for the repose of the person deceased."

My mistress' marble heart;
  Which epitaph containeth,
"Her eyes were once his dart."
    From so ungrateful fancy;
    From such a female frenzy;
    From them that use men thus,
    Good Lord, deliver us.

Alas! I lie: rage hath this error bred;
Love is not dead,
  Love is not dead, but sleepeth
In her unmatched mind:
  Where she his counsel keepeth
Till due deserts she find.
    Therefore from so vile fancy,
    To call such wit a frenzy:
    Who Love can temper thus,
    Good Lord, deliver us.

SONNET.

Thou blind man's mark; thou fool's self-chosen snare,
  Fond fancy's scum, and dregs of scatter'd thought:
Band of all evils; cradle of causeless care;
  Thou web of will, whose end is never wrought:

Desire! Desire! I have too dearly bought,
With price of mangled mind, thy worthless ware;
  Too long, too long, asleep thou hast me brought,
Who shouldst my mind to higher things prepare;

But yet in vain thou hast my ruin sought ;
In vain thou mad'st me to vain things aspire ;
In vain thou kindlest all thy smoky fire :
   For Virtue hath this better lesson taught,
Within myself to seek my only hire,
Desiring nought but how to kill Desire.

SONNET.

Leave me, O love! which reachest but to dust ;
  And thou, my mind, aspire to higher things :
Grow rich in that which never taketh rust ;
  Whatever fades, but fading pleasure brings.

Draw in thy beams, and humble all thy might
  To that sweet yoke where lasting freedoms be,
Which breaks the clouds, and opens forth the light,
  That doth both shine, and give us sight to see.

O take fast hold! let that light be thy guide,
  In this small course which birth draws out to death,
And think how evil becometh him to slide,
  Who seeketh heav'n, and comes of heav'nly breath.

   Then farewell, world, thy uttermost I see,
   Eternal Love, maintain thy life in me.

SPLENDIDIS LONGUM VALEDICO NUGIS.

SONNET.

The dart, the beams, the sting, so strong I prove,
   Which my chief part doth pass through, parch, and tie,
That of the stroke, the heat, and knot of love,
   Wounded, inflam'd, knit to the death, I die.

Harden'd and cold, far from affection's snare
   Was once my mind, my temper, and my life;
While I that sight, desire, and vow forbare,
   Which to avoid, quench, lose, nought boasted strife.

Yet will not I grief, ashes, thraldom change
   For others' ease, their fruit, or free estate;
So brave a shot, dear fire, and beauty strange,
   Bid me pierce, burn, and bind, long time and late,
And in my wounds, my flames, and bonds, I find
A salve, fresh air, and bright contented mind.

STANZAS TO LOVE.

Ah, poor Love! why dost thou live,
   Thus to see thy service lost;
If she will no comfort give,
   Make an end, yield up the ghost!

That she may, at length, approve
   That she hardly long believ'd,
That the heart will die for love
   That is not in time reliev'd.

Oh! that ever I was born!
   Service so to be refus'd;
Faithful love to be foreborn!
   Never love was so abus'd.

But, sweet Love, be still awhile;
   She that hurt thee, Love, may heal thee;
Sweet! I see within her smile,
   More than reason can reveal thee.

For, though she be rich and fair,
   Yet she is both wise and kind,
And, therefore, do thou not despair,
   But thy faith may fancy find.

Yet, although she be a queen,
   That may such a snake despise,
Yet, with silence all unseen,
   Run, and hide thee in her eyes:

Where if she will let thee die,
   Yet at latest gasp of breath,
Say that in a lady's eye
   Love both took his life and death.*

---

* For the two preceding poems we are indebted to the learning and unwearied research of Dr. Bliss. The first is contained in his Bibliographical Miscellanies, a small volume of literary curiosities which has long been completely out of print: the second is to be found in his elaborate, and, we may safely say, perfect edition of Wood's Athenæ Oxonienses, vol. i. col. 525.

SONNET.

Virtue, beauty, and speech, did strike, wound, charm,
My heart, eyes, ears, with wonder, love, delight;
First, second, last, did bind, enforce, and arm,
His works, shows, suits, with wit, grace, and vows' might.

Thus honour, liking, trust, much, far, and deep,
Held, pierc'd, possess'd, my judgment, sense, and will,
Till wrongs, contempt, deceit, did grow, steal, creep,
Bands, favour, faith, to break, defile, and kill.

Then grief, unkindness, proof, took, kindled, taught,
Well-grounded, noble, due, spite, rage, disdain :
But ah, alas! in vain my mind, sight, thought,
Doth him, his face, his words, leave, shun, refrain.
   For nothing, time, nor place, can loose, quench, ease,
   Mine own, embraced, sought, knot, fire, disease.*

---

* The above is reprinted from " England's Helicon ; " and is there entitled " An Excellent Sonnet of a Nymph." The same work contains thirteen other poetical compositions by Sidney; but they are all merely extracts from the Astrophel and Stella, the Arcadia, or the Sonnets, etc., at the end of the latter, which the reader will find included in the present volume under the head of Miscellaneous Poems.

WOOING-STUFF.

Faint amorist, what! do'st thou think
    To taste Love's honey, and not drink
One dram of gall? or to devour
    A world of sweet, and taste no sour?
Do'st thou ever think to enter
    Th' Elysian fields, that dar'st not venture
In Charon's barge? a lover's mind
    Must use to sail with every wind.

He that loves, and fears to try,
    Learns his mistress to deny.
Doth she chide thee? 'tis to show it,
    That thy coldness makes her do it:
Is she silent? is she mute?
    Silence fully grants thy suit:
Doth she pout, and leave the room?
    Then she goes to bid thee come:
Is she sick? why then be sure,
    She invites thee to the cure:
Doth she cross thy suit with "No?"
    Tush, she loves to hear thee woo:
Doth she call the faith of man
    In question? Nay, 'uds-foot, she loves thee than;*
And if ere she makes a blot,
    She's lost if that thou hit'st her not.

---

* "Than" and "then" were used as synonymous by our elder poets, whenever their rhyme required the interchange.

He that after ten denials,
 Dares attempt no farther trials,
Hath no warrant to acquire
 The dainties of his chaste desire.*

TWO PASTORALS,

Made by Sir Philip Sidney, upon his meeting with his two worthy friends and fellow poets, Sir Edward Dyer and M. Fulke Greville.†

JOIN mates in mirth to me,
 Grant pleasure to our meeting;
Let Pan, our good god, see
 How grateful is our greeting.
  Join hearts and hands, so let it be,
  Make but one mind in bodies three.

---

* This lively little poem is printed at the end of "Cottoni Posthuma," together with "Valour Anatomised in a Fancy," which will also be found in a subsequent part of this volume.

† This, and the following pastoral, are taken from the ably illustrated, and beautiful reprint of Davison's Poetical Rhapsody, edited by Nicholas Harris Nicolas, Esq. We have already seen the close intimacy that subsisted between Fulke Greville and our author; and Sidney's connection with Sir Edward Dyer appears not to have been less affectionate. They are styled by Gabriel Harvey the "Castor and Pollux of poetry;" and Spenser denominates them "The two very diamonds of her Majesty's court." The friendship of this illustrious trio seems only to have been dissolved by death; for Sir Philip, in his will, ordered his books to be divided between Sir Edward and Lord Brooke.

Ye hymns and singing skill
  Of god Apollo's giving,
Be press'd our reeds to fill
  With sound of music living.
    Join hearts and hands, so let it be,
    Make but one mind in bodies three.

Sweet Orpheus' harp, whose sound
  The stedfast mountains moved,
Let there thy skill abound,
  To join sweet friends beloved.
    Join hearts and hands, so let it be,
    Make but one mind in bodies three.

My two and I be met,
  A happy blessed trinity,
As three more jointly set
  In firmest band of unity.
    Join hearts and hands, so let it be,
    Make but one mind in bodies three.

Welcome my two to me,*
  The number best beloved,
Within my heart you be
  In friendship unremoved.
    Join hearts and hands, so let it be,
    Make but one mind in bodies three.

Give leave your flocks to range,
  Let us the while be playing;
Within the elmy grange,
  Your flocks will not be straying.

* On the margin are the initials, E. D. F. G. P. S.

Join hearts and hands, so let it be,
　　Make but one mind in bodies three.

Cause all the mirth you can,
　Since I am now come hither,
Who never joy, but when
　I am with you together.
　　Join hearts and hands, so let it be,
　　Make but one mind in bodies three.

Like lovers do their love,
　So joy I in you seeing:
Let nothing me remove
　From always with you being.
　　Join hearts and hands, so let it be,
　　Make but one mind in bodies three.

And as the turtle dove
　To mate with whom he liveth,
Such comfort fervent love
　Of you to my heart giveth.
　　Join hearts and hands, so let it be,
　　Make but one mind in bodies three.

Now joined be our hands,
　Let them be ne'er asunder,
But link'd in binding bands
　By metamorphosed wonder.
　　So should our sever'd bodies three
　　As one for ever joined be.

DISPRAISE OF A COURTLY LIFE.

WALKING in bright Phœbus' blaze,
Where with heat oppress'd I was,
I got to a shady wood,
Where green leaves did newly bud;
And of grass was plenty dwelling,
Deck'd with pied flowers sweetly smelling.

In this wood a man I met,
On lamenting wholly set;
Ruing change of wonted state,
Whence he was transformed late,
Once to shepherds' God retaining,
Now in servile court remaining.

There he wand'ring malecontent,
Up and down perplexed went,
Daring not to tell to me,
Spake unto a senseless tree,
One among the rest electing,
These same words, or this affecting;

"My old mates I grieve to see
Void of me in field to be,
Where we once our lovely sheep
Lovingly like friends did keep;
Oft each other's friendship proving,
Never striving, but in loving.

But may love abiding be
In poor shepherds' base degree ?
It belongs to such alone
To whom art of love is known :
Seely * shepherds are not witting
What in art of love is fitting.

Nay, what need the art to those
To whom we our love disclose ?
It is to be used then,
When we do but flatter men :
Friendship true, in heart assured,
Is by Nature's gifts procured.

Therefore shepherds, wanting skill,
Can Love's duties best fulfil ;
Since they know not how to feign,
Nor with love to cloak disdain,
Like the wiser sort, whose learning
Hides their inward will of harming.

Well was I, while under shade
Oaten reeds me music made,
Striving with my mates in song ;
Mixing mirth our songs among.

* In Todd's Johnson this word is described on the authority of Chaucer and Spenser to mean lucky, happy ; and likewise, agreeably to the usage of the latter writer, silly, inoffensive, harmless. Perhaps the instance in the text, as well as that in the next page, afford the best proof which can be adduced of the word being used synonymously with silly, ignorant, or simple. NICOLAS.

Greater was the shepherd's treasure,
Than this false, fine, courtly pleasure.

Where how many creatures be,
So many puff'd in mind I see ;
Like to Juno's birds of pride,
Scarce each other can abide :
Friends like to black swans appearing,
Sooner these than those in hearing.

Therefore, Pan, if thou may'st be
Made to listen unto me,
Grant, I say, if seely man
May make treaty to god Pan,
That I, without thy denying,
May be still to thee relying.

Only for my two loves' sake,*
In whose love I pleasure take ;
Only two do me delight
With their ever-pleas.ng sight ;
Of all men to thee retaining,
Grant me with those two remaining.

So shall I to thee always
With my reeds sound mighty praise :
And first lamb that shall befall,
Yearly deck thine altar shall,
If it please thee to be reflected,
And I from thee not rejected."

* The margin again gives the initials, Sir E. D. and M. F. G.

So I left him in that place,
Taking pity on his case;
Learning this among the rest,
That the mean estate is best;
Better filled with contenting,
Void of wishing and repenting.

THE LADY OF MAY,

A MASQUE.

The origin of the "Lady of May" possesses somewhat of political interest. In 1578, while Queen Elizabeth either was, or affected to be, still entirely undecided whether or not she should embrace the matrimonial proposals of the Duke of Alençon, she was invited by the Earl of Leicester to his splendid mansion of Wanstead-house, probably with the hope of recovering, in privacy, and when relieved from the counter-manœuvres of his rivals, that ascendancy over the royal mind, which seemed now on the point of being completely annihilated. The Queen accepted the invitation, and remained several days at the luxurious mansion of her favourite, where every pleasure was presented to her which ostentatious magnificence could devise, or prodigality collect. Even Sir Philip Sidney then condescended to flatter her vanity in the following Masque, which was written for the occasion, and performed in her Majesty's presence with all the adornments which the composition admitted of. Like the other similar productions of the same period, it is remarkable for little else than the nauseous seasoning of adulation in which that extraordinary woman took such exquisite delight.

The following are the names of the

DRAMATIS PERSONÆ.

The SUITER, mother of the May-Lady.
The MAY-LADY.
THERION, a forester } Suiters of the May-Lady.
ESPILUS, a shepherd }
ROMBUS, a schoolmaster.
LALUS, an old shepherd.
DORCAS, a shepherd.
RIXUS, a forester.

THE LADY OF MAY,

A MASQUE.

Her most excellent Majesty walking in Wanstead Garden, as she passed down into the grove, there came suddenly among the train one apparelled like an honest man's wife of the country; where crying out for justice, and desiring all the lords and gentlemen to speak a good word for her, she was brought to the presence of her Majesty, to whom, upon her knees, she offered a supplication, and used this speech.

THE SUITER.

OST fair lady! for as for other your titles of state, statelier persons shall give you, and thus much mine own eyes are witnesses of; take here the complaint of me, poor wretch! as deeply plunged in misery, as I wish to you the highest point of happiness.

Only one daughter I have, in whom I had placed all the hopes of my good hap, so well had she, with her good parts, recompensed my pain of bearing her, and care of bringing her up: but now, alas! that she is come to the time I should reap my full comfort of her, so is she troubled with that notable matter, which we in the country call matrimony, as I cannot choose but fear the loss of her wits, at least of her honesty. Other women think they may be unhappily cumbered with one master-husband; my poor daughter is oppressed with two, both loving her, both equally liked of her, both striving to deserve her. But now, lastly (as this jealousy, forsooth, is a vile matter) each have brought their partakers with them, and are, at this present, without your presence redress it, in some bloody controversy; now, sweet lady, help; your own way guides you to the place where they encumber her. I dare stay here no longer, for our men say in the country, the sight of you is infectious.

And with that she went away a good pace, leaving the supplication with her Majesty, which very formally contained this

SUPPLICATION.

Most Gracious Sovereign!

To one, whose state is raised over all,
   Whose face doth oft the bravest sort enchant;
Whose mind is such as wisest minds appal;
   Who in one self these divers gifts can plant:
How dare I, wretch! seek there my woes to rest,
Where ears be burnt, eyes dazzled, hearts opprest?

   Your state is great, your greatness is your shield;
Your face hurts oft, but still it doth delight;
   Your mind is wise, but still it makes you mild:
Such planted gifts enrich ev'n beggars' sight:

So dare I, wretch ! my bashful fear subdue,
And feed mine ears, mine eyes, my heart in you.

Herewith, the woman suiter being gone, there was heard in the wood a confused noise, and forthwith there came out six shepherds, with as many fosters, hauling and pulling to whither side they should draw the Lady of May, who seemed to incline neither to the one nor the other side. Among them was Master Rombus, a schoolmaster of a village thereby, who, being fully persuaded of his own learned wisdom, came thither, with his authority to part their fray; where, for answer, he received many unlearned blows. But the Queen coming to the place where she was seen of them, though they knew not her estate, yet something there was which made them startle aside and gaze upon her : till old Father Lalus stepped forth (one of the substantiallest shepherds) and making a leg or two, said these few words.

LALUS THE OLD SHEPHERD.

May it please your dignity to give a little superfluous intelligence to that, which, with the opening of my mouth, my tongue and teeth shall deliver unto you. So it is, right worshipful audience, that a certain she-creature, which we shepherds call a woman, of a minsical countenance ; but, by my white lamb, not three quarters so beauteous as yourself, hath disannulled the brainpan of two of our featiest young men. And will you wot how ? By my mother Kit's soul, with a certain frenzical malady they call love : when I was a young man they called it flat folly. But here is a substantial schoolmaster can better disnounce the whole foundation of the matter, although, in sooth, for all his loquence, our young men were nothing duteous to his clerkship. Come on, come on, master schoolmaster, be not so bashless ; we say, " that the fairest are ever the gentlest:" tell the whole case, for you can much better vent the points of it than I.

Then came forward Master ROMBUS, and, with many special graces, made this learned oration.

Now the thunder-thumping Jove transfund his dotes into your excellent formosity, which have, with your resplendent beams, thus segregated the enmity of these rural animals: I am " potentissima domina," a schoolmaster; that is to say, a pedagogue, one not a little versed in the disciplinating of the juvenile fry, wherein, to my laud I say it, I use such geometrical proportion, as neither wanted mansuetude nor correction: for so it is described

<blockquote>Parcare subjectos, et debellire superbos.*</blockquote>

* We hope the reader will hold us guiltless of the dog-latin which the rustic pedant is made to utter throughout the whole of this piece. The character of Master Rombus bears a striking resemblance to that of the erudite Holofernes in Love's Labour Lost. " He, too, draweth out the thread of his verbosity finer than the staple of his argument." No doubt they were both intended to ridicule the tortured English, called Euphuism, which John Lyly, and his followers, had succeeded in bringing into a temporary fashion; and the chief credit of discarding which from general use, Drayton has ascribed, in the following lines, to Sir Philip Sidney:

<blockquote>
The noble Sidney, with this last, arose,
That héroë for numbers and for prose,
That throughly pac'd our language, as to show
The plenteous English hand in hand might go
With Greek and Latin; and did first reduce
Our tongue from Lyly's writing then in use;—
Talking of stones, stars, plants, of fishes, flies,
Playing with words and idle similies.—
</blockquote>

Yet hath not the pulchritude of my virtues protected me from the contaminating hands of these plebeians; for coming, "solummodo," to have parted their sanguinolent fray, they yielded me no more reverence, than if I had been some "pecorius asinus." I, even I, that am, who am I? "Dixi; verbus sapiento satum est." But what said that Trojan Æneas, when he sojourned in the surging sulks of the sandiferous seas?

> Hæc olim memonasse juvebit.

Well, well, "ad propositos revertebo;" the purity of the verity is, that a certain "pulchra puella profectò," elected and constituted by the integrated determination of all this topographical region, as the sovereign lady of this dame Maia's month, hath been, "quodammodo," hunted, as you would say; pursued by two, a brace, a couple, a cast of young men, to whom the crafty coward Cupid had, "inquam," delivered his dire dolorous dart.

> But here the May-Lady interrupted his speech, saying to him,

Away, away, you tedious fool! your eyes are not worthy to look to yonder princely sight; much less your foolish tongue to trouble her wise ears.

> At which Master ROMBUS, in a great chafe, cried out,

"O Tempori, O Moribus!" in profession a child; in dignity a woman; in years a lady; "in cæteris" a maid; should thus turpify the reputation of my doctrine, with the superscription of a fool!—"O Tempori, O Moribus!"

But here again the May-Lady saying to him,

Leave off, good Latin fool, and let me satisfy the long desire I have had to feed mine eyes with the only sight this age hath granted to the world.

The poor schoolmaster went his way back, and the lady, kneeling down, said in this manner:

Do not think, sweet and gallant lady, that I do abase myself thus much unto you because of your gay apparel; for what is so brave as the natural beauty of the flowers? nor because a certain gentleman hereby seeks to do you all the honour he can in his house; that is not the matter, he is but our neighbour, and these be our own groves; nor yet because of our great estate, since no estate can be compared to be the lady of the whole month of May, as I am. So that since both this place and this time are my servants, you may be sure I would look for reverence at your hands, if I did not see something in your face which makes me yield to you: the truth is, you excel me in that wherein I desire most to excel, and that makes me give this homage unto you, as to the beautifullest lady these woods have ever received. But now, as old Father Lalus directed me, I will tell you my fortune, that you may be judge of my mishaps, and others' worthiness. Indeed so it is, that I am a fair wench, or else I am deceived, and therefore, by the consent of all our neighbours, have been chosen for the absolute lady of this merry month. With me have been (alas! I am ashamed to tell it) two young men, the one a forester named Therion, the other Espilus a shepherd, very long, even in love, forsooth. I like them both, and love neither: Espilus is the richer, but Therion the livelier. Therion doth me many pleasures as stealing me venison out of these forests, and many other such like pretty and prettier services; but withal, he grows to such rages, that sometimes he strikes me, sometimes he rails at me This shepherd Espilus, of a mild disposition, as his fortune hath not been to do me great service, so hath he never done me any wrong; but feeding his sheep, sitting under some sweet bush, sometimes, they say, he records my name in doleful verses. Now the question I am to ask you, fair lady, is, whether the many deserts and many faults of Therion, or the very small deserts and no faults of Espilus, be to be preferred? But before you give your judgment, most excellent lady, you shall hear what each of them can say for themselves in their rural songs.

Thereupon Therion challenged Espilus to sing with him, speaking these six verses.

THERION.

Come, Espilus, come, now declare thy skill;
  Show how thou canst deserve so brave desire:
Warm well thy wits, if thou wilt win her will;
  For water cold did never promise fire:
Great, sure, is she, on whom our hopes do live,
Greater is she who must the judgment give.

But Espilus, as if he had been inspired with the Muses, began forthwith to sing, whereto his fellow shepherds set in with their recorders, which they bare in their bags like pipes; and so of Therion's side did the foresters, with the cornets they wore about their necks, like hunting-horns, in baudrikes.

ESPILUS.

Tune up, my voice, a higher note I yield,
  To high conceits, the song must needs be high:

More high than stars; more firm than flinty field,
    Are all my thoughts, in which I live or die :
Sweet soul, to whom I vowed am a slave,
Let not wild woods so great a treasure have.

THERION.

The highest note comes oft from basest mind,
As shallow brooks do yield the greatest sound ;
    Seek other thoughts thy life or death to find,
Thy stars be fall'n, plow'd is thy flinty ground :
    Sweet soul, let not a wretch that serveth sheep,
    Among his flock so sweet a treasure keep.

ESPILUS.

Two thousand sheep I have, as white as milk,
Though not so white as is thy lovely face ;
    The pasture rich, the wool as soft as silk :
All this I give, let me possess thy grace :
    But still take heed, lest thou thyself submit
    To one that hath no wealth, and wants his wit.

THERION.

Two thousand deer in wildest woods I have ;
Them can I take, but you I cannot hold :
    He is not poor, who can his freedom save :
Bound but to you, no wealth but you I would :
    But take this beast, if beasts you fear to miss,
    For of his beasts, the greatest beast he is.

ESPILUS, *kneeling to the Queen*.

Judge you, to whom all beauty's force is lent :

THERION.

Judge you of love, to whom all love is bent.

But as they waited for the judgment her Majesty should give of their deserts, the shepherds and foresters grew to a great contention, whether of their fellows had sung better, and so whether the estate of shepherds or foresters were the more worshipful. The speakers were Dorcas, an old shepherd, and Rixus, a young foster, between whom the schoolmaster, Rombus, came in as a moderator.

DORCAS, THE SHEPHERD.

Now all the blessings of my old grandam (silly Espilus) light upon thy shoulders for this honeycomb singing of thine; now, of my honesty, all the bells in the town could not have sung better: if the proud heart of the harlotry lie not down to thee now, the sheep's rot catch her, to teach her that a fair woman hath not her fairness to let it grow rustish.

RIXUS, THE FOSTER.

O Midas! why art not thou alive now to lend thine ears to this drivel? By the precious bones of a huntsman, he knows not the blaying of a calf from the song of a nightingale; but if yonder great gentlewoman be as wise as she is fair, Therion, thou shalt have the prize; and thou, old Dorcas, with young master Espilus, shall remain tame fools, as you be.

DORCAS. And, with cap and knee be it spoken, it is your pleasure, neighbour Rixus, to be a wild fool!

RIXUS. Rather than a sheepish dolt.

DORCAS. It is much refreshing to my bowels, you have made your choice; for my share, I will bestow your leavings upon one of your fellows.

RIXUS. And art not thou ashamed, old fool! to liken Espilus, a shepherd, to Therion of the noble vocation of huntsmen, in the presence of such an one as even with her eye only can give thee cruel punishment?

DORCAS. Hold thy peace, I will neither meddle with her, nor her eyes; they feign in our town they are dangerous both; neither will I liken Therion to my boy Espilus, since one is a thievish prowler, and the other is as quiet as lambs that now came from sucking.

ROMBUS, THE SCHOOLMASTER.

"Heu! Ehem! Hei! Insipidum! Inscitium vulgorum et populorum!" Why, you brute nebulons, have you had my "corpusculum" so long among you, and cannot yet tell how to edify an argument? Attend and throw your ears to me, for I am gravidated with child, till I have endoctrinated your plumbeous cerebrosities. First, you must divisionate your point, "quasi" you should cut a cheese into two particles; for thus must I uniform my speech to your obtuse conceptions: for "prius dividendum oratio antequam definiendum; exemplum gratia," either Therion must conquer this dame Maia's nymph, or Espilus must overthrow her, and that "secundum" their dignity, which must also be subdivisionated into three equal species, either according to the penetrancy of their singing, or the meliority of their functions; or, lastly, the supremacy of their merits.

" De " singing "satis." " Nunc " are you to argumentate of the qualifying of their estate first; and then, whether hath more infernally, I mean deeply, deserved.

DORCAS. O poor Dorcas! poor Dorcas! that I was not sent in my young days to school, that I might have purchased the understanding of Master Rombus's mysterious speeches. But yet thus much I concern of them, that I must even give up what my conscience doth find in the behalf of shepherds. O sweet honey-milken lambs! And is there any so flinty a heart, that can find about him to speak against them, that have the charge of such good souls as you be, among whom there is no envy, and all obedience; where it is lawful for a man to be good if he list, and hath no outward cause to withdraw him from it; where the eye may be busied in considering the works of nature, and the heart quietly rejoiced in the honest using them? If templation, as clerks say, be the most excellent, which is so fit a life for templars as this is, neither subject to violent oppression, nor servile flattery? How many courtiers, think you, have I heard under our field, in bushes, making their woful complaints; some, of the greatness of their mistress's estate, which dazzled their eyes, and yet burned their hearts; some, of the extremity of her beauty mixed with extreme cruelty; some, of her too much wit, which made all their loving labours folly? O how often have I heard one name sound in many mouths, making our vales witnesses of their doleful agonies! So that with long-lost labour, finding their thoughts bare no other wool but despair, of young courtiers they grew old shepherds. Well, sweet lambs, I will end with you as I began : he that can open his mouth against such innocent souls, let him be hated as much as a filthy fox; let the taste of him be worse than musty cheese; the sound of him be more dreadful than the howling of a wolf; his sight more odible than a toad in one's porridge.

RIXUS.   Your life, indeed, hath some goodness.

ROMBUS, THE SCHOOLMASTER.

"O tace, tace!" or all the fat will be ignified; first let me dilucidate the very intrinsical marrowbone of the matter. He doth use a certain rhetorical invasion into the point, as if, indeed, he had conference with his lambs; but the truth is, he doth equitate you in the mean time, Master Rixus; for thus he saith, that the sheep are good, "ergo," the shepherd is good, an "Enthymeme a loco contingentibus," as my finger and my thumb are "contingentes." Again he saith, who liveth well, is likewise good; but shepherds live well, "ergo," they are good; syllogism in Darius, King of Persia, "a conjugatis;" as you would say, a man coupled to his wife, two bodies, but one soul; but do you but acquiescate to my exhortation, and you shall extinguish him. Tell him his "major" is a knave, his "minor" is a fool, and his conclusion both, "Et ecce homo blancatus quasi lilium."

RIXUS. I was saying, the shepherd's life had some goodness in it, because it borrowed of the country quietness something like ours: but that is not all; for ours, besides that quiet part, doth both strengthen the bodies, and raise up the mind with this gallant sort of activity.

O sweet contentation! to see the long life of the hurtless trees! to see how in straight growing up, though never so high, they hinder not their fellows! they only enviously trouble, which are crookedly bent. What life is to be compared to ours, where the very growing things are ensamples of goodness! we have no hopes but we may quickly go about them, and going about them, we soon obtain them; not like those that have long followed one, in troth, most excellent chase, do now, at length, perceive she could never be taken, but that, if she staid at any time near the pursuers, it was never meant to tarry with them, but only to take breath to fly farther from them. He, therefore, that doubts that our life doth not so far excel all others, let him also doubt, that the well-deserving and painful Therion is not to be preferred before the idle Espilus; which is even as much as to say, as that the roes are not swifter than sheep, nor the stags more goodly than goats.

ROMBUS. "Bene, bene, nunc de quæstione prepositus;" that is as much as to say, well, well, now of the proposed question; that was, whether the many great services, and many great faults of Therion, or the few small services, and no faults of Espilus, be to be preferred; incepted or accepted the former?

THE MAY-LADY.

No, no; your ordinary brains shall not deal in that matter: I have already submitted it to one, whose sweet spirit hath passed through greater difficulties; neither will I that your blockheads lie in her way.

Therefore, O Lady! worthy to see the accomplishment of your desires, since all your desires be most worthy of you, vouchsafe our ears such happiness, and me that particular favour, as that you will judge, whether of these two be more worthy of me? or, whether I be worthy of them? and this I will say, that in judging me, you judge more than me in it.

This being said, it pleased her Majesty to judge, that Espilus did the better deserve her; but what words, what reasons, she used for it, this paper, which carrieth so base names, is not worthy to contain. Sufficeth it, that upon the judgment given, the shepherds and foresters made a full concert of their cornets and recorders, and then did Espilus sing this song, tending to the greatness of his own joy, and yet to the comfort of the other side, since they were overthrown by a most worthy adversary. The song contained two short tales; and thus it was.

SONG.

SILVANUS, long in love, and long in vain,
   At length obtain'd the point of his desire;
Who being ask'd, now that he did obtain
   His wished weal, what more he could require?
Nothing, said he, for most I joy in this,
That goddess mine my blessed being sees.

When wanton Pan, deceiv'd with lion's skin,
   Came to the bed, where wound for kiss he got
To woe and shame the wretch did enter in,
   Till this he took for comfort of his lot;
Poor Pan, he said, although thou beaten be,
It is no shame, since Hercules was he.

Thus joyfully in chosen tunes rejoice,
   That such an one is witness of my heart,

Whose clearest eyes I bless, and sweetest voice ;
  That see my good, and judgeth my desert :
Thus woful I, in woe, this salve do find,
My foul mishap came yet from fairest mind.

The music fully ended, the May-Lady took her leave in this sort.

Lady, Yourself, for other titles do rather diminish than add unto you; I and my little company must now leave you: I should do you wrong to beseech you to take our follies well, since your bounty is such as to pardon greater faults. Therefore I will wish you good night, praying to God, according to the title I possess, that, as hitherto it hath excellently done, so henceforward the flourishing of May, may long remain in you, and with you.

VALOUR ANATOMIZED,

IN A FANCY.

This pleasing little Essay bears the date 1581; and originally appeared under the name of Sir P. Sidney, at the end of the small volume entitled "Cottoni Posthuma, being divers choice pieces of that renowned antiquary Sir Robert Cotton, Knt. and Bart.," published in the year 1651, and edited by James Howell, the popular writer of "Epistolæ Ho-Elianæ." Anthony Wood, in his Athenæ, inserts the "Valour Anatomized" in his summary of our author's compositions, but adds, that "others say it was written by Sir Thomes Overbury." It has been generally claimed, notwithstanding, on behalf of Sidney, by his biographers; though, as far as we can ascertain, it has never been hitherto reprinted with his Works.

VALOUR ANATOMIZED,

IN A FANCY.

ALOUR towards men is an emblem of ability towards women, a good quality signifying a better. Nothing draws a woman like to it. Nothing is more behoveful for that sex: for from it they receive protection, and in a free way too, without any danger. Nothing makes a shorter cut to obtaining; for a man of arms is always void of ceremony, which is the wall that stands betwixt Pyramus and Thisbe, that is, man and woman: for there is no pride in women but that which rebounds from our own baseness, as cowards grow valiant upon those that are more cowards; so that only by our pale asking we teach them to deny, and by our shamefacedness we put them in mind to be modest. Whereas, indeed, it is cunning rhetoric to persuade the hearers that they are that already which the world would have them to be. This kind of bashfulness is far from men of valourous disposition, and especially from soldiers; for such are

ever men, without doubt, forward and confident, losing no time lest they should lose opportunity, which is the best factor for a lover. And because they know women are given to dissemble, they will never believe them when they deny. Certainly before this age of wit, and wearing black, brake in upon us, there was no way known to win a lady, but by tilting, tourneying, and riding to seek adventures through dangerous forests; in which time these slender striplings with little legs were held but of strength enough to marry their widows. And even in our days, there can be given no reason of the inundation of serving-men upon their mistresses, but only that usually they carry their masters' weapons, and their valour. To be accounted handsome, just, learned, and well-favoured, all this carries no danger with it. But it is better to be admitted to the title of valiant acts: at least that imports the venturing of mortality; and all women delight to hold him safe in their arms, who hath escaped thither through many dangers. To speak at once, man hath a privilege in valour. In clothes and good faces we do but imitate women; and many of that sex will not think much, as far as an answer goes, to dissemble wit too. So then these neat youths, these women in men's apparel, are too near a woman to be beloved of her; they be both of a trade: but he of grim aspect, and such a one a lass dares take, and will desire him for newness and variety. A scar in a man's face is the same that a mole is in a woman's; and a mole in a woman's is a jewel set in white, to make it seem more white. So a scar in a man is a mark of honour, and no blemish; for it is a scar and a blemish in a soldier to be without one. Now as for all things else which are to procure love, as a good face, wit, clothes, or a good body, each of them, I must needs say, works somewhat for want of a better; that is, if valour corrive not therewith. A good face availeth nothing, if it be on a coward that is bashful; the utmost of it is to be kissed, which rather increaseth, than quencheth appetite. He that sendeth her gifts, sends her word also, that he is a man of small gifts otherwise: for wooing by signs and tokens implies the author dumb. And if Ovid, who writ the Law of Love, were alive, as he is extant, and would allow it as a good diversity; then gifts should be sent as gratuities, not as bribes; and wit would rather get promise than love. Wit is not to be seen, and no woman takes advice of any in her loving, but of her own eyes, or her waiting-woman's: nay, which is worse, wit is not to be felt, and so no good bedfellow. Wit applied to a woman makes her dissolve her simperings, and discover her teeth with laughter; and this is surely a purge for love; for the beginning and original of love is a kind of foolish melancholy. As for the man that makes his tailor his bawd, and hopes to inveigle his love with such a coloured suit, surely the same man deeply hazards the loss of her favour upon every change of his clothes. So likewise the other that courts her silently with a good body, let me tell him that his clothes stand always betwixt his mistress's eyes and him. The comeliness of clothes depends upon the comeliness of the body, and so both upon opinion. She that hath been seduced by apparel, let me give her to weet, that men always put off their clothes before they go to bed; and let her that hath been enamoured of her servant's body understand, that if she saw him in a skin of cloth, that is, in a suit made to the pattern of his body, she would discern slender cause to love him ever after. There are no clothes fit so well in a woman's eye as a suit of steel, though not of the fashion: and no man so soon surpriseth a woman's affections, as he that is the subject of whisperings, and hath always some twenty stories of his own achievements depending upon him. Mistake me not, I understand not by valour one that never fights but when he is backed by drink or anger, or hissed on by beholders; nor one that is desperate; nor one that takes away a serving-man's weapons, when perhaps they cost him his quarter's wages; nor one that wears a privy coat of defence, and therein is confident; for then such as make bucklers would be accounted the very scum of the commonwealth: I intend one of an even resolution, grounded upon reason, which is always even; having his power restrained by the law of not doing wrong.

LETTER

TO

QUEEN ELIZABETH,

ANNO 1580,

DISSUADING HER FROM MARRYING

THE DUKE OF ANJOU.

In addition to the extract from Miss Lucy Aikin's Court of Queen Elizabeth, which we have already given in the Life of our Author prefixed to this volume, we may here add two other commendations of this celebrated state document.

"It contains," observes Strype, in his Annals of the Reformation, "many brief, but bright sentences; showing the mature judgment of the writer, his wisdom in counsel, his skill in politics, his acquaintance with the Roman history, his knowledge of foreign states and kingdoms, and observations thence, his apprehension of the great danger from Papists, his concern for the Protestant interest abroad, (of which she was the only protectress, as well as of the religion at home,) the little or no advantage she was like to receive from France, her personal danger in case of a conclusion of this marriage with Monsieur, and how dear she was to her own people. So that, in short, this letter, abounding with such close application of arguments, seems to have swayed the Queen to decline this motion."

"Among other enemies to the match," says Mr. Hume, "Sir Philip Sidney, son to Sir Henry Sidney, Lord Deputy of Ireland, and nephew to Leicester, a young man the most accomplished of that age, used the freedom to write her a letter, in which he dissuaded her from her present resolution, with an unusual elegance of expression, as well as force of reasoning."

This courageous epistle was first printed in the "Scrinia Ceciliana," or "Supplement to the Cabala," p. 201. Lond. 1663.— It was afterwards inserted among the "Sidney Papers," vol. i. p. 287.

SIR PHILIP SIDNEY

TO

QUEEN ELIZABETH,

ANNO 1580,

DISSUADING HER FROM MARRYING THE DUKE OF ANJOU.

Most feared and beloved,
Most sweet and gracious sovereign,

O seek out excuses of this my boldness, and to arm the acknowledging of a fault with reasons for it, might better show I knew I did amiss, than any way diminish the attempt, especially in your judgment; who being able to discern lively into the nature of the thing done, it were folly to hope, by laying on better colours, to make it more acceptable. Therefore, carrying no other olive branch of intercession, than the laying of myself at your feet; nor no other insinuation, either for attention or pardon, but the true vowed sacrifice of unfeigned love; I will, in simple and direct terms (as hoping they shall only come to your merciful eyes), set down the

overflowing of my mind in this most important matter, importing, as I think, the continuance of your safety; and, as I know, the joys of my life. And because my words (I confess shallow, but coming from the deep well-spring of most loyal affection) have delivered to your most gracious ear, what is the general sum of my travelling thoughts therein; I will now but only declare, what be the reasons that make me think, that the marriage with Monsieur will be unprofitable unto you; then will I answer the objection of those fears, which might procure so violent a refuge.

The good or evils that will come by it, must be considered either according to your estate or person. To your estate, what can be added to the being an absolute born, and accordingly respected, princess? But, as they say the Irishmen are wont to call over them that die, "they are rich, they are fair, what needed they to die so cruelly:" not unfitly of you, endowed with felicity above all others, a man might well ask, " what makes you in such a calm to change course; to so healthful a body, to apply so unsavory a medicine: what can recompense so hazardous an adventure?" Indeed, were it but the altering of a well maintained and well approved trade: for, as in bodies natural, every sudden change is full of peril; so in this body politic, whereof you are the only head, it is so much the more dangerous, as there are more humours to receive a hurtful impression. But hazards are then most to be regarded, when the nature of the patient is fitly composed to occasion them.

The patient I account your realm; the agent Monsieur, and his design; for neither outward accidents do much prevail against a true inward strength; nor doth inward weakness lightly subvert itself, without being thrust at by some outward force.

Your inward force (for as for your treasures indeed, the sinews of your crown, your Majesty doth best and only know) consisteth in your subjects, generally unexpert in warlike defence; and as they are divided now into mighty factions (and factions bound on the neverdying knot of religion) the one of them, to whom your happy government hath granted the free exercise of the eternal truth; with this, by the continuance of time, by the multitude of them, by the principal offices, and strength they hold, and lastly, by your dealings both at home and abroad against the adverse party; your state is so entrapped, as it were impossible for you, without excessive trouble, to pull yourself out of the party so long maintained. For such a course once taken in hand, is not much unlike a ship in a tempest, which how dangerously soever it may be beaten with waves, yet is there no safety or succour without it: These, therefore, as their souls live by your happy government, so are they your chief, if not your sole, strength: these, howsoever the necessity of human life makes them lack, yet can they not look for better conditions than presently they enjoy: these, how their hearts will be galled, if not aliened, when they shall see you take a husband, a Frenchman and a Papist, in whom (howsoever fine wits may find farther dealings or painted excuses) the very common people well know this, that he is the son of a Jezebel of our age: that his brother made oblation of his own sister's marriage, the easier to make massacres of our brethren in belief: that he himself, contrary to his promise, and all gratefulness, having his liberty and principal estate by the Hugonots' means, did sack Lacharists,* and utterly spoil them with fire and sword. This, I say, even at first sight, gives occasion to all, truly religious, to abhor such a master, and consequently to diminish much of the hopeful love they have long held to you.

The other faction, most rightly, indeed, to be called a faction, is the Papists; men whose spirits are full of anguish, some being infested by others, whom they accounted damnable; some having their ambition stopped, because they are not in the way of advancement; some in prison and disgrace; some whose best friends are banished practisers; many thinking you are an usurper; many thinking also you had disannulled your right, because of the Pope's excommunication; all burthened with the weight of their conscience; men of great numbers, of great riches, because the affairs of state have not lain on them: of united minds, as all men that deem themselves oppressed naturally are; with these I would willingly join all discontented persons, such as want and disgrace keep lower than they have set their hearts; such as have resolved what to look for at your hands; such as Cæsar said, " quibus opus est bello civili," and are of his mind, " malo in acie, quam in foro cadere." These be men so much the more to be doubted, because, as they do embrace all estates; so are they commonly of the bravest and wakefulest sort; and that know the advantage of the world most. This

---

* Or rather, as it is written in some manuscript copies, La Charite, a town in France, situated upon the river Loire. The matins of Paris, equally disgraceful with the Sicilian vespers, were repeated at La Charite, one of the cautionary towns given to the Protestants, which was surprised, and the inhabitants abandoned to the rage of their enemies. DR. ZOUCH.

double rank of people, how their minds have stood, the northern rebellion, and infinite other practices, have well taught you; which, if it be said it did not prevail, that is true indeed; for if they had prevailed, it were too late now to deliberate. But, at this present, they want nothing so much as a head, who in effect needs not but to receive their instructions; since they may do mischief only with his countenance. Let the Singiniam * in Henry the Fourth's time, Perkin Warbeck † in your grandfather's; but of all, the most lively and proper is

* Such is the reading in the Supplement of the Cabala, and in the Sidney Papers. But in two MSS., one in the British Museum, the other in the library of Trinity College, Dublin, we read " the singing man," a proper appellation for a priest before the Reformation, when it was his principal employment to sing or chant the service of the Church. In 1400, John Magdalen, Chaplain to Richard the Second, and much resembling him in person, was supported in his attempts to gain the regal power by many of the English nobility. These conspiracies against King Henry the Fourth were defeated, and Magdalen, the Pseudo-Richard, flying into Scotland, was taken and sent to London, where he suffered death as a common traitor. See Stowe's Annals, p. 325. DR. ZOUCH.

† This mysterious personage made his appearance in the reign of Henry the Seventh, and represented himself to be Richard, Duke of York, the second son of Edward the Fourth, who, with his brother, was supposed to have been murdered in the Tower by their uncle, Richard the Third. Perkin first made a landing in Ireland, and was instantly supported by the Earl of Desmond, and other partisans of the white rose. He was afterwards invited to the court of France, and received as the rightful heir to the English throne. He had similar honours conferred upon him by the Duchess of Burgundy, and James the Fourth, then King of Scotland, who married him to his near relation, the Lady Catharine Gordon, daughter to the Earl of Huntley. For a minute account of his proceedings and final submission, see Lingard's Hist. of England, vol. v. p. 414. 8vo.

that of Lewis, the French King's son, in Henry the Third's time; who having at all no show of title, yet did he cause the nobility, and more, to swear direct fealty and vassalage; and they delivered the strongest holds unto him. I say, let these be sufficient to prove, that occasion gives minds and scope to stranger things than ever would have been imagined. If then the affectionate side have their affections weakened, and the discontented have a gap to utter their discontent; I think it will seem an ill preparative for the patient (I mean your estate) to a great sickness.

Now the agent party, which is Monsieur: whether he be not apt to work on the disadvantage of your estate, he is to be judged by his will and power; his will to be as full of light ambition as is possible; besides the French disposition, and his own education; his inconstant temper against his brother; his thrusting himself into the Low Country matters; his sometimes seeking the King of Spain's daughter; sometimes your Majesty; are evident testimonies of his being carried away with every wind of hope; taught to love greatness any way gotten; and having for the motioners and ministers of the mind, only such young men, as have showed they think evil contentment a ground of any rebellion; who have seen no commonwealth but in faction; and divers of which have defiled their hands in odious murders: with such fancies and favourites, what is to be hoped for; or that he will contain himself within the limits of your conditions; since, in truth, it were strange that he that cannot be contented to be the second person in France, and heir apparent, should be content to come to be a second person, where he should pretend no way to sovereignty. His power, I imagine, is not to be despised, since he is come into a country, where the way of evil-doing will be presented unto him; where there needs nothing but a head, to draw together all the ill-affected members: himself a prince of great revenues, of the most popular nation of the world, full of soldiery, and such as are used to serve without pay, so as they may have show of spoil; and, without question, shall have his brother ready to help him, as well for old revenge, as to divert him from troubling France, and to deliver his own country from evil humours. Neither is King Philip's marriage here any example; since then it was between two of one religion, so that only he in England, stood only upon her strength, and had abroad King Henry of France, ready to impeach any enterprise he should make for his greatness that way. And yet what events time would have brought forth of that marriage, your most blessed reign hath made vain all such considerations. But things holding in present state, I think I may easily conclude, that your country as well by long peace, and fruits of peace, as by the poison of division, wherewith the faithful shall by this means be wounded, and the contrary enabled, made fit to receive hurt; and Monsieur being every way likely to use the occasions to hurt, there can almost happen no worldly thing of more eminent danger to your estate royal. And as to your person, in the scale of your happiness, what good there may come by it, to balance with the loss of so honourable a constancy; truly, yet I perceive not. I will not show so much malice, as to object the universal doubt, the race's unfaithfulness; neither will I lay to his charge the ague-like manner of proceedings, sometimes hot and sometimes cold, in the time of pursuit; which always rightly is most fervent; and I will temper my speeches from any other unreverend disgracings of him, in particular; (though they might be never so true) this only will I say, that if he do come hither, he must live here in far less reputation than his mind will well brook, having no other royalty to countenance himself with; or else you must deliver him the keys of your kingdom, and live at his discretion; or, lastly, he must be separate himself, with more dishonour, and farther disuniting of heart, than ever before. Often have I heard you, with protestation, say, no private pleasure nor self-affection could lead you to it; but if it be both unprofitable for your kingdom, and unpleasant to you, certainly it were a dear purchase of repentance; nothing can it add unto you, but the bliss of children, which, I confess, were a most unspeakable comfort; but yet no more appertaining unto him, than to any other, to whom the height of all good haps, were allotted to be your husband; and therefore I may assuredly affirm, that what good soever can follow marriage, is no more his than anybody's; but the evils and dangers are peculiarly annexed to his person and condition. For, as for the enriching of your country with treasure, which either he hath not, or hath otherwise bestowed it; or the staying of your servants' minds with new expectations and liberality, which is more dangerous than fruitful: or the easing of your Majesty of cases, which is as much as to say, as the easing of you to be queen and sovereign: I think every one perceives this way to be full of hurt, or void of help. Now resteth to consider, what be the motives of this sudden change, as I have heard you in most sweet words deliver; fear of standing alone, in respect of foreign dealings; and in them, from whom you should have respect, doubt of contempt. Truly, standing alone, with good foresight of government, both in peace and warlike defence, is the honourablest thing that can be, to a well-established monarchy; those buildings being ever most strongly durable, which lean to none other, but remain from their own foundation.

So yet in the particulars of your estate at present, I will not altogether deny that a true Masinissa, were fit to countermine the enterprise of mighty Carthage: but how this general truth can be applied to Monsieur, in truth I perceive not. The wisest that have given best rules, where surest leagues are made, have said, that it must be between such as either vehement desire of a third thing, or as vehement fear, doth knit their minds together. Desire is counted the weaker bond, but yet that bound so many princes to the Holy Land. It united that invincible king, Henry the Fifth, and that good Duke of Burgundy; the one desiring to win the crown of France from the Dauphin, the other desiring to revenge his father's murder upon the Dauphin; which both tended to one. That coupled Lewis the Twelfth and Ferdinando of Spain to the conquest of Naples. Of fear, there are innumerable examples: Monsieur's desires, and yours, how they shall meet in public matters, I think no oracle can tell; for as the geometricians say, that parallels, because they maintain divers lines, can never join: so truly, two, having in the beginning contrary principles, to bring forth one doctrine, must be some miracle. He of the Romish religion; and if he be a man, must needs have that manlike property, to desire that all men be of his mind: you the erector and defender of the contrary, and the only sun that dazzleth their eyes: he French, and desiring to make

France great; your Majesty English, and desiring nothing less than that France should not grow great: he, both by own fancy and his youthful governors, embracing all ambitious hopes; having Alexander's image in his head, but perhaps evil painted: your Majesty with excellent virtue, taught what you should hope, and by no less wisdom, what you may hope; with a council renowned over all Christendom for their well-tempered minds, having set the utmost of their ambition in your favour, and the study of their souls in your safety.

Fear hath as little show of outward appearance, as reason, to match you together; for in this estate he is in, whom should he fear, his brother? alas! his brother is afraid, since the King of Navarre is to step into his place. Neither can his brother be the safer by his fall, but he may be the greater by his brother's; whereto, whether you will be an accessary, you are to determine. The King of Spain certainly cannot make war upon him, but it must be upon all the crown of France, which is no likelihood he will do: well may Monsieur (as he hath done) seek to enlarge the bounds of France upon this state; which likewise, whether it be safe for you to be a countenance to, any other way, may be seen: so that if neither desire nor fear be such in him, as are to bind any public fastness, it may be said, that the only fortress of this your marriage, is of his private affection; a thing too incident to the person, laying it up in such knots.

The other objection of contempt in the subjects: I assure your Majesty, if I had heard it proceed out of your mouth, which of all other I do most dearly reverence, it would as soon (considering the perfections of body and mind have set all men's eyes by the height of your estate) have come to the possibility of my imagination, if one should have told me on the contrary side, that the greatest princess of the world, should envy the state of some poor deformed pilgrim. What is there, either within you or without you, that can possibly fall into the danger of contempt, to whom fortunes are tied by so long descent of your royal ancestors? But our minds rejoice with the experience of your inward virtues, and our eyes are delighted with the sight of you. But because your own eyes cannot see yourself, neither can there be in the world any example fit to blaze you by, I beseech you vouchsafe to weigh the grounds thereof. The natural causes are length of government, and uncertainty of succession: the effects, as you term them, appear by cherishing some abominable speeches, which some hellish minds have uttered. The longer a prince reigneth, it is certain the more he is esteemed; there is no man ever was weary of well-being. And good increased to good, maketh the same good both greater and stronger: for it useth men to know no other cares, when either men are born in the time, and so never saw other; or have spent much of their flourishing time, and so have no joy to seek other; in evil princes, abuse growing upon abuse, according to the nature of evil, with the increase of time, ruins itself. But in so rare a government, where neighbours' fires give us light to see our quietness, where nothing wants that true administration of justice brings forth; certainly the length of time, rather breeds a mind to think there is no other life but in it, than that there is any tediousness in so fruitful a government. Examples of good princes do ever confirm this, who, the longer they lived the deeper they sunk into their subjects' hearts. Neither will I trouble you with examples, being so many and manifest. Look into your own estate, how willingly they grant, and how dutifully they pay such subsidies, as you demand of them: how they are no less troublesome to your Majesty in certain requests, than they were in the beginning of your reign; and your Majesty shall find you have a people more than ever devoted to you.

As for the uncertainty of succession, although for mine own part I have cast the utmost anchor of my hope; yet for England's sake, I would not say anything against such determination; but that uncertain good should bring a contempt to a certain good, I think it is beyond all reach of reason; nay, because if there were no other cause (as there are infinite) common reason and profit would teach us to hold that jewel dear, the loss of which would bring us to we know not what; which likewise is to be said of your Majesty's speech of the rising sun; a speech first used by Sylla to Pompey, in Rome, as then a popular city, where indeed men were to rise and fall, according to the flourish and breath of a many-headed confusion. But in so lineal a monarchy, wherever the infants suck the love of their rightful prince, who would leave the beams of so fair a sun, for the dreadful expectation of a divided company of stars: virtue and justice are the only bonds of people's love; and as for that point, many princes have lost their crowns, whose own children were manifest successors; and some that had their own children used as instruments of their ruin; not that I deny the bliss of children, but only to show religion and equity to be of themselves sufficient stays. Neither is the love borne in the Queen your sister's days, any contradiction hereunto; for she was the oppressor of that religion, which lived in many men's hearts, and whereof you were known to be the favourer; by her loss was the most excellent prince in the world to succeed; by your loss, all blindness light upon him, that sees not our misery. Lastly, and most properly for this purpose, she had made an odious marriage with a stranger (which is now in question whether your Majesty shall do or no) so that if your subjects do at this time look for any after-chance, it is but as the pilot doth to the ship-boat, if his ship should perish; driven by extremity to the one, but as long as he can with his life, tending the other. And this I say, not only for the lively parts that be in you; but even for their own sakes, for they must needs see what tempests threaten them.

The last proof in this contempt, should be the venomous matter, certain men imposthumed with wickedness should utter against you. Certainly not to be evil spoken of, neither Christ's holiness nor Cæsar's might, could ever prevent or warrant; there being for that no other rule than so to do, as that they may not justly say evil of you; which whether your Majesty have not done, I leave it in you, to the sincereness of your own conscience, and wisdom of your judgment in the world, to your most manifest fruits and fame throughout Europe. Augustus was told that men spake of him much hurt: "It is no matter," said he, "so long as they cannot do much hurt." And lastly, Charles the Fifth, to one that told him, "Les Hollandois parlent mal;" "Mais ils patient bien," answered he. I might make a scholar-like reckoning of many such examples; it sufficeth that these great princes knew well enough upon what way they flew, and cared little for the barking of a few curs: and truly in the behalf of your subjects, I durst with my blood answer it, that there was never monarch held in more precious reckoning of her people; and before God how can it be otherwise? For mine own part, when I hear some lost wretch hath defiled such a name with his mouth, I consider the right name of blasphemy, whose unbridled soul doth delight to deprave that, which is accounted generally most high and holy. No, no, most excellent lady, do not raze out the impression you have made in such a multitude of hearts; and let not the scum of such vile minds bear any witness against your subjects' devotions: which to proceed one point farther, if it were otherwise, could little be helped, but rather nourished, and in effect began by this. The only means of avoiding contempt are love and fear; love, as you have by divers means sent into the depth of their souls; so if anything can stain so true a form, it must be the trimming yourself, not in your own likeness, but in new colours unto them; their fear by him cannot be increased, without the appearance of French forces, the manifest death of your estate; but well may it against him, bear that face, which (as the tragic Seneca saith) "Metus in authorem redit," as because both in will and power, he is like enough to do harm. Since then it is dangerous for your state, as well because by inward weakness (principally caused by division) it is fit to receive harm; since to your person it can be no way comfortable, you not desiring marriage; and neither to person nor estate, he is to bring any more good than anybody; but more evil he may, since the causes that should drive you to this, are either fears of that which cannot happen, or by this means cannot be prevented: I do with most humble heart say unto your Majesty (having assayed this dangerous help) for your standing alone, you must take it for a singular honour God hath done you, to be indeed the only protector of his church; and yet in worldly respects your kingdom very sufficient so to do, if you make that religion, upon which you stand, to carry the only strength, and have abroad those that still maintain the same course; who as long as they may be kept from utter falling, your Majesty is sure enough from your mightiest enemies. As for this man, as long he is but Monsieur in might, and a Papist in profession, he neither can, nor will, greatly shield you; and if he get once to be King, his defence will be like Ajax's shield, which rather weighed them down, than defended those that bare it. Against contempt, if there be any, which I will never believe, let your excellent virtues of piety, justice, and liberality, daily, if it be possible, more and more shine. Let such particular actions be found out (which be easy as I think to be done) by which you may gratify all the hearts of your people: let those in whom you find trust, and to whom you have committed trust, in your weighty affairs, be held up in the eyes of your subjects: lastly, doing as you do, you shall be, as you be, the example of princes, the ornament of this age, and the most excellent fruit of your progenitors, and the perfect mirror of your posterity.

>Your Majesty's faithful, humble,
>and obedient subject,
>P. SYDNEY.

A DISCOURSE IN DEFENCE

OF THE

EARL OF LEICESTER.

The circumstances which led to the drawing up of this Defence of the Earl of Leicester, have been already briefly stated in our preliminary memoir, pp. 38, 39. It was first published by Arthur Collins in his Introduction to the Sidney Letters, and in his opinion was written in 1584, immediately after the appearance of Leicester's Commonwealth; which was originally circulated on the Continent in the commencement of that year. The MS. is still, we believe, among the family papers at Penshurst, which form altogether, as we have understood, no less than twenty volumes folio.

It was this Defence which Lord Orford affected to consider as infinitely the most valuable of all Sir Philip's writings. " By far the best specimen of his abilities," says his lordship, " to us who can judge only by what we see, is a pamphlet published amongst the Sidney Papers, being an answer to the famous libel called Leicester's Commonwealth. It defends his uncle with great spirit. What had been said in derogation to their blood seems to have touched Sir Philip most."

A

DISCOURSE IN DEFENCE

OF THE

EARL OF LEICESTER.

F late there hath been printed a book, in form of dialogue, to the defaming of the Earl of Leicester, full of the most vile reproaches, which a wit used to wicked and filthy thoughts can imagine. In such manner truly, that if the author had as well feigned new names, as he doth new matters, a man might well have thought his only meaning had been, to have given a lively picture of the uttermost degree of railing. A thing contemptible in the doer, as proceeding from a base and wretched tongue, and such a tongue, as, in the speaking, dares not speak his own name. Odious to all estates, since no man bears a name, of which name, how unfitly soever to the person, by an impudent liar, anything may not be spoken; by all good laws sharply punished, and by all civil companies like a poisonous serpent avoided. But to the Earl himself, in the eyes

of any men, who, with clear judgments, can value things, a true and sound honour grows out of these dishonourable falsehoods. Since he may justly say, as a worthy senator of Rome once in like case did, that no man, these twenty years, hath borne a hateful heart to this estate, but that, at the same time, he hath showed his enmity to this Earl; testifying it hereby, that his faith is so linked to her Majesty's service, that who goes about to undermine the one, resolves withal to overthrow the other. For it is not now, first that evil contented, and evil minded persons, before the occasion be ripe for them, to show their hate against the prince, do first vomit it out against his counsellors; nay certainly, so stale a device it is, as it is to be marvelled, that so fine wits, whose inventions a fugitive fortune hath sharpened, and the air of Italy perchance purified, can light upon no gallanter way, than the ordinary pretext of the very clownish rebellious. And yet that this is their plot of late, by name, first to publish something against the Earl of Leicester, and after, when time served, against the Queen's Majesty, by some of their own intercepted discourses, is made too manifest. He himself, in some places, brings in the examples of Gaveston, Earl of Cornwall, Robert Vere, Duke of Ireland, and Delapool, Duke of Suffolk. It is not my purpose to defend them, but I would fain know, whether they that persecuted those counsellors, when they had had their will in ruining them, whether their rage ceased, before they had as well destroyed the kings themselves, Edward, and Richard the Second, and Henry the Sixth? The old tale testifieth, that the wolves, that mean to destroy the flock, hate most the truest and valiantest dogs. Therefore, the more the filthy imposthume of their wolvish malice breaks forth, the more undoubtedly doth it raise this well-deserved glory to the Earl, that who hates England, and the Queen, must also withal hate the Earl of Leicester.

And as for the libel itself, such is it, as neither in respect of the writer, nor matter written, can move, I think, the lightest wits to give thereto credit, to the discredit of so worthy a person. For the writer (whom in truth I know not, and, loath to fail, am not willing to guess at) shows yet well enough, of what kennel he is, that dares not testify his own writings with his own name. And which is more base — (if anything can be more base than a defamatory libeller) he counterfeits himself, in all the treatise, a Protestant, when any man, with half an eye, may easily see he is of the other party; which filthy dissimulation, if few honest men of that religion will use, to the helping of themselves, of how many carats of honesty is this man, that useth it (as much as his poor power can) to the harm of another. And lastly, evident enough it is, to any man that reads it, what poison he means to her Majesty, in how golden a cup soever he dress it.

For the matter written, so full of horrible villanies, as no good heart will think possible to enter into any creature, much less to be likely in so noble and well-known a man as he is, only thus accused to be by the railing oratory of a shameless libeller. Perchance he had read the rule of that sycophant, that one should backbite boldly; for though the bite were healed, yet the scar would remain: but sure that schoolmaster of his would more cunningly have carried it, leaving some shadows of good, or, at least, leaving out some evil, that his treatise might have carried some probable show of it;

for as reasonable commendation wins belief, and excessive gets only the praiser the title of a flatterer; so much more in this far worse degree of lying, it may well rebound upon himself, the vile reproach of a railer, but never can sink into any good mind. The suspicion of any such unspeakable mischiefs, especially it being every man's case, even from the meanest to the highest, whereof we daily see odious examples, that even of the great princess, the dear riches of a good name are sought in such sort to be picked away by such night thieves. For through the whole book, what is it else, but such a bundle of railings, as if it came from the mouth of some half-drunk scold in a tavern, not regarding while evil were spoken, what was fit for the person of whom the railing was, so the words were fit for the person of an outrageous railer. Dissimulation, hypocrisy, adultery, falsehood, treachery, poison, rebellion, treason, cowardice, atheism, and what not, and all still so upon the superlative, that it was no marvel, though the good lawyer, he speaks of, made many a cross to keep him from such a father of lies, and in many excellent gifts, passing all shameless scolds; in one he passeth himself with an unheard-of impudence, bringing persons, yet alive, to speak things which they are ready to depose, upon their salvation, never came in their thoughts. Such a gentlewoman spake of a matter no less than treason, belike she whispered, yet he heard her; such two knights spake together of things not fit to call witnesses to, yet this ass's ears were so long that he heard them. And yet see his good nature all this while would never reveal them, till now, for secrecy's sake, he puts them forth in print; certainly such a quality in a railer, as I think never was heard of, to name persons alive, as not only can, but do disprove his falsehoods, and yet with such familiarity to name them. Without he learned it of Pace, the Duke of Norfolk's fool, for he, when he had used his tongue, as this heir of his hath done his pen, of the noblest persons, sometimes of the Duke himself, the next that came fitly in his way, he would say he had told it him, of abundance of charity, not only to slander but to make bate. What, therefore, can be said to such a man? Or who lives there, even Christ himself, but that so stinking a breath may blow infamy upon? Who hath a father, by whose death the son inherits, but such a nameless historian may say his son poisoned him? Where may two talk together, but such a spirit of revelation may surmise they spake of treason? What need more, or why so much? as though I doubted that any would build belief upon such a dirty seat, only when he, to borrow a little of his inkhorn, when he plays the statist, wringing very unluckily some of Machiavel's axioms to serve his purpose, then indeed — then he triumphs. Why then the Earl of Leicester means and plots to be king himself, but first to rebel from the prince to whom he is most bound, and of whom he only dependeth, and then to make the Earl of Huntingdon king, and then to put him down, and then to make himself. Certainly, sir, you shoot fair; I think no man, that hath wit and power to pronounce this word England, but will pity a sycophant so weak in his own faculty. But of the Earl of Huntingdon, as I think all indifferent men will clear him from any such foolish and wicked intent of rebellion, so I protest, before the majesty of God, who will confound all liars, and before the world, to whom effects and innocency will witness my truth, that I could never find in the Earl of Leicester any one motion of inclination toward any such pretended conceit in the Earl of Huntingdon. I say no wit future, for as for the present, or for drawing it to himself, I think no devil so wicked, nor no idiot so simple, as to conjecture; and yet, being to him as I am, I think I should have some air of that, which this gentle libel-maker doth so particularly and piecemeal understand, and I do know the Earls of Warwick, of Pembroke, my father, and all the rest he names there, will answer the like. And yet such matters cannot be undertaken without good friends, nor good friends be kept without knowing something; but the Earl's mind hath ever been to serve only and truly, setting aside all hopes, all fears, his mistress by undoubted right Queen of England, and most worthy to be the queen for her royal excellences, and most worthy to be his queen, having restored his overthrown house, and brought him to this case, that curs for only envy bark at. And this his mind is not only (though chiefly) for faith knit in conscience and honour, nor only (though greatly) for gratefulness, where all men know how much he is bound, but even partly for wisdom's sake, knowing, by all old lessons and examples, that, how welcome soever treasons be, traitors to all wise princes are odious, and that, as Mucius answered Tully, who wrote to him how he was blamed for showing himself so constant a friend to Cæsar, that he doubted not, even they that blamed him would rather choose such friends as he was, than such as they were. For wise princes well know, that these violent discontentments arise out of the parties' wicked humours, as in sick folks, that think, with change of places, to ease their evil, which indeed is inward, and whom nor this prince, nor that prince, can satisfy, but such as are led by their fancies, that is to say, who leave to be princes. But this gentle libel-maker, because he would make an evident proof of an unquenchable malice, desperate impudency and falsehood, which never knew blushing, is not content with a whole dictionary of slanders upon these persons living, but as if he would rake up the bones of the dead, with so apparent falsehoods toucheth their houses, as if he had been afraid else he should not have been straight found in that wherein he so greatly labours to excel. First, for Hastings, he saith, the Lord Hastings conspired the death of his master King Edward's sons; let any man but read the excellent treatise of Sir Thomas More, compare but his words with this libel-maker's, and then judge him, if he, who in a thing so long since printed, and, as any man may see by other of his allegations, diligently read, hath the face to write so directly contrary, not caring, as it seems, though a hundred thousand find his falsehood, so some dozens, that never read Sir Thomas More's words, may be carried to believe his horrible slanders of a nobleman so long ago dead. I set down the words of both, because, by this only lively comparison, the face of his falsehood may be the better set forth. And who then can doubt, but he that lies in a thing, which, with one look, is found a lie, what he will do, where yet there is though as much falsehood, yet not so easy disproof.

Now to the Dudleys, such is his bounty, that, when he hath poured out all his flood of scolding eloquence, he saith they are no gentlemen, affirming, that the then Duke of Northumberland was not born so; in truth, if I should have studied with myself of all points of false invections, which a poisonous tongue could have spit out against that duke, yet would it never have come into my head, of all other things, that any man would have objected want of gentry unto him; but this fellow doth like him, who, when he had shot off all his railing quiver, called one cuckold that was never married, because he would not be in debt to any one evil word. I am a Dudley in blood, that duke's daughter's son, and do acknowledge, though in all truth, I may justly affirm, that I am, by my father's side, of ancient, and always well-esteemed and well-matched gentry, yet I do acknowledge, I say, that my chiefest honour is to be a Dudley, and truly am glad to have cause to set forth the nobility of that blood whereof I am descended, which, but upon so just cause, without vain glory, could not have been uttered; since no man, but this fellow of invincible shamelessness, would ever have called so palpable a matter in question. In one place of his book, he greatly extolleth the great nobility of the house of Talbot, and truly with good cause, there being, as I think, not in Europe a subject house which hath joined longer continuance of nobility, with men of greater service and loyalty. And yet this duke's own grandmother, whose blood he makes so base, was a Talbot, daughter and sole heir to the Viscount L'Isle; even he, the same man, who, when he might have saved himself, chose rather manifest death, than to abandon his father, that most noble Talbot, Earl of Shrewsbury, of whom the histories of that time make so honourable mention. The house of Gray is well known; to no house in England in greater continuance of honour, and for number of great houses sprung of it, to be matched by none; but, by the noble house of Neville, his mother was a right Gray, and a sole inheritrix of that Gray of the house of

Warwick which ever strave with the great house of Arundel, which should be the first earl of England; he was likewise so descended, as that justly the honour of the house remained chiefly upon him, being the only heir to the eldest daughter, and one of the heirs to that famous Beauchamp, Earl of Warwick, that was Regent of France; and although Richard Neville, who married the youngest sister, because she was of the whole blood to him that was called Duke of Warwick, by a point in our law carried away the inheritance; and so, also, I know not by what right the title, yet in law of heraldry and descents, which doth not consider those quiddities of our law; it is most certain, that the honour of the blood remained upon him chiefly who came of the eldest daughter. And more undoubtedly is it to be said of the house of Berkeley, which is affirmed to be descended lineally from a King of Denmark, but hath ever been one of the best houses in England, and this duke was the only heir-general to that house, which the house of Berkeley doth not deny; howsoever, as sometimes it falls out between brothers, there be question for land between them.* Many other houses might herein be

* Elizabeth, Countess of Warwick, was the only daughter and heir of Thomas, fifth Baron Berkeley, by Margaret De L'Isle, daughter and heir of Warine, second Baron De L'Isle. The Countess of Warwick had issue three daughters, the eldest of whom, Margaret, became the wife of James Talbot, first Earl of Shrewsbury; and it was from being heirs to this lady, through the intermarriage of Edmund, the father of John Dudley, Duke of Northumberland, with the eldest daughter of Edward Gray, created Baron De L'Isle, fifteenth Edward IV. and subsequently Viscount L'Isle, on account of having married Elizabeth, sister and eventually heir of Thomas Talbot, the second Viscount L'Isle, that the Dudleys came to consider themselves heirs-general to the house of Berkeley.

mentioned, but I name these, because England can boast of no nobler, and because all these bloods so remained in him, that he, as heir, might (if he had listed) have used their arms and name, as in old time they used in England, and do daily, both in Spain, France, and Italy. So that, I think, it would seem as great news as if they came from the Indies, that he, who by right of blood, and so accepted, was the ancientest viscount of England, heir in blood and arms to the first or second earl of England; in blood of inheritance a Gray, a Talbot, a Beauchamp, a Berkeley, a L'Isle,* should be doubted to be a gentleman. But he will say, these great honours came to him by his mother, for these I do not deny they came so; and that the mother, being an heir, hath been,

* The ancient barony of L'Isle, which has long been in abeyance, was claimed in 1823, by Sir John Shelly Sidney, Bart. of Penshurst, the heir and representative of Sir Philip Sidney, being descended from his brother Robert, the first Earl of Leicester, of their name. A committee of the House of Lords, however, determined on the 25th of May, 1826, "that there did not appear sufficient ground to advise his Majesty to allow the claim of the petitioner." The principal reason for this decision appears to have been, that, while the peerage in question was created by writ, there was no direct and conclusive, though there was the strongest presumptive, evidence of either Gerard De L'Isle, the first baron, or Warine De L'Isle, the second baron, having ever sat in Parliament, in compliance with the various briefs of summons with which they were undoubtedly served, in the reigns of Edward the Third and his successor, a circumstance absolutely necessary to create a barony in fee in favour of themselves and their descendants. Lord Redesdale, in the course of the proceedings, went the length of maintaining that, according to the tenor of the law in the sixth year of Richard the Second, even this was insufficient to constitute a descendible right of peerage, a discovery for which we presume his lordship was more indebted to his fancy than his learning. See the valuable Report of the case, just published by Mr. Nicolas.

in all ages and countries, sufficient to nobilitate, is so manifest, that, even from the Roman time to modern times, in such case they might, if they listed, and so often did use the mother's name; and that Augustus Cæsar had both name and empire of Cæsar, only by his mother's right, and so both* moderns. But I will claim no such privilege; let the singular nobility of his mother nothing avail him, if his father's blood were not, in all respects, worthy to match with hers. If ancient, undoubted, and untouched nobility be worthy to match with the most noble house that can be: this house, therefore, of Dudley, which, in despite of all shamelessness, he so doth deprave, is, at this day, a peer, as we term it, of the realm, a baron, and, as all Englishmen know, a lord of the Parliament, and so a companion, both in marriage, Parliament, and trial, to the greatest duke that England can bear; so hath it been ever esteemed, and so, in the constitutions of all our laws and ordinances, it is always reputed. Dudley house is so to this day, and thus it hath been time out of mind; in Harry the Fifth's time, the Lord Dudley was his Lord Steward, and did that pitiful office in bringing home, as the chief mourner, his victorious master's dead body; as who goes but to Westminster, in the church may see. I think if we consider together the time which was of England the most flourishing, and the King he served, who, of all English kings, was most puissant, and the office he bare, which was, in effect, as great as an English subject could have, it would seem very strange; so that Lord Dudley, if he could out of his grave hear this fellow make question,

---

* i. e. both name and arms.

whether his lawful posterity, from father to son, should be gentlemen or no? But though he only had been sufficient to erect nobility to his successors, bringing, as the Romans termed it, so noble an image into the house, yet did he but receive his nobility from his ancestors, who had been lords of that very seignory of Dudley Castle, many descents before, even from King Richard the First's time; at which time, Sir Richard Sutton married the daughter and heir of the Lord Dudley; since which time all descended of him, as divers branches there be, left the name of Sutton, and have all been called Dudleys, which is now above four hundred years since; and both those houses of Sutton and Dudley, having been before that time of great nobility; and that Sutton was a man of great honour and estimation, that very match witnesseth sufficiently, it being a dainty thing in that time, that one of Saxon blood, as Sutton's name testifieth he was, should match with such an inheritrix as Dudley was; the like example whereof I remember none, but the great house of Raby, who matched with Neville, who of that match, as the Suttons were called Dudleys, so did they ever since take the name of Neville; so, as of a house, which, these four hundred years, have been still owners of one seignory, the very place itself, to any that sees it, witnessing; such as, for any that I know, in England none, but the noble house of Stafford hath the like, considering the name of the house, the length of time it hath been possessed, the goodliness of the seat, with pleasures and royalties about it; so, as I think, any, that will not swear themselves brothers to a reproachful tongue, will judge of his other slanders by this most manifest; since all the world may see he speaks against his own knowledge; for if either the house of Dudley had been great anciently, and now extinguished, or now great, and had not continued from old time, or that they had been unentitled gentlemen, so as men must not needs have taken knowledge of them, yet there might have been cast some veil over his untruth; but in a house now noble, long since noble, with a nobility never interrupted, seated in a place which they have, each father, and each son, continually owned, what should be said, but that this fellow desires to be known; suitable, having an untrue heart, he will become it with an untrue tongue. But perchance he will seem to doubt, for what will not he doubt, who will affirm that, which beyond all doubt is false, whether my great-grandfather, Edmond Dudley, were of the Lord Dudley's house, or no. Certainly, he might, in conscience and good manners, if so he did doubt, have made some distinction between the two houses, and not in all places have made so contemptible mention of that name of Dudley, which is borne by another peer of the realm; and even of charity sake he should have bestowed some father upon Edmond Dudley, and not leave him not only ungentled, but fatherless. A railing writer extant, against Octavius Augustus, saith, his grandfather was a silversmith; another Italian, against Hugh Capet, though with most absurd falsehood, saith his father was a butcher. Of divers of the best houses of England, there have been such foolish dreams, that one was a farrier's son, another a shoemaker's, another a milliner's, another a fiddler's; foolish lies, and by any that ever tasted any antiquities, known to be so. Yet those houses had luck to meet with honester railers, for they were not left fatherless clean, they descended from somebody; but we, as if we were of Deucalion's brood, were made out of stones, have left us no ancestors from whence we are come: but, alas! good railer, you saw the proofs were clear, and therefore, for honesty's sake, were contented to omit them; for, if either there had been difference of name, or difference of arms between them; or, if though in name and arms they agreed, yet, if there had been many descents fallen since, the separating of those branches (as we see in many ancient houses, it so falls out, as they are uncertain whether came out of other) then, I say yet, a valiant railer may venture upon a thing, where, because there is not an absolute certainty, there may be some possibility to escape; but, in this case, where not only name and arms, with only that difference which acknowledgeth our house to be of the younger brother, but such nearness of blood, as that Edmond Dudley's was no farther off than son to the younger brother of the same Lord Dudley, and so as he was to be Lord Dudley, if the Lord Dudley had died without heirs; and, by the German and Italian manner, himself was to have been also called Lord Dudley; that his father, being called John Dudley, married to the daughter and heir of Bramshot in Sussex; it was the only descent between him and the Lord Dudley, who was his grandfather; his great-grandfather being that noble Lord Dudley, whom before I mentioned, and no man need doubt that this writer doth not only know the truth hereof, but the proofs of this truth. This John, Edmond's father, being buried at Arundel Castle, who married Bramshot, and left that land to Edmond, and so to the duke in Sussex, which, after the duke sold, by confiscation came to the crown. This tomb any man at Arundel Castle may see. This Bramshot land I name, a thing not in the air, but which any man, by the ordinary course of those things, may soon know whether such land did not succeed unto Edmond from his father. So as where is this inheritance of land, and monuments in churches, and the persons themselves little more than in man's memory; truly this libeller deserves many thanks, that, with his impudent falsehood, hath given occasion to set down so manifest a truth.

As to the Dudleys, he deals much harder withal, but no whit truer: But therein I must confess, I cannot allege his uncharitable triumphing upon the calamities fallen to that house, though they might well be challenged of a writer, of whom any honesty were to be expected; but God forbid I should find fault with that, since, in all his book, there is scarce any one truth else. But our house received such an overthrow; and hath none else in England done so? I will not seek to wash away that dishonour with other honourable tears. I would this land were not so full of such examples; and I think, indeed, this writer, if he were known, might in conscience clear his ancestors of any such disgraces, they were too low in the mire to be so thunder-stricken; but this I may justly and boldly affirm, let the last fault of the duke be buried.

And, in good faith, now I have so far touched there, as any man that list to know a truth (if at least there be any that can doubt thereof) may straight be satisfied. I do not mean to give any man's eyes or ears such a surfeit, as by answering to repeat his filthy falsehoods, so contrary to themselves, as may well show how evil lies can be built with any uniformity. The same man in the beginning of the book, was potent, to use his term, in that the Queen had cause to fear him; the same

man, in the end thereof, so abject, as any man might
tread on him; the same man so unfriendly as no man
could love him: the same man so supported by friends,
that court and country were full of them; the same
man extremely weak of body, and infinitely luxurious,
the same man a dastard to fear anything: the same man
so venturous, as to undertake, having no more title, such
a matter, that Hercules himself would be afraid to do, if
he were here among us: in sum, in one the same man,
all the faults that in all the most contrary-humoured
men in the world can remain; that sure, I think, he
hath read the Devil's Roll of Complaints, which he
means to put up against mankind, or else he could never
have been acquainted with so many wretched mischiefs.
But hard it were, if every goose quill could any way
blot the honour of an Earl of Leicester, written in the
hearts of so many men through Europe. Neither for
me, shall ever so worthy a man's name be brought to
be made a question, where there is only such a nameless
and shameless opposer. But because that, though the
writer hereof doth most falsely lay want of gentry to my
dead ancestors, I have to the world thought good to say
a little, which, I will assure any, that list to seek, shall
find confirmed with much more. But to thee, I say,
thou therein liest in thy throat; which I will be ready
to justify upon thee, in any place of Europe, where thou
wilt assign me a free place of coming, as within three
months after the publishing hereof, I may understand
thy mind. And, as till thou hast proved this, in all con-
struction of virtue and honour, all the shame thou hast
spoken is thine own, the right reward of an evil-tongued
shelm, as the Germans especially call such people. So
again, in any place, whereto thou wilt call me, provided

that the place be such, as a servant of the Queen's majesty have free access unto; if I do not, having my life and liberty, prove this upon thee, I am content that this lie, I have given thee, return to my perpetual infamy. And this which I write I would send to thine own hands, if I knew thee; but I trust it cannot be intended, that he should be ignorant of this printed in London, which knows the very whisperings of the privy-chamber. I will make dainty of no baseness in thee, that art indeed the writer of this book. And, from the date of this writing, imprinted and published, I will three months expect thine answer.

LETTERS.

In the following collection will be found such familiar epistles of Sir Philip Sidney, as seem either calculated to interest the general reader, or to throw any light upon our author's character. The sixteen letters which are placed together, last in order, are now published for the first time from MSS. in the British Museum. These we have thought it better to reprint verbatim from the originals, only here and there presuming to supply, within brackets, the *lacunæ* which fire and damp have occasioned; since we are aware that many antiquaries have a strong prejudice against modernized versions, and those who entertain such an opinion cannot have access in regard to this part of our work, as was the case with the previous contents of the present volume, to other published copies more suited to their tastes.

Walpole has sneeringly observed that the letters of Sidney are but "poor matters." They are certainly the hurried and careless productions of a man deeply immersed in business, who takes up his pen solely because duty and necessity compel him to write; and not the laborious effusions of a secluded literary coxcomb, which, after having been dribbled out by syllables, and diligently pruned and adjusted into smooth and striking sentences, are addressed indirectly to the world through the medium of some gossiping friend.

LETTERS.

Sir Philip Sidney to Edward Molineux, Esq., Secretary to his father as Lord Deputy.*

[Reprinted from the Sidney Papers, vol. i. p. 256.]

Mr. Molineux,

Few words are best. My letters to my father have come to the eyes of some. Neither can I condemn any but you for it. If it be so, you have played

---

* This letter was not written to the steward, as Walpole falsely states, but to the secretary of Sir H. Sidney, Edward Molineux, Esq., of Nutfield in the county of Surrey. Sir Philip imagined, erroneously, as he afterwards confessed, that this gentleman had basely betrayed the confidence of his employer, and furnished the enemies of the aged Lord Deputy with matter of accusation against him. Though the above epistle, therefore, is sadly deficient in point of discretion and temper, it shows the intensity of our author's filial regard; and, whatever may be deducted from our estimation of the coolness of his head on account of it, an equivalent must, we apprehend, be substituted in our increased love and respect for the amiable qualities of his heart.

the very knave with me; and so I will make you know, if I have good proof of it. But that for so much as is past. For that is to come, I assure you before God, that if ever I know you do so much as read any letter I write to my father, without his commandment, or my consent, I will thrust my dagger into you. And trust to it, for I speak it in earnest. In the mean time farewell. From court, this last of May, 1578.

By me,

PHILIP SIDNEY.

Indorsed, Mr. Philip Sidney to me, brought 1578, by my Lord Chancellor; received the 21st of June.

Sir Philip Sidney to his brother Robert, the first Earl of Leicester of their name.*

MY GOOD BROTHER,

You have thought unkindness in me that I have not written oftener unto you, and have desired I should write unto you something of my opinion touching your

---

* This letter was probably composed about 1578; and originally appeared in a little volume, entitled, " Instructions for Travellers, by Robert Earl of Essex, Sir Philip Sidney, and Secretary Davison, 1633." It has been since reprinted in Seward's Biographiana, vol. ii. p. 370. A MS. copy of it is extant in Trinity College Library, Dublin; and another in the Library of University College, Oxon. For a transcript from the latter, we have been indebted to the courtesy of the Rev. Fred. Charles Plumptre, fellow and tutor of University.

travel; you being persuaded my experience thereunto be something, which I must needs confess, but not as you take it; for you think my experience grows from the good things which I have learned; but I know the only experience which I have gotten, is to find how much I might have learned, and how much indeed I have missed, for want of directing my course to the right end, and by the right means. I think you have read Aristotle's Ethics; if you have, you know it is the beginning and foundation of all his works, the end to which every man doth and ought to bend his greatest and smallest actions. I am sure you have imprinted in your mind the scope and mark you mean by your pains to shoot at: for if you should travel but to travel, or to say you had travelled, certainly you should prove a pilgrim to no purpose. But I presume so well of you, that though a great number of us never thought in ourselves why we went, but a certain tickling humour to do as other men had done, you purpose, being a gentleman born, to furnish yourself with the knowledge of such things as may be serviceable for your country and calling; which certainly stands not in the change of air, for the warmest sun makes not a wise man; no, nor in learning languages, although they be of serviceable use, for words are but words in what language soever they be, and much less in that all of us come home full of disguisements, not only of apparel, but of our countenances, as though the credit of a traveller stood all upon his outside; but in the right informing your mind with those things which are most notable in those places which you come unto.

Of which as the one kind is so vain, as I think ere it be long, like the mountebanks in Italy, we travellers shall be made sport of in comedies; so may I justly say, who rightly travels with the eye of Ulysses, doth take one of the most excellent ways of worldly wisdom. For hard sure it is to know England, without you know it by comparing it with some other country, no more than a man can know the swiftness of his horse without seeing him well matched. For you, that are a logician, know, that as greatness of itself is a quantity, so yet the judgment of it, as of mighty riches and all other strengths, stands in the predicament of relation; so that you cannot tell what the Queen of England is able to do defensively or offensively, but through knowing what they are able to do with whom she is to be matched. This, therefore, is one notable use of travellers, which stands in the mind and correlative knowledge of things, in which kind comes in the knowledge of all leagues betwixt prince and prince; the topographical description of each country; how the one lies by situation to hurt or help the other; how they are to the sea, well harboured or not; how stored with ships; how with revenue; how with fortification and garrisons; how the people, warlike, trained, or kept under, with many other such considerations, which as they confusedly come into my mind, so I, for want of leisure, hastily set them down; but these things, as I have said, are of the first kind which stands in the balancing one thing with the other.

The other kind of knowledge is of them which stand in the things which are in themselves either simply good, or simply bad, and so serve for a right instruction or a shunning example. These Homer meant in this verse, "Qui multos hominum mores cognovit et urbes." For he doth not mean by "mores" how to look, or put off one's cap with a new-found grace, although true behaviour is not to be despised; marry my heresy is, that the English behaviour is best in England, and the Italian's in Italy. But " mores " he takes for that from whence moral philosophy is so called; the certainness of true discerning of men's minds both in virtue, passion, and vices. And when he saith "cognovit urbes," he means not, if I be not deceived, to have seen towns, and marked their buildings ; for surely houses are but houses in every place, they do but differ " secundum magis et minus ;" but he attends to their religion, politics, laws, bringing up of children, discipline both for war and peace, and such like. These I take to be of the second kind, which are ever worthy to be known for their own sakes. As surely in the great Turk, though we have nothing to do with him, yet his discipline in war matters is, " propter se," worthy to be known and learned.

Nay, even in the kingdom of China, which is almost as far as the Antipodes from us, their good laws and customs are to be learned; but to know their riches and power is of little purpose for us, since that can neither advance nor hinder us. But in our neighbour countries, both these things are to be marked, as well the latter, which contain things for themselves, as the former, which seek to know both those, and how their riches and power may be to us available, or otherwise. The countries fittest for both these, are those you are going into. France is above all other most needful for us to mark, especially in the former kind ; next is Spain and the Low Countries ; then Germany, which in my opinion excels all others as much in the latter consideration, as the other doth in the former, yet neither are void of neither; for as Germany, methinks, doth excel in good laws, and well administering of justice, so are we likewise to consider in it the many princes with whom we may have league, the places of trade, and means to draw both soldiers and furniture thence in time of need. So on the other side, as in France and Spain, we are principally to mark how they stand towards us both in power and inclination; so are they, not without good and fitting use, even in the generality of wisdom to be known. As in France, the courts of parliament, their subaltern jurisdiction, and their continual keeping of paid soldiers. In Spain, their good and grave proceedings; their keeping so many provinces under them, and by what manner, with the true points of honour; wherein since they have the most open conceit, if they seem over curious, it is an easy matter to cut off when a man sees the bottom. Flanders likewise, besides the neighbourhood with us, and the annexed considerations thereunto, hath divers things to be learned, especially their governing their merchants and other trades. Also for Italy, we know not what we have, or can have, to do with them, but to buy their silks and wines; and as for the other point, except Venice, whose good laws and customs we can hardly proportion to ourselves, because they are quite of a contrary government; there is little there but tyrannous oppression, and servile yielding to them that have little or no right over them. And for the men you shall have there, although indeed some be excellently learned, yet are they all given to counterfeit learning, as a man shall learn among them more false grounds of things than in any place else that I know; for, from a tapster upwards, they are all discoursers in certain matters and qualities, as horsemanship, weapons, painting, and such are better there than in other countries; but for other matters, as well, if not better, you shall have them in nearer places.

Now resteth in my memory but this point, which indeed is the chief to you of all others; which is the choice of what men you are to direct yourself to; for it is certain no vessel can leave a worse taste in the liquor it contains, than a wrong teacher infects an unskilful hearer with that which hardly will ever out: I will not tell you some absurdities I have heard travellers tell; taste him well before you drink much of his doctrine. And when you have heard it, try well what you have heard, before you hold it for a principle; for one error is the mother of a thousand. But you may say, how shall I get excellent men to take pains to speak with me? truly in few words, either by much expense or much humbleness.

Sir Philip Sidney to his brother Robert.

[Reprinted from the Sidney Papers, vol. i. p. 283–5.]

MY DEAR BROTHER,

For the money you have received, assure yourself (for it is true) there is nothing I spend so pleaseth me, as that which is for you. If ever I have ability you will find it, if not, yet shall not any brother living be better beloved than you of me. I cannot write now to N. White, do you excuse me. For his nephew, they are but passions in my father, which we must bear with reverence; but I am sorry he should return till he had the circuit of his travel, for you shall never have such a servant as he would prove; use your own discretion therein. For your countenance I would for no cause have it diminished in Germany; in Italy your greatest expense must be upon worthy men, and not upon householding. Look to your diet (sweet Robin) and hold up your heart in courage and virtue, truly great part of my comfort is in you. I know not myself what I meant by bravery in you, so greatly you may see I condemn you; be careful of yourself, and I shall never have cares. I have written to Mr. Savile,* I wish you kept still together, he is an excellent man; and there may if you list pass good exercises betwixt you and Mr. Nevyle,† there is great expectation of you both. For the method of writing history, Boden hath written at large; you may read him, and gather out of many words some matter. This I think in haste, a story is either to be considered as a story, or as a treatise, which, besides that, addeth many things for profit and ornament; as a story, he is nothing but a narration of things done, with the beginnings, causes, and appendances thereof; in that kind your method must be to have "seriem temporum" very exactly, which the Chronologies of Melancthon, Tarchagnora, Languet, and such other, will help you to. Then to consider by that   as you not yourself, Zenophon to follow Thucydides, so doth Thucydides follow Herodotus, and Diodorus Siculus follow Zenophon: so generally do the Roman sto-

---

* Afterwards the celebrated Sir Henry Savile.

† Mr. Alexander Nevyle. For an account of this gentleman see Warton's History of Poetry, vol. iv., p. 208, edit. 1824.

ries follow the Greek, and the particular stories of present monarchies follow the Roman. In that kind you have principally to note the examples of virtue or vice, with their good or evil successes, the establishments or ruins of great estates, with the causes, the time, and circumstances of the laws then wrote of, the enterings and endings of wars, and therein, the stratagems against the enemy, and the discipline upon the soldier; and thus much as a very historiographer. Besides this, the historian makes himself a discourser for profit, and an orator, yea a poet, sometimes for ornament. An orator, in making excellent orations, "e re nata," which are to be marked, but marked with the note of rhetorical remembrances: a poet, in painting forth the effects, the motions, the whisperings of the people, which though in disputation, one might say were true, yet who will mark them well, shall find them taste of a poetical vein, and in that kind are gallantly to be marked; for though perchance they were not so, yet it is enough they might be so. The last point which tends to teach profit, is of a discourser, which name I give to whosoever speaks, "Non simpliciter de facto, sed de qualitatibus et circumstantiis facti;" and that is it which makes me and many others, rather note much with our pen than with our mind, because we leave all these discourses to the confused trust of our memory, because they being not tied to the tenor of a question, as philosophers use sometimes places; the divine, in telling his opinion and reasons in religion; sometimes the lawyer, in showing the causes and benefits of laws; sometimes a natural philosopher, in setting down the causes of any strange thing, which the story binds him to speak of; but most commonly a moral philosopher, either in the ethic part, when he sets forth virtues or vices, and the natures of passions, or in the politic, when he doth (as often he doth) meddle sententiously with matters of estate. Again, sometimes he gives precept of war, both offensive and defensive; and so, lastly, not professing any art, as his matter leads him he deals with all arts, which because it carrieth the life of a lively example, it is wonderful what light it gives to the arts themselves, so as the great civilians help themselves with the discourses of the historians; so do soldiers, and even philosophers and astronomers; but that I wish herein, is this, that when you read any such thing, you straight bring it to his head, not only of what art, but by your logical subdivisions, to the next member and parcel of the art. And so as in a table, be it witty words, of which Tacitus is full; sentences of which Livy, or similitudes whereof Plutarch; straight to lay it up in the right place of his storehouse, as either military, or more specially defensive military, or more particularly defensive by fortification, and so lay it up. So likewise in politic matters, and such a little table you may easily make, wherewith I would have you ever join the historical part, which is only the example of some stratagem, or good counsel, or such like. This write I to you in great haste, of method without method, but with more leisure and study (if I do not find some book that satisfies) I will venture to write more largely of it unto you. Mr. Savile will with ease help you to set down such a table of remembrance to yourself, and for your sake I perceive he will do much, and if ever I be able I will deserve it of him; one only thing, as it comes unto my mind, let me remember you of, that you consider wherein the historian excelleth, and that to note, as Dion Nicæus, in the searching the secrets of government; Tacitus, in the pithy opening the venom of wickedness, and so of the rest. My time, exceedingly short, will suffer me to write no more leisurely; Stephen can tell you who stands with me while I am writing. Now (dear brother) take delight likewise in the mathematicals; Mr. Savile is excellent in them. I think you understand the sphere, if you do, I care little for any more astronomy in you. Arithmetic and geometry, I would wish you well seen in, so as both in matter of number and measure you might have a feeling and active judgment; I would you did bear the mechanical instruments, wherein the Dutch excel. I write this to you as one, that for myself have given over the delight in the world, but wish to you as much, if not more, than to myself. So you can speak and write Latin, not barbarously, I never require great study in Ciceronianism, the chief abuse of Oxford, "qui dum verba sectantur, res ipsas negligunt." My toyful books I will send, with God's help, by February, at which time you shall have your money: and for 200*l.* a year, assure yourself, if the estates of England remain, you shall not fail of it; use it to your best profit. My Lord of Leicester sends you forty pounds, as I understand by Stephen, and promiseth he will continue that stipend yearly at the least, then that is above commons; in any case write largely and diligently unto him, for in troth I have good proof that he means to be every way good unto you; the odd 30*l.* shall come with the hundred, or else my father and I will jarl. Now, sweet brother, take a delight to keep and increase your music, you will not believe what a want I find of it in my melancholy times. At horsemanship when you exercise it, read Crison Claudio, and a book that is called "La Gloria del' Cavallo," withal that you may join the thorough contemplation of it with the exercise; and so shall you profit more in a month, than others in a year, and mark the bitting, saddling, and curing of horses. I would by the way your worship would learn a better hand; you write worse than I, and I write evil enough; once again have a care of your diet, and consequently of your complexion; remember "Gratior est veniens in pulchro corpore virtus." Now sir for news, I refer myself to this bearer, he can tell you how idle we look on our neighbours' fires, and nothing is happened notable at home, save only Drake's return, of which yet I know not the secret points; but about the world he hath been, and rich he is returned. Portugal we say is lost, and to conclude, my eyes are almost closed up, overwatched with tedious business. God bless you, sweet boy, and accomplish the joyful hope I conceive of you. Once again commend me to Mr. Nevyle, Mr. Savile, and honest Harry White, and bid him be merry. When you play at weapons, I would have you get thick caps and brasers, and play out your play lustily, for indeed ticks and dalliances are nothing in earnest, for the time of the one and the other greatly differs, and use as well the blow as the thrust; it is good in itself, and besides exerciseth your breath and strength, and will make you a strong man at the tourney and barriers. First, in any case practise the single sword, and then with the dagger; let no day pass without an hour or two such exercise; the rest study, or confer diligently, and so shall you come home to my comfort and credit. Lord! how I have babbled: once again farewell dearest brother.

    Your most loving and careful brother,
          PHILIP SYDNEY.
At Leicester-house, this 18th of October, 1580.

Letter to Sir Francis Walsingham.

[Reprinted from Lodge's Portraits and Memoirs of the most Illustrious Personages, No. 1.]

RIGHT HONOURABLE,

  I receive divers letters from you, full of the discomfort which I see, and am sorry to see, that you daily meet with at home; and I think, such is the good will it pleaseth you to bear me, that my part of the trouble is something that troubles you; but I beseech you let it not. I had before cast my count of danger, want, and disgrace; and, before God, sir, it is true in my heart, the love of the cause doth so far overbalance them all, that, with God's grace, they shall never make me weary of my resolution. If her Majesty were the fountain, I would fear, considering what I daily find, that we should wax dry; but she is but a means whom God useth, and I know not whether I am deceived, but I am faithfully persuaded, that if she should withdraw herself, other springs would rise to help this action: for methinks I see the great work indeed in hand against the abusers of the world, wherein it is no greater fault to have confidence in man's power, than it is too hastily to despair of

God's work. I think a wise and constant man ought never to grieve while he doth play, as a man may say, his own part truly, though others be out; but if himself leave his hold because other mariners will be idle, he will hardly forgive himself his own fault. For me, I cannot promise of my own course, no, not of the . . . . . because I know there is a higher power that must uphold me, or else I shall fall; but certainly I trust I shall not by other men's wants be drawn from myself; therefore, good sir, to whom for my particular I am more bound than to all men besides, be not troubled with my troubles, for I have seen the worst, in my judgment, beforehand, and worse than that cannot be.

If the Queen pay not her soldiers she must lose her garrisons; there is no doubt thereof; but no man living shall be able to say the fault is in me. What relief I can do them, I will. I will spare no danger, if occasion serves. I am sure no creature shall be able to lay injustice to my charge; and, for farther doubts, truly I stand not upon them. I have written by Adams to the council plainly, and therefore let them determine. It hath been a costly beginning unto me this war, by reason I had nothing proportioned unto it; my servants unexperienced, and myself every way unfurnished; but hereafter, if the war continue, I shall pass much better through with it. For Bergen up Zome, I delighted in it, I confess, because it was near the enemy: but especially having a very fair house in it, and an excellent air, I destined it for my wife; but, finding how you deal there, and that ill payment in my absence thence might bring forth some mischief, and considering how apt the Queen is to interpret everything to my disadvantage, I have resigned it to my Lord Willoughby, my very friend, and indeed a valiant and frank gentleman, and fit for that place; therefore I pray you know that so much of my regality is fallen.

I understand I am called very ambitious and proud at home, but certainly if they knew my heart they would not altogether so judge me. I wrote to you a letter by Will, my Lord of Leicester's jesting player, enclosed in a letter to my wife, and I never had answer thereof. It contained something to my Lord of Leicester, and counsel that some way might be taken to stay my lady there. I, since, divers times have writ to know whether you had received them, but you never answered me that point. I since find that the knave delivered the letters to my Lady of Leicester, but whether she sent them you or no I know not, but earnestly desire to do, because I doubt there is more interpreted thereof. Mr. Erington is with me at Flushing, and therefore I think myself at the more rest, having a man of his reputation; but I assure you, sir, in good earnest, I find Burlas another manner of man than he is taken for, or I expected. I would to God, Burne had obtained his suit. He is earnest, but somewhat discomposed with consideration of his estate. Turner is good for nothing, and worst for the sound of the hackbutes. We shall have a sore war upon us this summer, wherein if appointment had been kept, and these disgraces forborne, which have greatly weakened us, we had been victorious. I can say no more at this time, but pray for your long and happy life. At Utrecht, this 24th of March, 1586.

Your humble son,
PHILIP SYDNEY.

I know not what to say to my wife's coming till you resolve better; for if you run a strange course, I may take such a one here as will not be fit for any of the feminine gender. I pray you make much of Nichol. Gery. I have been vilely deceived for armours for horsemen; if you could speedily spare me any out of your armory, I will send them you back as soon as my own be finished. There was never so good a father found a more troublesome son. Send Sir William Pelham, good sir, and let him have Clerke's place, for we need no clerks, and it is most necessary to have such a one in the council.

LETTERS

OF

SIR PHILIP SYDNEY, KNIGHT.

From the unpublished originals in the British Museum.

LETTER I.

FROM THE COTTONIAN MS. GALBA, B. XI. F. 370.

N. B. The edges of this volume are so burnt, that some whole words at the ends of the lines are lost. These we have endeavoured occasionally to supply within brackets.

To the Right honorable and my singular vnkle, the earle of [*Leicester.*]

RIGHTE HONORABLE
 AND MY SINGULAR GOOD LORDE AND VNCLE,

 Allthoughe I haue at this presente .. little matter worthy the writinge vnto your Lordeshippe, yet beinge newlie returned frome my poll[ish] iournei, I woolde not omitt anie ocasion of humbly perfoorminge this dutie. Wherefore I hum[bly] beseeche your L. to take these few lines in good parte, Whiche I wryte rather to continew this [duty] I ow vnto yow, then for any other thinge they may conteine in them. The Emperour* as I wrate .. laste vnto your L. hathe these two yeeres continuallie pretended a iourney to Prage, wh[ich] it is

---

 * Maximilian the Second of Hungary.

thoughte shall in deede be perfoormed, to the greate contentacion of that kingedome, wh[ich] otherwise seemed to bende to disobedience. There it is thoughte his son shall very shortlie be [elected] kinge, whome likewise the Emperour seekes by all meanes possible to aduance to the kinged[om] of the Romaines, and for that purpose desyres to call an imperiall diett in Francfort, the [place] appointed for the elections, but it is thoughte the Electours will rather choose an other . . for this nexte ensuinge diett whiche is saide shall be sommer followinge at the fur[thest,] and then there is no hope of election. Not beinge at Francfort, it is likely it shal [be held] at Regenspurg, where I beleue the Emperour will demaunde fur greater summes of mo[ney] then will be grawnted unto him. Thoughe the peace betwixte the Turke and him [is not] as yet, as fur as it is knowne, perfittlie concluded, yet it is thought the Turke will rath[er] proceede by sea then this waie, and as the Frenche ambassadour hathe writtne, meane . . . . insite the Pope's territorie, perchaunce his conscience moueth him, to seeke the benefitt of . . . . Jubile. I hope as the Spanierdes allreddy begin to speake lower, so the Pope's holiness will haue lesse leasure to ministre suche wicked and detestable counceills to the chris[tian] princes as hetherto he dothe. Owt of Frawnce yowr L. hathe the aduertisements fu . . . . the Prince of Conde is retired to Basill where he liuethe in companie withe the Adr . . . . . . children, beinge frustrate of a greate hope he had conceaued of suckowr owt of Jerma[ny] wherein many and wise men do impute greate faulte to the prince Casimire, the Cow[nt] Palatines seconde son, in so muche that to write to yowr L. plainely, he is heauilie sus[pected] to be corrupted by the frenche. His father

certainely is as vertuous a prince as liuethe [but] he sufferethe him selfe to much to be gouerned by that son. This I thoughte my dut[ie to] write as hauinge hearde it in a very good place and muche affectioned to the tr[ew] cawse. The Polakes hartily repente their so fur fetcht election, beinge now in suche case [that] neither they haue the kinge, nor any thinge the kinge, withe so many othes, had promised . . . . besides that their is lately sturred up a very dangerous Sedition, for the same ca[use] that hathe bredde suche lamentable ruines in France and Flandres. Now the [sedition] is reasonably wel appeased, but it is thoughte it will remaine so but a while. I have no othre thinge worthy the writinge at this presente to yowr L. wherefore I humbly ceasse withe my dailie and moste boundne praier, that it please the eternall to continew and encreace yow in all prosperitie. Frome Vienne, This 27 of Nouembre, 1574.
     Yowr L. moste
      obedi . . . . . .
         PHILIPPE SIDNEY.

LETTER II.

Ibid. ff. 387-8. not the original.

Sir Philip Sydney to Sir Francis Walsingham.

RIGHTE HONORABLE,

  I receiued in commandement from her Matie that in my waye to the Emperor, I should deliver her Maties

letters to the brethren Palatins, and withall giue them to vnderstand how greatly, and in what good respectes her Matie was sorry for the death of the late Elector, and yet withall somewhat comforted by the assured expectation her Matie had of their succeeding vnto him in all his vertues, I should, according as I sawe cause, perswade them to brotherly loue, necessary for the publique weale, and their owne preseruation. Afterwards to Casimire in particular, I should so much the more expresse her Maties good fauor towards him, as he was the son most deere vnto his father, and had allready giuen very good shew of his princely vertues. Lastly I should learne of him, whether the mony deliuered were as yet receiued, which her Matie would be content to leaue there in some place of that country *in deposito*. For the first I could not yet doe it, but only to prince Casimir, the Electour being at a towne of his in the upper Palatinate called Amberg, whether I meane to goe vnto him, being not much out of the waye for Prage, where the Emperour lyes, if I doe not meete him by the way, as it is thought I shall, but to Prince Casimire I said according to mine instructions, and to that purpose so much more, as the course of speech, and the framing of the time did give occasion. His answer was that her Matie in deed had great reason to be sorry for the losse of his father, hauing bene in truth so trew a friend and servant vnto her, of his other good partes he left to be witnessed by the things he hath done in the aduancement of vertue and Religion. For himselfe he could not thinke himselfe bound enough to her Matie for this signification of her goodnes towards him, and in the vertues of his father, there was none he would seeke more to follow, then his duty and good will to her Matie.

This he did in very good termes, and with a countenance well witnessing it came from his hart.

For the second, I founde no cause to perswade him to vnity with his brother, he being, as he saith, fully perswaded so to embrace it, as nothing more, yet found I in him great miscontentment that his brother beginnes to make alteration in Religion, for hauing two principall gouerments the vpper Palatinate which lyes in Bauaria, and this which they calle the nether, by the Rhine, the Elector hath already in the vpper established Lutheranisme, and as it is feared is comming shortly to doe the like here. He hath vsed great perswasions to his brother in it, and of late hath sett out in print his father's Confession in his owne name, to the end as I perceiue, by him, to auoyde all suspicion, that eyther flattery in his father's time, or feare now, did or may moue him, either to embrace, or leaue, that which concernes his conscience. This confession he hath sent to all the Electors, and most part of the Princes of Germany. He is resolved, if his brother doe drive away from him the learned men of the true profession, that he will receiue to him, and hereof something may breed gall betwixt them, if any doe; but the best is to be hoped, considering Prince Lodouick is of a soft nature, ledde to these things only thorough conscience, and Prince Casimir wise that can temper well with the others weaknes.

For the third, which was to shew her Maties speciall good liking of Prince Casimir, I did it with the first, and his answere was the same protestation of his good harte, as before I wratte.

In the last, touching her Maties money, his answer was the K. of France had falsefied his promise, and therefore neither her Matie nor the Ritters who doe greatly cry for it, could as yet have their dew. I told him it would be a cause to make her Matie withdraw from like loanes, as the well paying would give her cause to doe it in greater somes. He was greeved with my vrging of him, and assured me, that if he could gett the payement, he wolde rather dye then not see her Matie honorably satisfied. Then I pressed him for certeine iewells and ostages I had learned he had in pawne of the King; he told mee, they were allready the Rittreses, but if her Matie would buy any of them she might haue a good bargaine.

In fyne, this I find, that of nyne Monthes was dew to the Soldiers, they are paied but to and an halfe, for other the Duke of Lorrayne and Vaudemont are bound, of which they make perfect account. Their Jewells and ostages they valew a little more then at halfe a Moneths paye, so that there is due vnto them yet foure Moneths pay, which according to their gentle allowance comes to aboue a $\frac{1}{2}$ Million of Frankes: vntil most part of this be payed, I do not think her Matie can receiue her dew. The best is, a thing well employed is halfe paied, and yet truly by that I find in the Prince, I doe hold my selfe in good beleefe, that her Matie within a yeare or two shalbe honorably answered it.

Now touching the particularities her Ma^tle willed me to learne of him, as of the Emperors, both in matters of State and Religion, how the Princes of Germany are affected in French and Low Country matters, what forces there are preparing here, and what he himselfe meanes to be.

For the Emperor, he knows very little of him, but such generall pointes euerywhere knowen, of his papistry or Spanish grauity. But this I understand by men of good iudgement, that he is left poore, the Diuision with his brethren not yet made, warres with the Turke feared, and yet his peace little better, considering the great tributes he paies, and the continuall spoiles his subieƌes suffer vppon the Frontiers.

The other Princes of Germany haue no care but how to grow riche and to please their senses; the Duke of Saxony so carried away with the vbiquity, that he growes bitter to the true Lutherians. The rest are of the same mould, thinking they should be safe, though all the world were on fire about them, except it be the Landgraue William, and his brethern, and this Prince Casimire, who wisheth very earnestly, that her Matie would writte of purpose vnto the Landgraue, being a Prince both religious, wise, and very much addiƌed to her Matie.

Forces there are none publiquely preparing. Casimir the only man, the Ritters and soldiors doe looke and depend vppon him, he temporises a little staying till he gathers of the K. of France and K. of Nauarre 3 Months paye for such an army, as he will bring, and then in deed he saith, I shall heare, that he is dead, or that he hath left a miserable France of the Papishe syde. I haue sent the Princes confession in Dutch. The Prince did giue of a meaning Don John * should haue

---

* Don John of Austria, natural brother to Philip the Second of Spain. Hume says, referring to Camden and Grotius as his authorities, that this prince "had projeƌed to espouse the Queen of Scots, and to acquire in her right the dominion of the British kingdoms." He was afterwards killed by poison in the Low Countries, at the instigation, as was generally supposed, of his brother, who dreaded his ambition.

to marry the Quene of Scotts, and so to sturr troubles in England.

There is none of the Princes like to enter into any League (and that rather as it were to serue the Quene, then any way ells) but the Prince Casimir, the Landgraue, and the Duke of Brunswick.

The Bohemians which were earnest in Maximilians time to haue Churches of the true Religion granted them, doe now grow cold only being content to haue the freedom in their houses. I will not furder trouble you, but with my humble commendations vnto you leaue you to the Eternall. From Heidelberg this 22. of Marche 1576.

Yours to doe you any seruice
PHILIPP SYDNEY.

LETTER III.

Ibid. f. 363, 4.

The direction of this letter, to Secretary Walsingham, is lost with the envelope.

RIGHTE HONORABLE.

The Nexte day I dispatched away Woodall be... 22 of Marche I departed frome Heidelberge, and not findinge the [Electour] at Amberg as I hoped to haue done came to Prague uppon Maun... uppon Easter Monday afterwardes I had Audience, where accord-[ing to] her Maties commawndemente, I was to make

knowne unto him, [how] greatlie Her Maiestie was
grieued withe the losse of so worthy a [Prince as] the
Emperour * his father was, her Matie hauinge so greate
cawse.... as bothe the publicke losse of suche a prince
(the fruites of whose..... gouernement were well
founde, bothe in the Mainteining the empir.... and
staijng the Turkes inuasion) and the Particular goodwill
.... euer betwixte Her Maiestie and him, coolde not
but greatly gr[ieve] her.

Secondly Her Maties good hope of him, that he woolde
seconde his fath[er] in his uertues and the manner of
his gouernemente. And [the advice of] her Maties
cownsaile unto him to auoide the turbulent cowncells,
of.... guyded withe pryuate passions whereof the issue
is uncertaine, [the bene]fittes none, and the harmes
manifeste.

Besides these, as ocasion shoolde serue, I shoolde
giue him to undrest [and how] nobly her Matie had pro-
ceeded in the low countrey matters, and upp[on] good
growndes. The 3 firste I did declare together unto
him.... other reasons as bothe ye instructions did more
largely specify, and [opportunity] it selfe did ministre.

He awnswered me in Latin withe very few wordes,
to the firste, t.... persuade him selfe so of her Matie as
it pleased her to signify un[to him] for wch signification
he gave her Serenitie (for y^t was ye tearme he [used])
uery greate thankes, and therewithall added a certaine
speeche of.... the praises her Matie gaue his father he
saide he woolde not stande.... becawse he mighte
seeme to deryue parte of the glory to him selfe....

* Maximilian the Second died in 1576, and was succeeded by
Rodolphus the Second.

his goodwill towardes her Matie of wch he was left uery good wi[tness,] hauinge by many meanes knowne his fathers minde therein.

To the seconde, and thirde, he awnswered together, that as God had pr[otection] of the Empire, so he woolde prouyde him withe cownceile how to [govern] it, but y^t he did in most gratefull manner accepte her Matie .... and y^t ye rule he woolde follow chiefly, shoolde be his fathers imita[tion] after y^t he fell into dyuerse other particuler demandes and speeches .... to longe to recyte, but that I uppon ocasion of Don Jhon D Hustro .... twise or thryse to giue him to vndrestande how her Matie had pr .... those thinges, but his allowance thereof was so generall y^t I coolde .... tyme passe no furdre.

The nexte day I deliuered her Maties lettres to the Empresse, withe the singular signification of her Maties greate good will unto her, and her Maiesties wisshinge of her to aduise her son to a wyse and peaceable gouernemente ; of the Emperour deceassed I used but few wordes, becawse in trothe I saw it bredd some troble unto her to heere him mentioned in that kinde ; she awnswered me withe many cowrteowse speeches, and greate acknowledging of her owne beholdingenes to her Matie. And for her son, she saide she hoped he woolde do well, but that, for her owne part, she saide she had giuen her selfe frome ye worlde and woolde not greatly sturr frome thence forwarde in it. Then did I deliuer the queene of Frawnce [her] letter, she standinge by the Empresse, usinge suche speeches as I thou[ght] were fitt for her double sorrow, and her Maties good will unto her, confirm[ed] by her wyse and noble gouerninge of her selfe in the tyme of her beinge in

Frawnce. Her awnswere was full of humblenes, but she spake so low y[t] I coolde not undrestande many of her wordes. Frome them I wente to the yonge princes, and paste of eache syde certaine complementes, w[ch] I will leaue becawse I feare me I haue allreddy bene ouer longe there[in]. The reste of the daies y[t] I lay there, I enfourmed my selfe as well as I coolde of suche particularities as I receaued in my enstructions, as of the 1. Emperours disposicion and his brethren. 2. By whose Aduise he is directed. 3. When it is lykely he shall marry. 4. What princes in Jermany are moste affected to him. 5. In w[t] state he is lefte for reuenews. 6. w[t] good agreement there is betwixte him and his brethren. 7. And what partaye they haue. In these thinges I shall at my returne more largely be hable, and wth more leysure, to declare it: now, only thus muche I will troble yow withe.

1. That the Emperour is holy by his inclination giune to the warres, few of wordes, sullein of disposition, very secrete and resolute, nothinge the manner his father had in winninge men in his behauior, but yet constant in keepinge them. And suche a one, as thoughe he promise not muche owtwardly, hathe, as the Latines say, *Aliquid in Recessu.*

His Brother Earnest, muche lyke him in disposition, but y[t] he is more franke and forwarde, w[ch] perchawnce y[e] necessity of his fortune dryues him to. Bothe Extreemely Spaniolated. Matthias and Maximilian lykew[ise] broughte upp togeather, but in Jermany, and in their behauiour fram[ing] of them selues to the lykinge of this contrey people, especially Maximilian, who seemes in deede to promise some greate worthines, but their yowthe, and education, as yet under gouernement, makes ye iudgem[ent] ye harder.

Albertus and Wenceslaus are in Spaine. Albertus, of late made Card[inal], of the beste witt of them all, and uppon him it is thoughte t[he Archbishoprick] of Toledo shall be bestowed. Wenceslaus is of a very quick spi[rit], as yet very yonge, and made putt on a Spanishe grauity .... upp to be seruantes to the pope, and y^t is lyke to be their h[ighest] Ambition.

2. The Emperour is most gouerned by one Diet .... greate m^r of his howse, beares ye redde crosse of Spaine and .... a professed seruante to ye crowne and inquisitors gouernemente. The nuntio of ye Pope y^t is now there is lykewise great u .... and followed by him, so y^t w^t cownceills suche authors giue m[ay be] easily imagined, thoughe ye effectes be longe in bringing forthe.

3. He dothe kepe him unmarried till the Daughter of Spaine be .... is now eleauen yeere olde, there was lyke to haue growen some .... becawse the kinge of Spaine seemed rather to have lyked of the K .... Portugall, but it is now hoped that y^t kinge will haue ye Don.... Frawnce, and so the Emperour to strengthen the holinesse of t .... muche ye more, will become bothe son, brother, nephew, and .... the kinge of Spaine.

4. How the princes of Jermany are affect .... him, and what authority the howse of Austriche dothe daily g[et over] them by their carelesnes, and whylst as you wrate they are .... in securitie, I will if it please yow referr till my returne .... 5. thereuppon hanges dyuerse thinges, and I haue allreddy bene .... His reuenewes are greate, but his enemy the Turke so muche ab .... greatnes, that he can not turne muche of them to other

use. . . . . The Empire of late at ye Dyet of Ratisbone did graunte his fath[er a loan] of six million of florins to be paide in six yeere. He hat . . . . nothinge of it as yet, but makes perfitt accompte not only to . . . . it, but to continew it, wch if it be so will be a matter of greate . . . . consideringe he is bounde to no other thinge for it but ye defence . . . . òwne patrimony. I will bringe yow a particular of his reuenews . . . . gesse in a thinge yeerly allmoste changinge may suffer.

6. The brethren do agree very well, and so certainly are lyke to doe . . . . suttlety of the worlde is conspyred to unite them, and more agreate n . . . . . . y^t sorte, to some terrible ende. This is certaine that none is loked o . . . . . . Ma^tle and the poore reliques of Frawnce and Flawndres, as the . . . . . . to her state, for as for iermany, I assure yow they make accown . . . . . . them in effecte allreddy at leaste hurtlesse enemies. 7. Their pa . . . . . . as yet made Austriche is ye only thinge y^t can be diuyded. I am of . . . . will be contented withe Pensions. Earnestus especially hauing as h . . . . . . absolute gouernement of Hungary and Austriche ye Emperour will keep his . . . . . . in . . . . I am ashamed I haue trobled yow so longe. But I will leaue the Emperours acceptacion of ye low contrey matters till I may my selfe say it unto yow, and so, his speeches at my farewell, wch I am afraide I was in the beginninge of these scribbles to longe in. Hether I came the last of Aprill, and had Audience the nexte day. I had frome her Ma^tle to condole wth him and to perswade him to vnitie withe his brother; he made his vizchancelour to awnswere me, whiche he did in a very longe speeche, withe thanks to her Ma^tle and prayses of ye worthy prince y^t is dead; the pointe of Concorde wth his brother, he thanked her

Maiestie for remembringe, And fell into a common place of ye necessitie of brothers loue, but descended nothinge into his own particularitie, or w^t he thoughte of him.

One thinge I was bolde to adde in my speeche, to desyre him, in her Maiesties name, to haue mercyfull consideration of the churche of the religion, so notably established by his father as in all Jermany there is not suche a number of excellente learned men, and truly woolde rue any man to see the desolation of them. I laied before him as well as I coolde the dangers of the mightiest princes of Christendome by entryng into lyke vyolente changes, the wronge he shoolde doe his worthy father utterly to abolishe y^t he had instituted, and so as it were condemne him, besydes the example he shoolde giue his posterity to handle him ye lyke. This I emboldened my selfe to doe, seinge as me thoughte greate cawse for it, either to moue him att least to haue some regarde for her Ma^{tis} sake, or if that followed not, yet to leaue y^t publicke testimony wth the churche of Jermany that her Ma^{ty} was carefull of them, besides y^t I learned Prince Casimir had used her Maties authoritie in perswadinge his brother from it. This I hope will be takne for sufficiente cawse therein, of my boldenes. My Awnswere was at firste none, so longe as m^r Vizchanceilour stode by. After I had an other interpretour he made me this answere, that for her Maties sake he woolde doe muche, he mislyked not of the men, but must be constrained to doe as the other princes of the Empyre. In the mean time he is gone to the bathes for the laste remedy of his infirmity.

Whow his brother and he stande I will lykewise referr till my returne, and that I haue spokne withe Prince Casimir. Frome who ... so to ende this longe troblinge of yow, I meane to goe wth her Ma^tles letter to the Langraue, who is the only prince Casimir makes accownte of.

What I shall fynde amonge these princes truly I know not till I haue spokne wth prince Casimir, [to wh]ome I go to morrow to Caisarlautar, but I see their proceedinges suche y^t my ho[pe] dothe euery day grow lesse and lesse. I beseeche yow pardon me for my longe troblinge of yow. I most humbly recommende my selfe unto yow, and leaue yow to the Eternalls most happy protection. Frome Heidelberg, this 3^d. of May, 1577.*

Yours humbly at commawndem[ent,]

PHILIPP SIDNEY.

LETTER IV.

BURGHLEY PAPERS, MS. LANSD. XXXIX., No. 29.

Endorsed, " Sr Ph. Sidney to my L. His suite to be ioined in Patents with ye E. of Warwick.

> . . . . *the right honorable*
> . . . . *gular good Lord*
> . . . . *L. Threasorer of*
> *England, etc.*"

RIGHT HONORABLE MY SINGULAR GOOD LORD,

Without carrijng with me any furdre reason of this boldnes, then yowr welknown goodnes [unto] me,

* The last of these four figures appearing more like an ordinary 2 than 7, occasioned the following note by Planta in the Catalogue :

I humbly craue of yowr L. yowr good word to her Matie, for the confirming y^t grawnt she once made vnto me, of ioining me pattent with my L. of Warwick: whose desyre is y^t it shoold be so. The larger discoursing hereof I will omitt, as superfluous to yowr wisdome, neither will I vse more plenty of wordes, till God make me hable to print them in som seruiceable effect, towardes yowr L. in the mean tyme I will prai for yowr Long and prosperows life, and so humbli take my leaue. At Ramsbury. This 20th of Juli, 1583.

Yowr Lps. most humbli at comandment,
PHILIP SIDNEJ.*

LETTER V.

FROM THE MS. GALBA, C. VIII. f. 213–4.

The direction is lost with the envelope; the edge, as in all these Cottonian MSS. is much burnt.

RIGHT HONORABLE MY SINGULAR GOOD LORD,

Vppon Thursday we came into this Town driuen to Land at Ramekins,† becaws the wynd began to ryse in such sort as our M^rs durst not anker befo[re] ye town,

---

" N. B. This date must be a mistake, since Maxim. II. died in 1576." But Sir Philip's " 22 " at the beginning is very different from the last numeral in the date 1572.

* The small red seal of arms belonging to this letter is in excellent preservation, wrapt in paper.

† The castle of Rammikins in Walcheren.

and from thence came with as durty a waulk as euer poor gouernor entred his charge withall.

I fynd the people very glad of me, and promis my self as much surety in keeping this town as .... popular goodwill gottne by light hopes and .... by a .... as slight conceites maj breed me, for indeed the garrison is far to weak to comand by .... autority, which is pitty, for how great a iew[el], this is to the crown of England and the queenes safety, I need not wryte it to yow[r] L. who knows it so well. Yet I must need saj the better I know it the more I fynd the preciowsnes of it. I haue sent to m^r Norreis for my cosin Scots company, for Coronel Morgans, and my brothers (which I mean to put in the Ramekins), but I dout I shall but change, and not encrease, the enseignes by any more then myne own company, for fear of breeding iealowsies in this people, wch is carried more by shews then substance, and therefore the waj must be rather to encreace the nombers of men in each company, then the companies, and y^t maj be done easily inough, withe their good lyking; but I mean to innovat as little as may be till yowr Lps comming which is hee longed for as Messias is of the iews, but indeed most necessary it is y^t your L. make great speed to reform both the Dutch and English abuses.

I am more and more perswaded that with y^t proportion wch her Ma^{tt} alloweth, the contrei is fully hable to maintain the wars, if what thei do be well ordred, and not abused, as it is by the states: and y^t thej look for at your L. handes, it beeing strange that the people shew them selues far more carefull then the gouernors in all thinges touching the publick.

The taking of the sconses by M^r. Norris was of good

moment, but now his lying before Numeyhen* is greatly feared will both wast his men (besydes the danger of the enemy, who very strongli marcheth y^t waj) and little preuail, there beeing a great riuer between him and the citti. But the great sufficiency of the gentleman maj ouerwaj other coniectures.

M_r. Edward Norrice deliuered the companies heer vnto me, whome he had very well and souldierly gou_rned, but the companies indeed very sikkly and miserable. Good my L. hast away, if yow do come, for all thinges considered, I had rather yow came n[ot] at all, then came not quikkli, for oncle by yo[ur] own presence these cources may be stopped, whic[h] if thei run on, wil be past remedy. Heer is Aldegond, a man greatli suspected, but by no man charged. He liues restrained to his hows, and for ought I can fynd deales wit[h] nothing oneli desyring to haue his cau[se w]holy referred to your L. and therefore with [the] best heed I can to his proceedings, I will leau hi[m] to his cleering, or condemning, when yowr L. sha[ll] heer him. I think truli if my coming ha[d] been longer delaied, som alteration woold ha[ve] followed, for the truth is ye people is weery of war, and if they do not see such a cource takne as maj be lykeli to defend them, the[y] wil in a suddain giue ouer the caws. Thei Ho[llanders have] newli made Count Morrice† gouernour of Hola[nd] and Zealand, which oneli grew by the delaies of your Lps

---

* Nimeguen.

† Maurice was the second son of the late Prince of Orange. He was invested by the States with the full power and authority of stadtholder, and appointed captain-general of Holland, Zealand, and Friesland.

coming, but I can not perceau o .... meaning of either diminishing or crossing your Lps autority. but rather y^t the Count meanes holy to depend vppon your Lps autority.

With 3000^{ti} charges, I coold fynd meanes so to lodge my self and souldiers in this Town, as woold in an extremity comand it where now we are at their mercie .... [The] enemy threatnes dyuers places as Ostend, Sluse, Bergen, and Bomel, but yet we haue no certain news what he will attempt, but what so euer it be, there is great lykelihod he will endanger it, the souldiers are so euill paied and prouyded of euery thing y^t is necessary. I haue delt earnestli with the States of Zealand, for the releef of Ostend, but yet can obtain nothing but delaies.

To conclude, all will be lost if gouernment bee not presently vsed. M^r. Dauison is heer very carefull in her Maties cawses, and in your Lps; he takes great paines therein, and goes to great charges for it. I am yet so new heer y^t I can not wryte so important matters as perhaps heerafter I shall, and therefore I will not any furdre tryflingli trouble your L. but humbli leau yow to the blessed protection of the Almighti. At Flushing, This 22nd of Nouember, 1585.

    Yowr Lps most humble
      and obedient neuew,
         PHILIP SIDNEj.

M^r. Edward Norrice, as lykewise his brother, put great hope in your L. which I haue thought good to nourishe, becaws I think it fitt for your Lps seruice. M^r. Edward woold faine haue charge of horses and for caws will seek to erect a company heer. I am beholding to this bearer, captain Fenton.

LETTER VI.

FROM THE HARLEIAN MS. 285, f. 162–4.

The seal is not quite perfect. It is thus directed to Secretary ~~Walsingham~~. Davison

" *To the right honorable her Maties. Embassadour in the low contreis.*"

SIR,

By the inclosed yow maj perceau what my request was, and what the generals answer. I desyred Coronal Morgans regiment might be brought to som part heeraboutes, becaws thei might be refreshed before being receaued into the Town: yow see what reason is made against it, but the Count Hollok fyndes my request reasonable, and accordingli hath writtne to ye states, with whome I prai yow for my sake in good sort deal for it, for I perceau I shall be driuen to this extremity, either to keep these stille, or to bring them in very miserabli. Besydes, if those men wear once in these quarters, I shoold haue ocasion to do seruice, and woold not be resty when I wear requyred in som tyme of need, and for any abuse of ye contrei I wil take it vppon me. I think Captain Huntlei goes to daj to Middelbourg; I praie God the general vse him well.

The Thre[asurer] takes a strange cource. M^r. Morgan assures me he hath receaued yet but 1200 gildrenes of 3 monthes. Truli, since ye kynd cource is not accepted, yow shall do well according to the nature of your office to deal thorowli in it, and for my part, I will stick to yow in it, and each thing els, and prai for yowr happy lyfe. At Flushing, Thes 7th of December.

Yowr Louing cosin and
frend,
Ph. Sidnej.

LETTER VII.

HARL. 286, f. 72–3. with seal; directed

*"To the right honorable
Sir Francis Walsingham,
knight, principal secretary."*

RIGHT HONORABLE,

I haue takne vp three hundred poundes of Hans Barnard at vsance, who very frendli hath vsed me in it. be caws yow giue me leau to be thus bold, I humbli beseech yow the daj maj be obserued, y^t I maj preseru my creddit in these partes, and I dout not by Gods grace to keep my self wth in my bowndes, and yet to proceed honorabli. And so I humbli take my leaue praijng for your long and happy Lyfe. At Middelbourg. This 1. of December, 1585.

Your humble son
Philip Sidnej.

LETTER VIII.

FROM THE HARLEIAN MS. 285, F. 164-5;

Thus partly directed,

> "*right honorable*
> *ıcis Walsing a*
> *principal Secretary.*"

RIGHT HONORABLE,

I haue receaued som lettres from yow, most of them in recomending the bearers, which shall bee as well performed as I can. *Turner* I hope will serue my *turn* well.

My company I look and long for, and am sorry the Leuy is not made of the hole number of 200, for we want supply of men exceedingli, and although I had not kept them all in myne own hand, yet might I very well haue helpe[d] my other copanies with them, and therefore if it maj yet be redrest, I humbli beseech yow lett it.

As concerning vittuailers, for ought I can yet perceau I mai better furnish my self either heer or in England, then by tying my self to any one. and for Brown and Bruin I assure yow sir, thei do as yet but badli satisfy the souldiowrs, and in my opinion are mereli hurtfull, after a Gomortha fashion by meanes of frendship of the officers forcing the poor men to take it deerer then heer they might prouyde them selues. Great abuses haue been heer wch I hope now my L. of Lester will reform: a very euill turn it is y^t Sir William Pellam and Mr.

Killigrew cam not with him, For, as for Doctor *Clerk*, he is of those great *clerkes* y^t are not alwaies the wysest, and so my Lord now to late fyndes him; and indeed the beginnings heer are so intricate, both in matters martiall, and politik, that if thei come not before ordres be sett down, thei will come to far les purpose. Mr. Dauison doth him good seruice heer; I woold he might be suffred to remain heer a month or two longer. The Thr[easurer] heer paies our Zealand souldiers in Zealand money, wch is 5 in the 100 loss to the poor sowldiers, who God knows want no such hindrances, beeing scarce hable to keep lyfe wth their entier pay. if the comodity thereof be truly answered the queen, yet truly is it but a poor encreace to her Ma^tt, considering what loss it is to the Miserable Souldier; but if priuat Lucre be made, it hath to hurtfull a proportion to other such abuses heer. For my self I am in a garrison as much hable to com- and Flushing, as the Towr is to answer for London, and for ought I can yet learn it is hardli to be redrest, for the articles intend y^t there must be fyue thowsand kept for the defence of the contrei besydes the garrisons, so as out of them w^thout som ado thei maj be hardli drawn. I mean truli, if I can not haue it helpt heer, to wryte a protestation thereof both to her Ma^tt and the Lordes of the Cownceill, as a thing y^t I can no waj take vpon me to answer, if I be not encreast by, at the least, 400 men more than yet I haue. I woold gladli know what my old frend, the Baron of Ausperg, did in England, for he landed iust when I embarked. Coronal Morgan whom I fynd indeed a sufficient man in gouerne- ment, humbli beseecheth yow for God's sake, y^t where- as his brother is dead in her Maties seruice, who was deepli bownd for him lykewise seruing her Ma^tt, and y^t

his son and heir, yowr seruante, is now also wth Sir
Francis Drake, y^t one Cooper, to whome Edward Mor-
gan was bownd for his brother, maj not be suffred to
take aduantage, by extentes or otherwise, of his Landes
till som reasonable end maj be made for him. I know
yow fauor your seruant, for the yong gentleman deserues
it, and it now standes vppon his vtter vndoing. And
lett me add my humble request y^t yow will deal carefulli
in it: if there be a general comandment giuen y^t none
trouble his landes till the yong gentlemans return, I
think it will be a very good cource. Burnam is come
to me whome I long longed for, and fynd my self much
steeded by him. I humbli beseech yow to end the mat-
ter for him wch yow promist him, for he hath and wil
deserue it, besydes yowr promis. yow told me sir I
shoold be free of excises for my own hows and haue
access to the town assembli as an assistant, but as yet I
fynd neither, they affirming y^t none but the general and
ye Earles y^t come with him, haue to enioy y^t priuiledg.
my Lord of Lester wil needs haue me with him to help
his settling, I leau ye best ordre I can, hauing great good
assistance of Mr. Burlace, whome I beseech yow com-
fort with som lettre. I am solicited to desyre the dis-
patch of the salt suit, wch is affirmed wil be worth fyue
hundred markes a yeer to me. but by the waj for Brown,
euen now I receaued lettres and beer, 12 ton, from him,
with lettres to Griffin y^t it was my lordes pleasure he
shold seru me, but I haue refused it and can assure
yow sir y^t I am better serued by the one haulf by my
mans prouision; now iudg yow sir how poor men are
delt with. I must euer remember yow for poor Steuen.
yow know sir it toucheth my creddit to haue my man so
long a prisoner, if by my industry it maj be helped; but

I leau y' and my self to your good care and fauour, hoping thereon as greatly as indeed I want his seruice. I will now end with my most humble comendacions to my best mother, and my praier for your long and happy lyues. At Middelbourg This 14th of December, 1585.

Yowr humble Son,

PHILIP SIDNEj.

LETTER IX.

IBID. F. 169–170.

The red seal is in perfect preservation. The direction is this,

" *right honorable*
" *Walsinga*
Knight, Principal Secretary."
N.   *etc.*

RIGHT HONORABLE,

This gentleman had the charge of Flushing till I came, where in trothe I must needes affirm I found no one greef grown between anj of them and ani burgess, which I prai yow sir acknowledg vnto him, becaws I perceau he especially relies vpon your good opinion and fauour. He is very desyrows to be emploied in seruice this waj and most of horsmen wch if it might be obtained he woold emploi him self with great diligence and care in it, and indeed he proffits in the vnderstanding of this art very much. And so hauing no more at this tyme, I

humbli take my leau, praijng for your long and happy
lyfe. At Middlebourg, This 16th of December.
Your humble Son.

PH. SIDNEj.

This letter is endorsed on the fold,

" 1585

Decemb. 16,

S^r. Ph. Sydney.

Mr. Edw. Norris."

(apparently the bearer.)

LETTER X.

IBID. 286. F. 74–5.

Endorsed on the fold thus, " 29 Januarie, 1585, From S^r. Phillippe, Sydney, by Mr. Arondell." The seal is perfect, and this direction,

" *To the right hono-
rable Sir Francis
Walsingam Knight,
principal secretary.*"

RIGHT HONORABLE,

   My cosin Arundel was loth to return withowt my lettres to yowr honowr, and I, willing to take any ocasion to remember my duty vnto yow, am glad with all to signefy my goodwill to this gentleman in crauing your good cowntenance towardes him, as one indeed exceedingli well qualefied, and, as far as I any way can fynd, earnestli and hartili affected to his contreis good: of all other he is especialli desyrows to be kept in yowr good fauor, wch beeing the sum of this letter, hauing writtn more at larg by sir Robert Stapleton, I humbli take my Leau, praijng for yowr long and happy lyfe. At Hage, This 29th of Jan. 1586.

Yowr humble son,
PHILIP SIDNEJ.

LETTER XI.

FROM THE COTTONIAN MS. GALBA, C. IX. f. 56–7.

Thus directed,

"*To his Ex^{ci}*
my Singular good Lord
The Earl of Leaster."

RIGHT HONORABLE MY SINGULAR GOOD LORD,

I haue sent this bearer, my Cornett, to yowr Excellency, whome I do most humbly beseech yow to dispatch again vnto me, becaws it standes me much vppon to know what I shall resolution, becaws my charges dyuers waies, and particularly of my horsmen, grows greater then I am hable to prow thorow withall. I had of the Cownt Hollock a patent for them of Somedick to Lodg me certain nomber of hors till my company wear sufficient to be mustred: there som of them wear, and now they haue gottne, vppon what caws I know not, an Act from your Excellency to be free from any, whereuppon so courteously those Bowres* delt, as to arrest my horses the very daj y‍ᵗ I had sent for them, thinking truly I shold haue had ocasion to haue ventred my lyfe, and wold not releas them till I had paid them two hundred flourins for the charges as thei pretended. I humbli beseech yowr Ex^cl becaws I know my lieutenant hath been at the sea syde almost this month to my great expence, that I may haue either a quarter assygned me, or els y‍ᵗ to this place thei maj bring such prouision as the encreacing of the number will requyre; for, els I beeing not to demand pay till thej be mustred, nor to be mustred till my nomber be complett, it will [be] to heauy a burden for me to bear, who I protest to your Ex^cl am so fur from desyring gain, y‍ᵗ I am willing to spend all y‍ᵗ I can make; onely my care is y‍ᵗ I maj be hable to go thorow with it to your honour and seruice, as I hope in God I shall.

For these men, they are of the richest yle of these partes, and neuer touched with the war, but so do the rich still putt of all matters by fynding som frend or other of theirs in y‍ᵉ cownceill y‍ᵗ may lighten them, to burden others. I humbli beseech yowr Ex^cl my Cornett may return with such resolution as I maj either go thorow or giue ouer my cornett; for my part I hope and am almost assured to do yow good seruice and my hart burnes to do it, if onely my hability do not fall me in the waj.

For Roger Williams also, I wold it wold pleas yowr Ex^cl to dispatch his sergeant maiorship vniuersalli ouer

---

* Boors.

all horsmen, and in y⁴ nature yow maj better allow him som good pension, then by beeing only ouer the English: and so also for his Cornett, the gentleman deserues much.

Heerwith I will no furdre trouble yowr Ex^{cl}, but humbli take my Leau, and pray to God for yowr long and prosperows Lyfe, with wictory. At Berghen, This 2 of February, 1586.

Yowr Ex^{cies}
most humble and
obedient neuew,
PH. SIDNEJ.

LETTER XII.

IBID. F. 44–5. Directed thus,

[*To*] "*His Ex^{ci}*
my singular
good lord."

RIGHT HONORABLE MY SINGULAR GOOD LORD.

The manner of ver j . . . . . . death, and my intent, I haue imparted to Mr. Tutty at large to deliuer to yowr Ex^{cl}; now I am onely to beseech yowr Ex^{cl} and if I maj preuail with yowr Ex^{cl} to persuade yow, that if the iournej into Freesland be but vppon such general growndes as thei wear when I came awaj, which maj as easily be done heerafter as now, y⁴ it will pleas yow to send forces to the beseeging of Steenberg wth 2000 of yowr footmen, besydes them that these quarters maj spare, and 300 of your hors with them heer abowt, I will vndertake vppon my lyfe either to win it, or to make the enemy rais his seeg from Graue, or, which I most hope, both. And it shall be done in the sight of the world, which is most honorable and profitable. For these matters of practises, I assure yowr Ex^ct thei are dainty in respect of ye doublenes which almost euer fals in them, and of the many impedimentes y^t fall in them, that if notable seasons guyde not, or som worthi person answer for it, thei are better omitted than attempted. Bredaj vndoutedli, at least I think vndoutedly, was but a trapp, for owr poor Englishmen might haue been suffred to take a place, which thei woold neuer haue striun to put them out of, till thej might haue cutt both them and vs in peeçes, who shoold come to seaz it. But as for Graueling, I will neuer stur till I haue La Mote himself, or som principal officers of his in hand. Therefore if it pleas yowr Ex^ci to let Old Tutty and Read, with sir William Stanley, and sir William Russel, with the 200 hors, com hether, I dout not to send yow honorable and comfortable news of it, for I haue good vnderstanding thereof, by this shew I made, and I know what the enemy can do shall not seru if this maj be done; 500 pyoners with munition and vittail according, must be done, and if God will, I will do yow honour in it. It greeues me very much, the souldiours are so hardli delt with in your first beginning of gouernment, not only in their paies, but in taking booties from them, as by yowr Ex^cies Letters I fynd: when souldiours grow to despair and giue vpp townes, then it is late to buy y^t with hundred thowsandes wch might haue been saued with a tryfle.

I think to write a French lettre to yowr Ex^cl, becaws yowr Ex^cj wrate to me in y^t Language, which if it pleas yow, maj be shewd to your cownceill, for, by my troth, they are euen in their old train, and maj do that safely vnder yowr cullour now, wch before they did the more sparingli for fear of hatred. I humbli beseech yowr Ex^cl y^t Morbais maj fynd him self comforted for this seruice he hath done vppon one of the best Captaines ye prince of Parma had. I am now departing toward Flushing, and ye tyde cals me awaj, I will therefore humbli kiss yowr handes and referr the rest to my next. praijng God to prosper yowr Ex^cl, as I dout not he will, and so humbli take my leau. At Berghen, This 2 of Feb. 1586.

    Yowr Ex^cies
     most humble and
     obedient
        Ph. Sidnej.

LETTER XIII.

IBID. C. XI. f. 265-6; directed

Monseig^r
Monseig^r le Conte
  de Leicestre etc.

RIGHT HONORABLE MY SINGULAR GOOD LORD,

The Baron of Greanye desyres me to remember yowr Excellency for his dispatch for the hydutch regiment, which I the willinger do becaws I think him a good honest gentleman, and know yᵗ he hath greatly blamed the Cownt Hollok* for his late drunken folly. If yowr Excellency mean to leuy of yᵗ contrej, I think he will well seru yowr turn: I perceau he wold fain be answered, becaws accordingli he might rule him self. Heer are no news in Roterdam, but yᵗ yowr band is of very handsom men, but meerly, and vnarmed, spending monej and time to no purpos. I humbli kis yowr handes and prai for your long and happy lyfe. At Roterdam, This 12ᵗʰ of Feb. 1586.

Your Excellencies most humble
PH. SIDNEJ.

---

* Count Hollok, or Hohenlo, the Lieutenant-General of Prince Maurice, was the head of a party in the Netherlands which was formed against the Earl of Leicester. These two enemies, however, were in part reconciled through the intervention of Sir P. Sidney, for whom the Count entertained a sincere and permanent affection. When the latter was told by the surgeon, after the skirmish before Zutphen, that the wound which Sidney had there received was likely to endanger his life, he exclaimed, "Away, villain, never see my face again, till thou bring better news of that man's recovery, for whose redemption many such as I were happily lost."

LETTER XIV.

IBID. C. IX. f. 93–4, thus directed,

"...... *he right honorable*
...... gular good Lord
the Earl of Leicester
lord general and gouernor
etc."

RIGHT HONORABLE MY SINGULAR GOOD LORD,

This bearer, Martin Droger, is a man known alreddi to your Excellenci, a man vndoutedly very hable to serue, but in the past time of want of gouernment, I think he was content to go with the stream of making commodity among the rest, whereof now he is charged, but in revenge thereof he vttereth such fowl abuses in the Magistrates heer, as is very horrible. For my part I haue not autority to redress it, but to speak of it and seek ye best amendes I can of it, it fitts properly next vnder your Ex^{cl} to the Cownt Norrice,* whome I woold to God yow woold send into these partes with ample autority, I am sure he woold heer aduyce, and I am persuaded together we shold do yow seruices of importance. for dyuers things come in my waj which, becaws thej belong not indeed to my charge, I am fain to lett pass.

It is assuredli thought that Sluce will be beseeged by cutting of the commodity of the sea; onely to be preuented by building the fort Grunfelt spake for, a matter of greater consequence a great deal than Barge: thei

---

* Sic in MS. It is most probably a mistake for Morrice.

make such store of Cables and other such furniture at Bruges, as it is almost apparent y^t it is so intended. I haue sent Burlas thither; at his coming back I will more particularli aduertis your Excellency.

I am in great hope to light vppon som good ocasions to do yow honour and seruice. The enterprises are still hopefull, but not yet fully rype, which till thei bee it wear hable to mar all if I shold be far absent. Roger Williams beseecheth your Excellency to pass him his sergeant-maiorship general, with such allowance as shall seem good vnto yow. Of all nations they do desyre him. he is fain to be at charge at Berghen. Yowr Eccellency shall take care of few men y^t more bravely deseru it, as I hope he will. For my self, I will hasten, as soon as I can possibly, to yowr Excellency, when I haue but a little settled the matters of these partes, especially of my regiment, ouer whome since it hath pleased yowr Excellency to appoint me, and that thei are most ioifull of it, if euer I may deserue any thing of yow, I humbli beseech yow that that thei mai fynd them selues so much the more tendred.

If it pleas your Ex^{ci} but to speak with Valk and Tellin, thei will aduertis your Ex^{ci} of the particular cace, becaws thei best vnderstand it.

There is with your Ex^{ci} Coronel Piron, one y^t hath serued as well as any man in these partes, in deed a most vaillant man, and of better iudgment than vttrance. He and I haue enterprises to be done vppon Flanders syde, of good importance; I beseech your Ex^{ci} to dispatch him awaj; it shall I hope turn to your seruis.

The Enemy sturs of euery syde, and your syde must not be ydle, for if it bee, it quickly looseth reputation. I beseech your Ex^{ci} be not discouraged with the queenes discontentmentes, for the euent beeing ani thing good, your glory will shyne thorow those mistes; onely if it pleas yow to haue daily cownceill taken of your meanes, how to encreace them, and how to husband them: and when all is said, if thei can seru, yow shall make a noble war; if not, the peace is in your hand, as I fynd well by Aldegend, of whome I keep a good opinion and yet a suspiciows ey.

It maj pleas yow to send awaj for the Scotts out of Berges, for Roger Williams standes in great dout of them. I humbli beseech your Eccellency to giue present order for y^t point indeed, and if in their steed it pleased yow to send your Welshmen thither, thei shold haue a good place of training, and care shold be had of them, to yowr good lyking: it maj pleas your Ex^{cl} to send presently awaj a placard of the prohibition and punishment of them y^t vittail the enemy, for yet there is nothing published, in my opinion, where now they maj carry marchandis to Calleis, and vittail to Roan. Roan should be the next place for marchandis, and Nantes for vittail; but that as yowr Ex^{cl} shall fynd good; but great expedition of sending the placard is exceeding necessary.

I will no furdre troble yowr Ex^{ci} for this tyme, but with my daily praier for yowr long and happy Lyfe, and victory ouer yowr enemies. At Flushing, this 19th of Feb: 1586.

   Yowr Ex^{cies}
     most humble and
     obedient nephew,
         PH.˙ SIDNEJ.

LETTER XV.

IBID. C. X. f. 75–6, directed, to

"*The right worshipful
my especial good cosin
and frend, Mr. Dauison* *
at Cowrt."

MY GOOD COSIN,

I loue to heer from yow: vppon my hauing the Zeland regiment, wch yow know was more yowr persuasion then any desyre in me, the Cownt Hollok cawsed a many handed supplication to be made, y^t no stranger might haue any regime[nt,] but presently after, with all the same handes, protested thei ment it not by me, to whome thei wished all honowr, etc. The Cownt Morrice shewd him self constantli kynd toward me therein, but M^r. Paul *Bus* hath to many *Busses* in his hed, such as yow shall fynd he will be to God and man abowt one pitch: happy is the coniunction with them y^t ioin in the fear of God. Medekerk far shynes aboue him in all matters of cownceill and faith[ful] dealing. I prai yow wryte to me and loue me, and farewel. At Flushing, where I thank God all is well, and my garrison in good ordre. This 24th of Feb: 1586.

Yowr louing cosin and
frend,

PH. SIDNEJ.

---

* We beg leave to correct an error which we have been inadvertently led into at p. 362. The VI. Letter is said to be addressed to Mr. Secretary Walsingham, instead of Mr. Davison, who was the English ambassador to the Low Countries.

LETTER XVI.

IBID. C. IX. f. 101.

The direction, to the Earl of Leicester, has been torn off.

RIGHT HONORABLE MY SINGULAR GOOD LORD,

I am so loth to trouble your Ex^{cl} with any thing concerning my self, that I am fain to be vrged vnto it by others, becaws the necessity of the seruice requyres it.

The Cownceill of Zeland haue all, with great earnestnes, vrged me, to beseech your Ex^{cl} that the regiment it hath pleased yow to appoint vnder my charge, maj be paid according to the manner heertofore obserued, for it is douted that now all beeing brought to one foot, they shall be paid but according to the manner of others, which though it maj seem iust, becaws it is equall, it is most vniust, becaws of the great difference of the pryzes. I humbli beseech yowr Ex^{cl}, indeed most humbli and earnestly, y^t it will pleas yow to haue graciows consideration thereof. The prince of Orange euer had y^t regard, as well for that reason of the contreis Dearth, as for the necessity of the places where thei are to be trusted, wch are both first to be attempted, when so euer the enemy makes any great forces, and yet are indeed to be esteemed owr last strength.

Becaws I know not how long these Letters shall be before they com to your Ex^{cl}, I will add nothing but my praier for your long and prosperous lyfe, with victory

ouer those whom your vertew makes your enemies. At Berghes. This 25th of February, 1586.
>Your Ex^{cies}
>>most humble and obedient,
>>>PH. SIDNEJ.

THE END.

www.ingramcontent.com/pod-product-compliance
Lightning Source LLC
Chambersburg PA
CBHW031413230426
43668CB00007B/301